THE COMMENTATORS' AL HANISSIM

Insights of the Sages on Purim and Chanukah

PURIM

by

RAV YITZCHAK SENDER

DESIGN EDITOR
DAVID C. ZARETSKY

FIRST EDITION

FELDHEIM PUBLISHERS
JERUSALEM • NEW YORK

THE COMMENTATORS' AL HANISSIM

First Edition
January 2000

ISBN 1-58330-411-8

Address of the Author:
Rabbi Yitzchak Sender
6620 North Whipple
Chicago, IL 60645

Feldheim Publishers, POB 35002 / Jerusalem, Israel

Feldheim Publishers, 200 Airport Executive Park, Nanuet, NY 10954

www.feldheim.com

Printed in Israel

ברכה

מהגאון הגדול, פאר הדור,
מרן ר' שלמה זלמן אויערבאך זצוק"ל
ראש הישיבה "קול תורה" בירושלים
ומחבר ספר "מעדני ארץ" ב"ח ועוד

ב"ה

כבר איתמחי האי גברא יקירא ידידי הרה"ג המופלא והמהולל
מוה"ר יצחק אייזיק סנדר שליט"א ונודע לתהלה בספריו היקרים
שזכה לחבר על הרבה ענינים חשובים וגדולי תורה נתנו עליהם
עדותם ויהללו אותם. אשר על כן גם יקרתו של ספר חשוב זה
תעיד על ערכו החשוב וכל מכתב תהלה אך למותר הוא. רק מברך
אני את ידידי הרה"ג המחבר שנותן התורה יהא בעזרו וימלא
משאלות לבו להיות שבתו כל הימים באהלה של תורה ולהרביץ
תורה לרבים מתוך הרחבה ושמחה וגם יפוצו מעינותיו חוצה להג-
דיל תורה ולהאדירה כאות נפשו ונפש ידידו ומוקירו.

שלמה זלמן אויערבאך

CONTENTS

. . . .

☙

STORIES

. . . .

☙

Foreword

Both Purim and Chanukah were ordained by *Chazal,* our Sages, after the other holidays had already been established. Earlier generations of Klal Yisrael found adequate spiritual sustenance in the three Pilgrimage Festivals of Pesach, Shavuos and Succos — the שלש רגלים — on which all Jewish males were required to ascend to the Bais HaMikdash in Yerushalayim three times a year, "שלש פעמים בשנה". It was these *"three times a year"* that gave the people the spiritual strength to carry on the rest of the *"year"*.

In later generations, however, they were unable to sustain this level of inspired dedication without the additional spiritual support provided by Purim and Chanukah. For these two holidays served to reinforce our commitment to Torah and mitzvos and to strengthen our faith in Hashem and His direct intervention in human affairs — השגחה פרטית.

The miracle of Purim reaffirmed the promise that Hashem had made to His chosen people — the promise that He would be responsive to their needs whenever they called upon Him (*Dvarim* 4:6):

"כי מי גוי גדול אשר לו אל-הים קרובים אליו כה' אלקינו בכל קראנו
אליו".

"For which is a great nation that has a God who is close to it as is Hashem, our God, whenever we call to him."

Purim is celebrated in proximity to Pesach. In past generations, Pesach was a time when the feared and cruel "blood libel" against the Jewish people was perpetrated each year. It was claimed that the Jewish people used the blood of gentile children to bake their matzos, and a body was often planted in a Jewish home or synagogue to add "substance" to this monstrous claim. The miracle of Purim gave us the courage to strengthen ourselves in the knowledge that just as the evil decrees of Haman the wicked were overcome, so too would we overcome the evil decrees of our present-day enemies and their false claims would come to naught.

The symbol of what was achieved on Chanukah — the miracle of the light which burned in the Bais HaMikdash for eight days, reflecting Hashem's abiding watchfulness over the Jewish people — was intended to serve as an inspiration for those Jews who eventually found themselves in exile. Unlike Purim with its Diaspora background, the events of Chanukah took place in the Land of Yisrael. We can understand this if we consider that the miraculous light of Chanukah alludes to the miracle of the *"eternal Jew"* who keeps the flame of Judaism alive, even when he finds himself in the far-flung corners of the world, in a *"land not his own"*.

The celebration of Purim, on the other hand, even though its events took place in the Diaspora, centers around the Land of Yisrael. For when we celebrate Purim on the fifteenth of Adar in walled cities, we determine this by reference to those cities that were walled in Eretz Yisrael at the time of Yehoshua ben Nun. This was meant to illuminate the hope of Klal Yisrael to be restored to their homeland with the rebuilding of the Bais HaMikdash.

Chanukah is celebrated in proximity to their "feast of lights". This phenomena is not accidental. The Master Plan here was to give courage to the Jew in exile. Although surrounded by "their" colorful lights, we feel reassured that our lights shall prevail. Although at present only a small light is seen illuminating our homes, in the near future the lights of Moshiach shall burn ever so brightly, brighter than all the lights ever lit.

When we study the laws of Purim and Chanukah, we find a peculiar situation. For in the *Shulchan Aruch* the laws of Chanukah precede those of Purim, whereas in the *Mishnah Torah* of the Rambam both holidays are presented together and Purim is placed before Chanukah.

Historically, the Rambam's order seems more logical, for the events of Purim occurred many years before those of Chanukah. Yet from the standpoint of the calendar, the order set down by the *Shulchan Aruch* seems to make more sense. Yet we might explain and defend the rationale of the Rambam, who not only deals with the laws of Purim before those of Chanukah but also joins them together. The common element here, which was ordained by our Sages, is that in both cases we express gratitude for the miracles wrought on our behalf.

This expression of thanks, הודאה, justifies adding these two holidays to our yearly calendar, even though we are normally very careful not to add any mitzvos to the Torah. The reason for this is that even though the Torah forbade adding new mitzvos to those already existing, yet the concept of the Jew expressing gratitude to Hashem preceded even the giving of the Torah itself. For example, "Yehudah" was given his name by his mother, Leah, for she yearned to express her deep feelings of gratitude to Hashem for His benevolence to her in giving her a son. Our Patriarchs, throughout their lives, built altars in order to offer sacrifices which expressed their gratitude for Hashem's kindness to them.

Thus the addition of these two holidays of Purim and Chanukah exemplified what the Jew has been taught from the very beginning of time, to express gratitude to the Almighty for the benevolence He has bestowed upon us. This explains why the Rambam dealt with these two holidays together, for in both of them the main emphasis is on thanksgiving, הודאה, which is expressed in the prayer of "על הנסים", inserted on both days in the thanksgiving section, הודאה, of our Amidah prayer.

Once again, I wish to express my sincere and heartfelt gratitude to all those contributors who have made this publication possible. I am grateful not only for their generosity in material terms, but also the generosity of spirit evident in the gracious manner in which their contributions were given.

I also offer my heartfelt thanks to my editor and friend, **Mrs. Wendy Dickstein**, who has as always given of herself above and beyond the call of duty. Her talents and dedication has made this volume what it is.

To my good friends: **Rabbi Ben-Zion Rand**, for his efforts in reviewing drafts of this sefer and for his technical input and helpful suggestions, and **Rabbi Chaim Twerski**, for his time and assistance in preparing the volume for production.

4

A special thank you to **David Zaretsky** for his talented contribution to the final layout and acknowledging his technical abilities.

Finally, and most importantly, my gratitude to my dear wife, נחמה תחי׳, who has seen to it that I be afforded the time and opportunity to work on this sefer. May Hashem bless her and our children and grandchildren with the strength, health and dedication to continue the teachings of His Torah and Mitzvos to His people.

The Mitzvos of Chodesh Adar

The first Mishna in *Mesechtas Shekalim* reads:

"באחד באדר משמיעין על השקלים ועל הכלאים"

"On the first day of Adar they make proclamations about the payment of the shekalim and about kilayim."

"Shekalim" refers to the payment of half a shekel by each member of Klal Yisrael, and "kilayim" refers to the prohibition against mixing two kinds (of animals, seeds, certain fabrics, etc.). The Admor of Ostrov (ר' מאיר יחיאל, זצ"ל) asks, what is the common bond between these two proclamations? And he suggests the following answer:

The Shelah HaKodesh (של"ה הקודש) explains that the Torah obligated us to give only half a shekel rather than a whole shekel — in order that each one of us should feel that he is incomplete and that we need the companionship of other Jews. Thus we naturally seek out the friendship of other Jews to satisfy this need. However, we are being warned here to be careful. For we might fall into the wrong company, "the company of scorners", as the first Psalm warns us to keep far away from such companions who can lead to our spiritual downfall. Similarly, the idea of "*kilayim*" alludes to the prohibition against "mixing" with people of a "different kind", who can bring us down spiritually and lead us astray.

We might suggest yet another homiletic interpretation of the appropriateness of this connection between *shekalim* and *kilayim* which

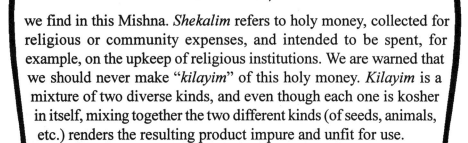

we find in this Mishna. *Shekalim* refers to holy money, collected for religious or community expenses, and intended to be spent, for example, on the upkeep of religious institutions. We are warned that we should never make "*kilayim*" of this holy money. *Kilayim* is a mixture of two diverse kinds, and even though each one is kosher in itself, mixing together the two different kinds (of seeds, animals, etc.) renders the resulting product impure and unfit for use.

Thus, we can derive no benefit from our *shekalim*, the money collected for religious purposes, if we "mix" this money with anything that is not holy. And so we must be extremely careful not to waste or squander that money. We must not make "*kilayim*" of our "*shekalim*".

CHAPTER ONE

Rejoicing when Adar Comes

I

UNDERSTANDING THE CONCEPT

The Gemara in *Ta'anis* 29a states that when Adar arrives, joy increases among the Jewish people:

"אמר רב יהודה ברי' דרב שמואל בר שילת משמי' דרב :כשם שמשנכנס
אב ממעטין בשמחה כך משנכנס אדר מרבין בשמחה."

"Rav Yehudah, the son of Rav Shmuel bar Shilas, said in the name of Rav: Just as when the month of Av begins we curtail joy, so too, when the month of Adar begins we increase joy."

The Gemara continues:

"אמר רב פפא :הילכך בר ישראל דאית ליה דינא בהדי נכרי לישתמיט
מיניה באב דריע מזליה ולימצי נפשיה באדר דבריא מזליה"

Rav Papa said: "Therefore a Jew who has a lawsuit with a gentile should avoid him in the month of Av and make himself available in the month of Adar. For in Av the luck of the Jew is not good; whereas in Adar it is good."

This saying, that "When Adar begins, we increase joy", has become a catchphrase in the Jewish world, and it ushers in the festive mood of the month in which Purim occurs. With the advent of Rosh Chodesh Adar, colorful posters adorn our homes, classrooms and synagogues, proclaiming this joyful message.

But where does this tradition come from? For neither the Rambam nor the Shulchan Aruch mentions this aspect of the month of Adar in any of their writings. And even Rav Papa, in his statement recommending that a Jew go to court with a gentile in Adar but not in Av, emphasizes merely the fortunate aspect of the month rather than our obligation to increase joy in it. How, then, is this the theme of the month, if the major poskim do not give any significance to this aspect?

Rashi's question: why mention Pesach?

The matter becomes even more puzzling when we consider that Rashi comments on this statement of "משנכנס אדר" by mentioning Pesach. He writes as follows:

"ימי נסים היו לישראל פורים ופסח"

"Adar begins the period in which many miracles were performed for Bnai Yisrael: Purim and Pesach."

The commentators all ask why we mention Pesach here when we are speaking about Adar. For indeed, if Nissan and Pesach contribute to the reason for joy during this period, why are we not required to *"increase joy"* during the month of Nissan?

How do we increase joy?

This leads us to ask: What exactly are we required to do in order to increase joy? One can understand what is meant when we are told to temper our festivities,"ממעטין בשמחה", we simply abstain from those activities which give us joy. But how in practical terms are we to *increase* our joy, "מרבין בשמחה"?

Good things happen on an auspicious day

The Ba'alei Tosafos, commenting on the statement of Rav Papa that we should avoid litigation in the month of Av and seek it out in Adar, maintain the Rav Papa's advice is based on a concept previously discussed on page 29a prior to the idea here of "משנכנס אב". This concept was that "good things happen on an auspicious day, whereas bad things happen on an inauspicious day."

If so, ask the commentators, why was Rav Papa's statement, cited previously in conjunction with the concept of "מגלגלין זכאי ליום זכאי וכו'" placed here, only after the statement of "משנכנס אב וכו'"?

Using the term "כשם" to mean different things

When the term "כשם" ("as") is used, it generally serves to connect two statements. However, it can have very different connotations in different contexts. For example, the statement is made (כריתות ו,ב):

"**כשם** שהדיבור רע ליין, כך הדיבור יפה לבשמים"

"Just as speech [that is, speaking while wine is being prepared] is harmful to wine, so is it beneficial to spices."

Here the word "as", "כשם", indicates that a single cause (namely, *speech*) may have very different effects. In other instances, though, the same term, "כשם", can suggest that a comparison is being made between two unrelated subjects. Yet the same law applies to both of them. An example of such use of "כשם" can be found in ברכות מח,ב:

"**שכשם** שמברך על הטובה, כך מברך על הרעה."

"Just as one makes a blessing for good things which happen, so too should one make a blessing for bad things which happen."

Even though "good" and "bad" are opposite concepts, the common element of *making a blessing*, is appropriate for both. And so in this case as well, the term "כשם", "as", serves to connect two opposites.

A third use of the term "כשם" is to compare something expected with something unexpected. An example of this can be found in the description of the *sotah*, the rebellious wife, who is tested with the "bitter waters". Chazal tell us (*Sotah* 27b):

"כשם שהמים בודקין את האשה כך המים בודקין אותו."

"In the same way as the bitter waters test the wife for unfaithfulness, so too do they test the husband."

It would seem that from what the Torah writes concerning the usage of the "bitter waters", it was meant as a test only for the woman. Therefore, we are told here that the husband is also tested.

With these three examples in mind, how are we to apply the term "כשם" to the Gemara regarding the months of Av and Adar? For here we do not have a single cause leading to two opposite effects. But rather it was the destruction of the Holy Temple, חורבן בית המקדש, which obligates us to curtail our joy in the month of Av, the time when that tragedy occurred. Whereas during the month of Adar, the commemoration of the Jewish people's salvation obligates us, on the contrary, to display increased joy.

We do not have "similar results" in this case, nor do we find that the element of the expected versus the unexpected applies here. Where, then, does the use of the term "כשם" fit in here, where we read: "**כשם** שמשנכנס אב...**כך** משנכנס אדר וכו'"?

II

THE CHASAM SOFER EXPLAINS THE RAMBAM

The Chasam Sofer, in his sefer, שו"ת חתם סופר (חלק אור"ח, סימן קס), questions why the Rambam omitted this statement of "משנכנס אדר". The answer he gives is based on the Gemara in *Ta'anis* 29b, which presents three opinions as to when the prohibitions which are in effect during the month of Av (such as bathing, washing clothes, cutting hair, eating meat and drinking wine) commence. These three opinions can be outlined as follows:

The prohibitions apply:
1) According to Rav Meir: from Rosh Chodesh until Tisha B'Av.
2) According to Rav Yehudah: Throughout the entire month of Av.
3) According to Rabban Shimon Ben Gamliel: Only during the week of Tisha B'Av itself.

The Gemara then gives the sources for each of these opinions. Rav Yochanan said: All three of these opinions were derived from one verse:

"והשבתי כל משושה חגה חדשה ושבתה" (הושע ב,יג)

"I will bring all of her joy to an end: her festivals, months and Sabbaths."

Rav Meir, who maintained that these prohibitions were to take effect from Rosh Chodesh Av until Tisha B'Av, derived his opinion from the word, "חגה", "her festival", which refers to Rosh Chodesh, the day which is celebrated as a festival.

Rav Yehudah, who forbade the above activities throughout the entire month of Av, based his opinion on the word "חדשה", "her months".

And finally, Rabban Shimon ben Gamliel, who forbade these activities only during the week of Tisha B'Av, based his opinion on the word "שבתה", "her Sabbaths".

Rav, author of the statement "משנכנס אב", holds the same opinion as Rav Yehudah, namely that these prohibitions which serve to curtail joy must be in effect throughout the entire month of Av, commencing with Rosh Chodesh. Thus Adar, which the *Megillah* characterizes as a month in which sadness was transformed into joy: "והחדש אשר נהפך להם מיגון "לשמחה (*Esther* 9:22), is considered a time for demonstrating happiness, שמחה. The Chasam Sofer gives other proofs to substantiate this claim that Rav subscribes to the opinion of Rav Yehudah. But since the halacha does not follow the opinion of Rav and Rav Yehudah here, this might be the reason the Rambam omitted the phrase "משנכנס אדר מרבין בשמחה" from his explanation of this practice.

III

THE FIFTEENTH OF AV AND THE DESTRUCTION OF THE TEMPLE

We can answer the questions raised here, based on the following insight, expanded upon elsewhere, in *The Commentators' Seder* (pp. 235-238). The halacha states that with the destruction of the Second Temple all the holidays mentioned in the *Megillas Ta'anis* (which chronicled all the holidays observed during the time of the Second Temple) were discontinued. This raises a question about The fifteenth of Av, which was articulated by Ha Gaon Rav Bezalel HaKohen of Vilna in his sefer

(עמ' צ-צב) "ראשית בכורים". There he asks, since Tu B'Av is among those holidays listed in *Megillas Ta'anis*, one would think that it should no longer be celebrated. However, the *Shulchan Aruch,* in סימן קלא סעיף י' (and also the *Magen Avraham*, ס"ק טו שם) maintains that even today the fifteenth of Av is considered to be a holiday of sorts, since on that day Tachanun is never said.

The Mishna at the end of *Mesechtas Ta'anis* states: "Rabban Shimon ben Gamliel said: Yisrael has no days as festive as the fifteenth of Av and Yom Kippur." The Gemara then gives six reasons for the festivities which took place on the fifteenth of Av, when the young girls of Yerushalayim would go out into the fields and dance in borrowed white dresses, and they would invite the young men to choose brides from among them. The six reasons specified in the Gemara are:

1) The fifteenth of Av was the day that the ban on intermarriage among the tribes of Yisrael was lifted.

2) On this day the tribe of Benjamin was allowed to re-enter the congregation of Yisrael, after they had been banned by the rest of the Jewish nation because of the incident of the concubine in Gevah (described in the *Book of Judges* 19-26).

3) On this day the decree of death was lifted from the surviving members of the Generation of the Desert, *Dor HaMidbar*.

4) Hoshea ben Elah removed the sentries Yeroboam had stationed along the roads to prevent the pilgrimage to Yerushalayim, *Aliyas HaRegel*.

5) The cutting down of trees used as wood on the altar of the Bais HaMikdash ceased.

6) On this day the Romans allowed the Jews killed in the uprising at Betar to be buried.

When we examine this list, some interesting issues emerge. For example, how are we to determine when this holiday of the Fifteenth of Av was established? For if it was initiated as a result of the first three reasons, then it would seem that this holiday had been instituted even before the building of the first Bais HaMikdash. On the other hand, if it was initiated as the result of the incident at Betar, then we could assume that it had been established *after* the destruction of the second Bais HaMikdash.

We might suggest that the celebration of the fifteenth of Av as a holiday was established at the time of the second Bais HaMikdash. It became a day set aside for the arrangement of matches, *shidduchim*. This particular day was selected because of its association with many positive events which had taken place on this day throughout history. As we have discussed, it is said that on auspicious days good things are bound to happen, "מגלגלין זכות ליום זכאי". Thus, even after the Destruction, this day has remained an auspicious day for Jews throughout history, a "יום סגולה", and therefore Tachanun is not recited on this day.

This also applies to the days of Rosh Chodesh Av and Adar. On Rosh Chodesh Av we need not curtail joy by abstaining from certain practices which we normally associate with happiness, such as cutting our hair, eating meat and drinking wine. And similarly, on Rosh Chodesh Adar we are not obligated to engage in acts which increase joy. Rather there exists here, in relation to these two days, a special sensitivity which calls upon Klal Yisrael to act appropriately. History has affected Klal Yisrael on these two days, and we are expected to behave as if these are not ordinary days. We are called upon to act with the understanding that momentous occurrences took place on these days. And so on Rosh Chodesh Av, though we are not expressly commanded to do so, it is expected of us that we have the sensitivity to curtail joy and on Rosh Chodesh Adar, to increase joy.

With this insight in mind, we can now attempt to answer all our previous questions.

1) We can now understand why the Rambam and the Shulchan Aruch did not mention this concept of increasing joy on Adar. For the Gemara

is not here stipulating an absolute requirement, but rather it is suggesting the need for sensitivity. As a general rule, both the Rambam and the Shulchan Aruch are careful to cite what is absolutely required by the halacha by our Sages, and because this was only a suggestion — a call for sensitivity — and not a halacha, this practice of increasing joy when the month of Adar begins is omitted from their formulations.

2) We can now also understand why Rashi associated Purim and Pesach when he described this period as a time of miracles, a period when we are expected to be sensitive to the special atmosphere which prevails. We are not obligated to fulfill any specific practices on these two special days, but rather we should be aware of the unique spiritual forces which surround us, and we should respond by increasing our joy in Adar and curtailing it in Av.

3) We can now also appreciate the use of the term "כשם" here and understand its intention. It equates two seeming opposites, Av and Adar. We must be sensitive to the particular spiritual forces of each of these periods of time, and we should understand intuitively that Av is a time to diminish joy and Adar a time to increase it.

4) Being aware of this special sensitivity which infuses time accounts for the statement made here by Rav Papa, that one should avoid litigation during the month of Av and seek it out in the month of Adar. This is not a directive or a halacha to be strictly followed, but rather a deduction we make, that we should enter into litigation with a gentile only when it is an auspicious time for the Jewish people. In a similar vein, Haman, when he sought to implement his diabolical plan against the Jews, chose the month of Adar, for he mistakenly believed that it was an auspicious month or the enemies of the Jewish people, since this was the month in which Moshe Rabbenu had died.

And therefore, Rav Papa explained the statement in the Mishna: "משנכנס אב ממעטין בשמחה ומשנכנס אדר מרבין בשמחה", to mean that we must be sensitive to the times and act accordingly. It was appropriate to quote this statement of Rav Papa here rather than on the preceding page, which deals with the concept of auspicious periods of time: "מגלגלין זכות ליום זכאי".

For although it is true that Rav Papa's statement here is based on that concept, yet in addition to showing us a practical application, what he says sheds light on how we are to understand the Mishna's statement about increasing joy in Adar and decreasing it in Av. Thus Rav Papa's statement rightfully belongs here on page 29b rather than in the previous discussion on page 29a regarding auspicious days.

IV

A NEW PERSPECTIVE ON RASHI

As we have seen, according to Rashi both Adar and Nissan should be a time for increasing joy, "מרבין בשמחה". However, only in Adar are we obligated to act on that requirement. The שאילת יעב"ץ (ח"ב תשובה פח) offers a new perspective on how to understand what Rashi means here.

1) It would seem logical that if increased joy is required whenever a miracle has been performed for the Jewish people, then the month of Kislev should also call for increasing joy. But Rashi specifically mentioned only Adar and Nissan, and not Kislev, to emphasize that only these two months and their accompanying miracles require us to increase joy.

2) Rashi here was alluding to a halachic consequence, which was that in a leap year, when there are two months of Adar, we should concentrate in increasing joy in the Adar month which falls closest to the month of Nissan, with its atmosphere of redemption. This is why Rashi mentioned both Adar and Nissan: "מסמך גאולה לגאולה".

The פרי צדיק (לר"ח אדר) suggests a reason why we are required to increase joy in Adar, but not in Nissan. He points out that there was a great difference between the miracles which the Almighty performed for the Jewish people in Nissan and in Adar. The miracle which occurred on Pesach, in the month of Nissan, came about only because of Heavenly intervention in the fate of the Jewish people, "אתרועעת דלתתא". For they had sunk to the lowest level of spiritual impurity, and they did not deserve to be redeemed, since they took no initiative to bring about their own redemption. Therefore, in the month of Nissan we are not called upon to display increased joy, since the Jewish people did not merit that redemption.

The miracle of Purim, on the other hand, came about as a result of the initiative of the Jewish people: "אתרועעת דלתתא". The spirit of self sacrifice displayed at that time by Mordechai and Esther, together with all of Bnai Yisrael, brought about the miracle of Purim. When we recall our merits and the concerted spiritual effort we made, this is a reason to increase our joy in the month of Adar.

MOSHE RABBENU'S FACE SHONE WITH A HEAVENLY RADIANCE

We would expand on the above concepts and thereby answer the question why we celebrate on Adar and not Nissan, based on what we have discussed elsewhere (See *The Commentators' Gift of Torah*, pp. 46-47).

Chazal tell us that the extraordinary radiance which shone from Moshe Rabbenu's face came from the "extra ink" which was left in his pen after he wrote the Ten Commandments. He rubbed this ink on his forehead and it illuminated his countenance. This prompts the Bais HaLevi to ask, how are we to understand that there was extra ink left in his pen? He goes on to explain the difference between the first and the second set of Tablets. The first set contained, in a miraculous manner, both the Written and the Oral Law. The second set, however, given after the sin of the Golden Calf, contained only the Written Law. Moshe, who anticipated that he would write the second set of Tablets as he did the first, had "extra ink", which was the ink he would have used to write the Oral Law.

Perhaps we should try to understood this concept metaphorically, rather than literally. Thus, since Moshe was now not able to write down the Oral Law, he must exert the greatest possible effort to learn and remember it. His supreme effort of mind and soul as he toiled in Torah study is what is meant by "rubbing ink on his forehead". When a person puts his heart and soul into studying the Torah, the results can be seen by the radiance which shines from his face. Such a person becomes a more spiritually refined human being. This is how we are to understand the rays of splendor, "קרני הוד", which illuminated Moshe Rabbenu's countenance.

This concept helps us understand why increased joy, "מרבין בשמחה", is called for in the month of Adar but not in Nissan. It is a matter of developing a particular sensitivity towards spiritual potentialities. No specific act is required, but rather we are encouraged to feel joy when we consider what transpired during this period in our national history. We remember that it was as a result of our own spiritual efforts that we were granted miraculous salvation in Shushan, Persia, so many generations ago.

As the פרי צדיק reminds us, only in Adar are we able to experience this deep inner joy and pride when we remember that we merited the miracle because of our worthy actions. In the month of Nissan, on the other hand, we can feel gratitude towards the Almighty for having brought us forth from slavery, but since it was a gift we did not deserve, this knowledge serves to dampen our joy somewhat rather than increase it.

Mordechai knew Haman's true worth

We read in the Megillah (*Esther* 5:9) that after being invited to the private feast Esther was hosting for the king, Haman was elated. However, as soon as he saw Mordechai sitting at the king's gate and he once again refused to bow down to him, all Haman's joy turned to ashes, and he remarked:

"וכל זה איננו שוה לי"

"All the honor and glory mean nothing to me as long as I see Mordechai the Jew sitting at the king's gate."

We might think that Haman was over-reacting here, for surely someone with so much prestige could overlook one unimportant commoner when he, Haman, of all the great ministers and courtiers in the kingdom, had been singled out for this special honor. The reason behind his reaction was once explained to me by HaRav Ben Zion Brook, of blessed memory. At the time HaRav Brook visited the United States, Dwight Eisenhower was president, and he used him to make a point about this statement of Haman's.

HaRav Brook remarked, what kind of fool was Haman to declare that all the honors bestowed on him meant nothing? Suppose, for example, that President Eisenhower were to open the "Chicago Tribune" one morning and read: "Eisenhower is an idiot." Would he sit down and cry? Hand in his resignation? Of course not! What person in power does not have enemies and critics? Why, then, after Haman had been

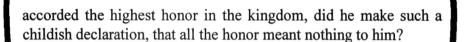

accorded the highest honor in the kingdom, did he make such a childish declaration, that all the honor meant nothing to him?

HaRav Brook gave the following reason for Haman being so devastated by Mordechai's disrespect. When Mordechai looked him straight in the eye and refused to budge, he was saying in effect that even though everyone in the entire kingdom bows down to you and thinks you are a great man, I know and you know who you really are — a nobody! Haman was shaken to his very core; for deep down he had to admit that Mordechai was right and he really was a nobody. His true essence surfaced, and because Mordechai knew it, Haman had to grudgingly admit to the truth. This was why he sought to destroy Mordechai. For as long as there was a voice in the world, however small, which whispered that Haman was a nobody, Haman had to hang his head in submission. If he could only silence this voice forever, no one would know his secret shame.

We can learn something from this. For it is true of every human being, that the unpleasant truth about oneself is always hard to face, especially if it contradicts what the world thinks is the truth. It is for this reason that we say in our prayers, "לעולם יהא אדם ירא שמים...ומודה על האמת" — *"May a person always acknowledge the truth in his heart."*

To be able to do this a person must have fear of heaven, and he must admit that there is a higher Being in the world who sees and knows all. If one has the courage to face the truth, he will be able to rise to great spiritual heights.

CHAPTER TWO

Parashas Zachor

I

Uprooting Amalek

In the First Book of Samuel, 15:1-3, the Prophet Samuel tells Saul that he has come to anoint him and to tell him of his divinely ordained mission.

"ויאמר שמואל אל שאול אתי שלח ה' למשחך למלך על עמו על ישראל ועתה שמע לקול דברי ה'. כה אמר ה' צבאות פקדתי את אשר עשה עמלק לישראל אשר שם לו בדרך בעלתו ממצרים. עתה לך והכיתה את עמלק והחרמתם את כל אשר לו ולא תחמול עליו והמתה מאיש עד אשה מעולל ועד יונק משור ועד שה מגמל ועד חמור."

"Samuel said to Saul: Hashem has sent me to anoint you king over His people, over Yisrael; so now hear the sound of Hashem's words. So said Hashem, Master of Legions: 'I remembered what Amalek did to Yisrael, the ambush he set for him along the way as he went up from Egypt. Now go and strike down Amalek and destroy everything he has; have no pity on him; kill man and woman alike, infant and suckling, ox and sheep, camel and donkey.' "

Amalek is also mentioned again in *Parashas Ki Tetze*, 25:17-19, where we read:

"זכור את אשר עשה לך עמלק...תמחה את זכר עמלק מתחת השמים לא תשכח."

"Remember what Amalek did to you...you shall blot out the remembrance of Amalek from under the heavens; you shall not forget."

We might wonder why it was necessary for Samuel the Prophet to call this to the attention of the soon-to-be king, Saul. For wasn't the commandment to eradicate Amalek already established as a fundamental principle of the Torah and a primary mitzva? Why did he need to remind him?

Chazal, in *Mesechtas Sanhedrin*, 20b, seems to present a straight-forward reason for this.

"תניא רבי יוסי אומר: שלש מצות נצטוו ישראל בכניסתן לארץ, להעמיד
להם מלך, ולהכרית זרעו של עמלק, ולבנות להם בית הבחירה."

"It has been taught, Rav Yose said: Three commandments were given to Yisrael when they entered the land: to appoint a king, to destroy the seed of Amalek, and to build the Holy Temple."

These three mitzvos were meant to be followed in the order in which they were set down here. Thus, since Saul had been appointed king, the Prophet Samuel was reminding him that he was now obligated to take the next step, which was to destroy Amalek.

The Radak, in his commentary to this pasuk, takes a similar approach. He comments on this verse by saying:

"ועתה שמע, כלומר, כיון שנמשחת למלך על ישראל, צריך שתעשה מה
שמצוה עליך לעשות והוא מלחמת עמלק."

"And now listen, as it is said, after you will become king over Yisrael, you must fulfill the mitzva which is incumbent upon you now, and that is to uproot Amalek."

The Rambam presents an astonishing explanation of what is actually happening here. He writes, in the *Sefer HaMitzvos (Mitzva 189)*:

"היא שצונו לזכור מה שעשה לנו עמלק בהקדימו להרע לנו. ולשנונא
אותו בכל עת ועת ונעורר הנפשות במאמרים להלחם בו ונזרז העם
לשנוא אותו עד שלא תשכח המצוה. ולא תחלש שנאתו ותחסר מהנפשות
עם אורך הזמן. והוא אמרו יתעלה 'זכור את אשר עשה לך עמלק' יכול,
בלבבך כשהוא אומר 'לא תשכח' הרי שכחת הלב אמור. הא מה אני
מקיים, זכור 'שתהא שנאתו, בפיך.' הלא תראה שמואל בהתחילו לעשות
במצוה הזאת איך עשה שהוא זכר תחלה מעשהו הרע ואחר כך צוה
להרגו. והוא אמרו יתברך, פקדתי את אשר עשה עמלק לישראל."

"Wherein He has commanded us to remember what Amalek did unto us in his eagerness to injure us, we are to reaffirm it

at all times and arouse the people by means of public orations, to make war upon him, admonishing them to hate him, to the end that the commandment may not be forgotten and our hatred for him may not be weakened or lessened with the passage of time... Thus you see that Samuel, in proceeding to fulfill this commandment, first recalled the wicked deeds of Amalek, and afterwards commanded [the king] to slay him."

This shows that the prophet's purpose here was not to remind Saul of the mitzva, but rather to arouse the people against the wicked Amalek and to call their attention to the hatred we must harbor towards him, so that we never forget what the Amalekites did to us and the evil they plot against us in every generation.

II

TWO VIEWS: THE HAGRIZ HALEVI AND THE ROGATCHOVER

The *HaGriz HaLevi* postulates that the Prophet Samuel's calling upon King Saul to initiate this mitzva of going to war against Amalek is a prerequisite to his fulfilling this mitzva. For it is only after the prophet instructs him with the command of: "כה אמר ה'...עתה לך והכיתה את עמלק"

that the mitzva of going to war against Amalek comes into being. The HaGriz HaLevi explains this idea as follows:

"ויאמר שמואל אל שאול...ועתה לך והכיתה את עמלק וגו', ונראה מוכרח מזה שאע"פ שמלחמת עמלק הוא אחד מג' המצוות שנצטוו ישראל בכניסתן לארץ, **אין מחויבין רק בנבואה** שילחמו אתם, דאל"כ למה נצטרכו כאן לצווי מיוחד. ומבואר בזה בקרא דכתיב (בשלח יז:טז), מלחמה ה' בעמלק, דמלחמה עפ"י הי היא..."

He explains here that it is only because the prophet conveys his divine revelation to him, that he is obligated to go to war against Amalek.

The Rogatchover offers a similar insight, in his Torah commentary on verse 15 in the First Book of Samuel, which says: *"and has not fulfilled my word"* — "ואת דברי לא הקים".

According to Chazal, "דברי ה'" alludes to prophecy (See *Shabbos* 138b). Thus what the verse in Samuel is saying is that King Saul did not fulfill the directive of the prophet to completely destroy Amalek.

The Rambam appears to support this position of the HaGriz HaLevi. In his introduction to his Mishnah Commentary, the Rambam writes as follows:

"גם המתנבא בשם ה' נחלק לשני חלקים... והחלק השני שיקרא לעבודת ה'... ויצוה צוויים ויזהר אזהרות שלא בעניני הדת כגון שיאמר הלחמו על עיר פלונית או על אומה פלונית עכשיו, כמו שצוה שמואל את שאול להלחם בעמלק..."

"The second category is exemplified by a prophet calling people to worship Hashem, commanding them to obey His precepts...He also prescribes ordinances, and decrees prohibitions on a subject which is not in the Torah, such as if he says, 'Wage war with such and such a town or people now', as Samuel commanded Saul to wage war with Amalek..."

From this we can see clearly that in the episode of King Saul and the Prophet Samuel, the Rambam also postulates that a prophet's command is required. However, we might claim that there is no proof from the Rambam's words here that a prophet's command is required in order to fight Amalek. And furthermore, we might even contend that the Rambam's position here actually goes against the contention of the HaGriz HaLevi. For the Rambam here is describing a situation in which we must listen to the prophet even in such matters which represent mitzvos not dictated by the Torah, and failure to do so brings about severe punishment.

If this is the Rambam's point, why did he set out to prove this point by reference to the incident of Samuel and Saul and the command to wage war against Amalek, which is a mitzvah from the Torah?

And why did he compare it to a situation where one is commanded to wage war against "a town or a people now", which is not dictated by the Torah?

III

Remembering Amalek in times of peace

Why did the Prophet Samuel exhort King Saul regarding the mitzva of eradicating the name of Amalek? Perhaps we can understand his motivation by examining the Torah portion which depicts that mitzva. The Torah tells us (*Dvarim* 25:17):

"והי' בהניח ה' אלקיך לך מכל אויביך מסביב...תמחה את זכר עמלק...
לא תשכח."

"And when Hashem, your God, lets you rest from all your surrounding enemies...you must erase the memory of Amalek...do not forget."

From this verse we discern a prerequisite which must be met before one can perform this mitzva of going to war against Amalek: the land of Yisrael must be in a state of peace and security. At the time of Saul's reign, this condition was not met. It was only later, after Jerusalem was annexed, during the reign of King David, that Bnai Yisrael and Eretz Yisrael experienced an era of peace and security. This indicates that the period of Saul's reign was not an opportune time to engage in a war against Amalek, according to the Torah's definition. And yet in his role as prophet, Samuel nevertheless called upon King Saul to initiate a war against Amalek. But this was only a suggestion, not a strict obligation ordained from the Torah at this time.

This may well have been the reason why the Rambam used this incident as an example of how one should listen to a prophet even in matters which are not biblically ordained, מדאורייתא. Thus the war Saul was encouraged to wage against Amalek by the Prophet Samuel was only a suggested action, מלחמת רשות, rather than an obligation on his part.

However, the Rambam himself seems to contradict this principle elsewhere in his writings. For in the first chapter of *Hilchos Melachim*, Halacha 5, he says:

"דמינוי מלך קודם למלחמת עמלק מדכתיב, אותי שלח ה' למשחך למלך
עתה לך והכיתה את עמלק."

"The appointment of a king should precede the war against Amalek. This is evident from the charge to King Saul: 'Hashem sent me to anoint you as king...Now go and smite Amalek.' "

From this we see that Saul's war against Amalek, which was ordered by the prophet Samuel, fulfilled the mitzva of eradicating the name of Amalek as called for in the Torah. But this confuses the issue, since the Rambam used this very example to illustrate a mitzva which is not called for by the Torah under certain circumstances, and yet we are nevertheless obligated to follow the prophet's injunction to do the mitzva.

To resolve this complication we might suggest a novel approach, which is employed by the מנחת חינוך in מצוה תרד. He writes that here in the Book of Samuel we are told that King Saul was commanded to "destroy Amalek completely...kill every man... ox and sheep alike, camel and donkey alike." Yet when the Rambam describes the war against Amalek he does not mention the necessity of killing all Amalek's animals.

Thus, contends the מנחת חינוך, destroying the animals of Amalek is not biblically ordained, but is rather only a mitzva articulated by the Prophet Samuel. And so we might contend that the prophet was needed here, not for the purpose of fulfilling the mitzva of eradicating Amalek — which was already known as a result of the Torah's injunction — but rather for his suggestion that the people set out to destroy all Amalek's animals, which is a condition they would not have extrapolated from the Torah alone.

Consequently, we might suggest that what the Rambam means here, in his commentary on the Mishna, is not that the war against Amalek during the reign of King Saul was not biblically ordained, but rather that the requirement of destroying Amalek's animals was not to be found in the Torah injunction but came instead from the divine inspiration of the prophet.

With this in mind, we can now understand why the Rambam compared a war against a people to the call of the prophet to wage war against the animals, for under the circumstances neither situation was biblically ordained.

Yet if we examine this rationale, it seems rather far-fetched, since the comparison which the Rambam makes is between *a city or a people* and *the war against Amalek.* There is no specific reference made to the animals, and so the simple reading seems to indicate that we are speaking about a war against the nation of Amalek. And so we are still left with the puzzling question as to why the Rambam compared the war against Amalek to a מלחמת רשות, a war that was permissible, though not obligatory.

IV

LISTENING TO THE PROPHET IS A MITZVA IN AND OF ITSELF

We might suggest a possible solution based on the following rationale. If a prophet were to approach someone during the holiday of Succos, for example, and command him to take the lulav, or to put on tefillin, and the person complied, he would be fulfilling the mitzva of lulav or tefillin. However, he would not necessarily be credited with fulfilling the mitzva of listening to a prophet. For it would be evident that the person was obligated on his own to take the lulav or to lay tefillin, and the directive of the prophet adds no new element here.

On the other hand, if the prophet were to command the person to take the lulav or put on tefillin *this very moment,* and the person were to comply, then we could say that the person has fulfilled two separate mitzvos: the mitzva of tefillin or lulav, and the mitzva of listening to the prophet.

For now the person has the option of fulfilling the mitzva of tefillin or lulav all day. And the fact that he hastened to fulfill it now indicates that he only did so in order to obey the dictate of the prophet. Thus he receives additional credit for doing this. This is a possible explanation of what the Rambam meant in his commentary to the Mishna when he said that the prophet ordered a war against a certain city *right now!* — "הלחמו על עיר פלונית...עכשיו."

This then explains the comparison made with the situation in which the Prophet Samuel commanded King Saul to wage war against Amalek *now*, rather than at the time the Torah ordained that it was absolutely imperative. "**עתה**— לך והכיתה את עמלק" — *"Go **now** and destroy Amalek."*

Had King Saul gone to war against Amalek, he would have fulfilled the mitzva of destroying Amalek, מחיית עמלק. Yet because he was also prepared to do it right away, as the prophet enjoined him — even though this was not immediately incumbent upon him according to the Torah — he was now credited with two mitzvos: one, the mitzva of going to war against Amalek, and two, that of listening to the command of a prophet.

Consequently, we can now understand why the prophet is mentioned in this episode, even though מלחמת עמלק does not usually require the intervention of a prophet as a prerequisite to the mitzva. For here the role of the prophet Samuel adds another dimension to the mitzva, that of listening to a prophet at the moment he commands that the king go to war against Amalek.

This accounts for the Rambam's comparison of listening to a prophet in matters that are not biblically ordained to the incident of Samuel commanding King Saul to destroy Amalek. For the comparison here by the Rambam is not in regards to the actual war against Amalek, but rather as said to that aspect of embarking on a war *now.* And that element is not used as biblically dictated, but only as a mitzva to listen to the prophet.

V

THE HAFTORAH OF PARASHAS ZACHOR
THE SINS OF THE GREAT: FACING UP TO ONE'S MISTAKES

Commenting on the events that transpired here in the Book of Samuel 1:15, Chazal offer the following insights (*Ecclesiastes* VII:16):

‎" 'וירב בנחל'. אומר רב מני: על עסקי נחל בשעה שאמר לו הקב"ה לשאול‎
‎'לך והכית את עמלק' אמר, מה נפש אחת אמרה תורה הבא עגלה‎
‎ערופה, כל הנפשות הללו על אחת כמה וכמה. ואם אדם חטא בהמה מה‎
‎חטאה, ואם גדולים חטאו קטנים מה חטאו. יצאת בת קול ואמרה לו: אל‎
‎תהי צדיק הרבה..."‎

"Rav Mani said: 'Because of what happened in the valley! When the Holy One, Blessed be He, said to Saul: Now go and smite Amalek, he said: If on account of one person the Torah said perform the ceremony of the Heifer, whose neck is to be broken; how much more consideration should be given to all these persons. And if human beings sinned, what sin has the cattle committed? And if the adults have sinned, what have the little ones done? A Divine voice came forth said: 'Be not overly righteous.'"

And the Gemara continues (*Yoma* 22b):

‎"אמר רב הונא: כמה לא חלי ולא מרגיש גברא דמריה סייעיה. שאול באחת‎
‎ועלתה לו, דוד בשתים ולא עלתה לו. שאול באחת מאי היא, מעשה דאגג..."‎

"Rav Huna said: How little does he whom Hashem supports need to grieve or trouble himself. Saul sinned once and it brought him down. David sinned twice and did not bring him down. What was the one sin of Saul? The affair with Agag..."

The Gemara comments further:

‎"'בן שנה שאול במלכו.' אמר רב הונא: כבן שנה שלא טעם טעם חטא."‎

" 'Saul was a year old when he began to reign'. Rav Huna said: Like an infant of one year, who had not tasted the taste of sin."

This raises two questions:

1) Saul's wrongdoing cost him his kingdom. But why was he so severely punished; whereas King David committed two sins and he was not so severely punished?

2) There seems to be a contradiction here regarding the personality of Saul. For on the one hand, he is compared to a year-old child who had not tasted sin; yet on the other hand, he committed a sin so grievous that it caused him to lose his throne.

The commentators attempt to answer these questions in several different ways. The "ספר העקרים" by Rav Yosef Albo (in מאמר ד' פרק כ'ו) writes:

> *"According to my opinion, the difference is that David's sin did not involve a specific commandment given to him after he became king or a specific commandment given in the Torah which concerned his role as king. Rather his sin involved a commandment which he had been given in common with all men...therefore it was fitting that his punishment should be like that of common men. Saul, on the other hand, sinned regarding a specific commandment given to him by Samuel **after** he became king [and which involved his status as king]."*

There is another possible explanation for this, which is given by other classical commentators. They maintain that Saul committed a misdeed involving a kingly act, whereas David's sin did not involve a kingly act, and that is the reason he was forgiven.

The commentators compare this to a case involving two scribes, one of whom is found guilty of forging a document and the other of contracting an incestuous marriage. When the king comes to punish these two men for their crimes he will punish in a fitting manner the one who entered into a prohibited married. He will punish him, for example, with the requisite number of lashes, but he will not remove him from his post as scribe, since his crime has nothing to do with the performance of his task. The other scribe, however, in addition to being appropriately punished for his transgression, will be removed from his position as scribe, since his sin directly involved a misuse of that position. Similarly, when King Saul spared the life of Agag and thus did not succeed in cutting off the seed of Amalek, as he had been strictly commanded to do, he committed a sin which was directly related to his position as king. Therefore he deserved to be punished by being removed from office.

The Chachamei Mussar explain why Saul was punished in this way whereas David was not by pointing out that Saul did not have the moral insight to admit his wrongdoing, but rather he tried to shift the blame to others. King David, on the other hand, readily admitted his transgression when it was pointed out to him by the Prophet Nathan. His eyes were opened to his sin and he declared, "חטאתי" — "I have sinned."

This behavior exemplifies an important principle: that a leader must be prepared to admit his mistakes and make amends for them, like David did, rather than making excuses to justify his wrongdoing, as Saul attempted to do. Thus, as a result of his behavior, Saul demonstrated that he was not fit to rule; whereas David, by facing up to his failings, showed that he was prepared to receive his due punishment. Only then was he able to resume his role as leader of the Jewish nation.

KING SAUL'S SIN: HE RATIONALIZED THE MITZVOS

Saul's personality is analyzed in the preface to the שו"ת עונג יום טוב, in his commentary to *Divrei Hayamin*, I:13-14, where he writes:

"וימת שאול במעלו אשר מעל בה' על דבר ה' אשר לא שמר..."

"Saul died because of the faithlessness with which he acted towards Hashem, in that he did not obey the commands of Hashem..."

The verse here, in describing Saul's sin, uses the term "במעלו". This prompts the עונג יום טוב to ask why this particular expression was used. To answer this question, he cites the Rambam, in הלכות מעילה (פרק ח' הלכה ח') where he discusses a situation in which one has transgressed by improperly using an article that was dedicated exclusively to the service of God.

"בא וראה כמה החמירה תורה במעילה, ומה אם עצים ואבנים זעפר ואפר כיון שנקרא שם אדון העולם עליהם בדברים בלבד. נתקדשו, וכל הנוהג בהם מנהג חול מעל בה, ואפילו היה שוגג. צריך כפרה, ק"ו למצוה שחקק לנו הקב"ה שלא יבעט האדם בהן מפני שלא ידע טעמן, ולא יחפה דברים אשר לא כן על השם, ולא יחשוב בהן מחשבתו כדברי החול..."

"It is fitting for a person to meditate upon the laws of the Holy Torah and to comprehend their full meaning to the extent of his ability. Nevertheless, a law for which he finds no reason and understands no cause should not be trivialized in his eyes . . . Come and consider how strict the Torah was concerning the laws of trespass. Now if sticks and stones and earth and ashes become hallowed by words alone as soon as the Name of the Master of the Universe was invoked upon them, and anyone who treated them as profane committed a trespass and required atonement, even if he acted unwittingly. How much more so, should a person be on guard not to rebel against a commandment decreed upon us by the Holy One, Blessed be He, only because he does not understand its reason; or to heap words that are not right against the Lord. This will cause him to regard the commandments in the manner he regards ordinary affairs."

From this statement we see that the Rambam equates the situation of one who rationalizes the reason for a mitzva with one who transgresses by treating a holy article as if it were profane. This was the failure of Saul, who rationalized and made his own reckoning about the meaning and ultimate effect of the mitzvos. He failed to accept the commandments at face value, without applying his own rationale. And for this fault he was removed from serving as king and leader of the Jewish people.

This explanation might help us appreciate the directive given to King Saul by the Prophet Samuel when he told him to *"go and smite Amalek"* — "**עתה** לך והכיתה את עמלק".

Here the prophet was admonishing the king by saying in effect: "I know you very well. You have the tendency to contemplate things and apply your own reasoning to my commandments. For example, when I once told you to wait until I appear before you to offer a sacrifice, you failed to wait for me, and you offered the excuse that you saw that the people had scattered and you claimed that I did not come at the appointed time (*Samuel I* 13:11). Therefore I tell you, 'עתה', go *now*, do exactly as you are told, and do not look for logical conclusions as you did before."

But Saul did not listen and continued to apply his own rationale to the mitzvos, and for this he was severely punished.

This tendency to rationalize, which is always inappropriate when one comes to obeying the will of God, was also at work in the case of Esther. This helps us appreciate the reprimand which Mordechai gave to his niece, when he directed her to approach the king and ask him to intercede on behalf of the Jewish people, and she retorted; "I have not been summoned by the king nor has he extended to me the gold scepter"(*Megillas Esther* 4:11). By adopting this approach, said Mordechai, I see that you are following in the footsteps of your grandfather, King Saul, who also procrastinated. Therefore, you and your father's house will perish (*op. cit.* 14).

What Mordechai was really telling Esther was that now she had an opportunity to correct the blunder her grandfather Saul had made; but if she did not act, both she and her ancestor would be held accountable. When Klal Yisrael is in jeopardy, if one does not act to save them, he or she will be considered as having failed their people, and they will be held responsible for failure throughout history.

This perhaps is the reason why the Haftorah, in which the Prophet Samuel calls upon King Saul to act, is read just before the festival of Purim, for it spells out for us the challenge Esther faced, which was not to make the same mistake her grandfather Saul made by rationalizing Hashem's commands, but rather to have complete faith in Him and to act promptly to save the Jewish people.

This was the approach adopted by the R' Yisroel, the Rebbe of Rizhin. The story is told that once, the Chidushei HaRim, who was then a young man, came to the visit the holy Rebbe of Rizhin, and he asked him the following question.

We are told by the Midrash that King Saul, by allowing Agag to live, caused Haman to threaten the very existence of the Jewish people. How did Saul rationalize his decision to let Agag live? And how did he then have the audacity to ask the Prophet Samuel: "הקימותי את דבר ה'?" — "Have I fulfilled Hashem's words?"

The Rebbe of Rizhin answered as follows: We know that at the time of Mordechai and Esther, Bnai Yisrael accepted the Torah once again. This time they did so with a complete commitment of their own, which was not the case at Mt. Sinai, where they were coerced to accept the Torah by Hashem holding the mountain suspended over their heads and threatening to lower it upon them — "כפאו עליהם הר כגיגית".

This new commitment which they now demonstrated, a result of their goodwill, arose as a response to the evil designs of the wicked Haman. Thus, one could claim that Haman was influential in causing Bnai Yisrael to accept the Torah most willingly. Therefore, this was how Saul defended his actions to the Prophet Samuel: "I saw by means of divine inspiration that a Haman would descend from this Agag and he would be the cause of Bnai Yisrael accepting the Torah again."

This was the way the Rebbe of Rizhin explained the statement made by Saul: "הקימותי את דבר ה'" — "*I have **caused** the **word** of Hashem to be now accepted most willingly.*" In this way Saul justified what he had done and pleaded that he should not be judged harshly for his actions.

The Chidushei HaRim responded to this interpretation of the Rizhiner Rebbe by asking: If this is so, then why was Saul punished? The Rebbe answered as follows:

One is obligated to do what he was commanded to do by Hashem. He must not seek to apply divine inspiration in order to ascertain through prophecy what future results will eventuate from his actions. In keeping with this, we find in the Gemara in *Berachos* 9a that King Hezekiah was reprimanded for making this very mistake. And so, too, when Saul was commanded to kill Agag, he should have done so immediately without trying to justify or defend his actions.

Were Esther's words redundant?

I n the Megillah we read : "וצומו עלי ואל תאכלו ואל תשתו" — *"And fast for me, do not eat or drink."* (*Esther* 4:16)

Why the redundancy, we may ask? For surely, if Esther commanded that the Jews of Shushan fast, doesn't this mean that they should neither eat nor drink?

There is a possible answer to this question, if we consider something the Apter Rebbe once said about fasting. In general, he was not a great advocate of fasting, and on one occasion he remarked: "If it were up to me, I would nullify all fasts except for Tisha B'Av and Yom Kippur. For who could possibly bring himself to eat on Tisha B'Av; and who would want to eat on Yom Kippur?"

Similarly, in this spirit we can understand the meaning behind Esther's words. When she asked her fellow Jews to fast, she was pleading with them not to merely follow by rote the ritual of fasting, but rather she wanted then to sense the seriousness of the situation, and to engage in the deepest repentance. If they succeeded in doing this, then who could eat, and who would wish to drink at such a time? For at this crucial moment, their lives hung in the balance, and they had to turn to the Heavenly King to save them.

This suggests an answer to a similar question. After Esther proclaimed that all the Jews should neither eat nor drink, she adds (*Esther* 4:16): "גם אני ונערתי אצום כן" — *"And I along with my maids, will also fast."*

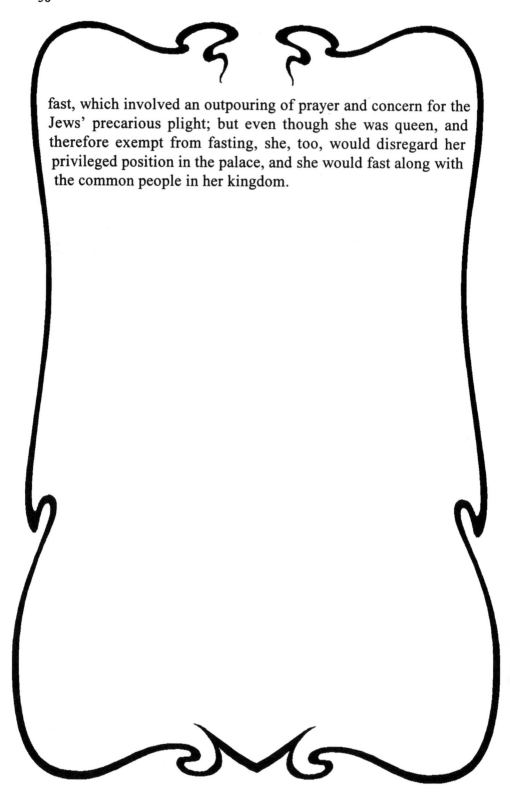

fast, which involved an outpouring of prayer and concern for the
Jews' precarious plight; but even though she was queen, and
therefore exempt from fasting, she, too, would disregard her
privileged position in the palace, and she would fast along with
the common people in her kingdom.

CHAPTER THREE

Ta'anis Esther

I

ESTHER FASTED FOR THREE DAYS IN NISSAN

The *Megillas Esther* (4:15-16) relates how Esther instructed Mordechai to "assemble all the Jews in Shushan and fast on my behalf for three days; neither eat nor drink, and my maidens and I will do the same."

”ותאמר אסתר להשיב אל מרדכי: לך כנוס את כל היהודים הנמצאים בשושן וצומו עלי ואל תאכלו ואל תשתו שלשת ימים לילה ויום גם אני ונערתי אצום כן...“

From here we see that the Fast of Esther continued for three days. Today, when we commemorate that fast, why do we fast for only a single day, rather than three days? Indeed, we know from *Mesechtas Sofrim* 21:1, that those who lived in Eretz Yisrael customarily fasted for three days:

”מפסיקין לפורים כמנהג רבותינו שבמערב להתענות שלשת ימי צום מרדכי ואסתר פרודות ולאחר פורים שני וחמישי ושני.“

"It is the custom of our Rabbis in the west [Eretz Yisrael] to fast the three days of the fast of Mordechai and Esther intermittently, that is, after Purim on Monday, Thursday and Monday."

The question arises: if we are to emulate the Fast of Esther, why do we not fast for three days, and why do we not commemorate the fast *after* Purim, as the early Rabbis did?

The *Shulchan Aruch*, in אור"ח סימן תרפ"ו ס"ק ב', specifies that we are to fast for one day on the thirteenth of Adar: "מתענין בי"ג באדר". But why do we fast in the month of Adar at all? For in the above-mentioned *Mesechtas Sofrim* 2:2, we find that the Fast of Esther took place, not in Adar, but in Nissan.

”ולמה אין מתענין אותן בחודש ניסן. מפני שבאחד בניסן הוקם המשכן וי"ב נשיאים הקריבו קרבנות לי"ב יום, יום לכל שבט ושבט, וכל אחד הי' עשה ביומו יום טוב. וכן לעתיד לבא עתיד המקדש להבנות בניסן לקיים מה שנאמר (קהלת א') אין כל חדש תחת השמש.“

"And why do they [in Eretz Yisrael] fast in the month of Nissan? Because on the first of Nissan the Tabernacle was erected and the twelve princes offered their sacrifices during the first twelve days of the month; a day for each tribe, and everyone held a festival on their day. Furthermore, in the days to come the Sanctuary will be rebuilt in the month of Nissan, to confirm that which is stated: 'There is nothing new under the sun.' "

This solves the problem of why the fast is not observed in Nissan, as was the Fast of Esther, yet the question still remains why we fast for only one day rather than three.

II

THE PEOPLE GATHERED TO FAST ON THE THIRTEENTH OF ADAR

This one-day fast on the thirteenth of Adar, which we call the Fast of Esther, is not explicitly mentioned in *Kisvei HaKodesh*, the Scriptures, nor in the Talmud. It is, however, mentioned in the שאילתות דרב אחאי גאון (שאילתא ס"ז) where we find the following:

"אבל תענית...כולן מתענין בשלשה עשר באדר. דאמר שמואל בר רב
יצחק: שלשה עשר זמן קהילה לכל הוא, שנאמר: ושאר היהודים אשר
במדינת המלך נקהלו ועמדו על נפשם ביום שלשה עשר לחודש אדר. מאי
'קהילה'? יום תענית ומאי 'יום כניסה' שמתכנסין בו ויושבין בתענית
ומבקשין רחמים."

"The fast day was observed on the thirteenth of Adar, as Shmuel, the son of Rav Yitzchak said: 'The thirteenth is a time of gathering for everyone.' What is meant by 'gathering'? A fast day; a day on which the people gathered to observe a fast and to petition for mercy."

Thus, although this fast of the thirteenth of Adar is not mentioned explicitly in the Gemara, yet it is alluded to in the Mishna at the beginning of *Mesechtas Megillah*, where we read:

"מגילה נקראת בי"א, בי"ב, בי"ג, בי"ד, בט"ו לא פחות ולא יותר."

*"The Megillah may be read on the eleventh, twelfth, thirteenth,
fourteenth and fifteenth of Adar, but not earlier or later."*

Although only the fourteenth and fifteenth of Adar are spelled out in
the *Megillah* as being the appropriate time for reading the *Megillah*, yet
Chazal explain that one may read the *Megillah* on two additional two
days as well. They derive this from the verse in *Esther* (יט:לא) which
states:

"לקיים את ימי הפורים האלה בזמניהם."

"To observe this holiday in its appropriate time."

Thus the fourteenth and fifteenth of Adar are explicitly mentioned as
appropriate days for reading the Megillah, whereas the appropriateness
of the eleventh and twelfth is derived from this phrase, "בזמניהם". As for
the thirteenth, the Gemara tells us that this day requires a separate verse
to teach us that the *Megillah* may be read on that day as well. This day is
referred to as a day when all the people gathered to fast and pray:
"י"ג, זמן קהילה לכל היא" — *"For on this day all gathered for the purpose
of fasting."* This shows that the thirteenth of Adar, too, was an appropriate
time for the *Megillah* to be read.

An explicit reference to the thirteenth of Adar as the day on which to
observe *Ta'anis Esther* is made by Rabbenu Tam, cited in the commentary
of the Rosh (דף ב' אות א'). There we read the following:

"ופירש רבינו תם 'זמן קהלה לכל היא' שהכל מתאספין **לתענית אסתר**
ובאים בני הכפרים לעיירות לומר סליחות ותחנונים לפי שבו נקהלו
לעמוד על נפשם והיו צריכים רחמים. וכן מצינו במשה שעשה תענית
כשנלחם בעמלק דכתיב ומשה ואהרן עלו ראש הגבעה ודרשינן במסכת
תענית מכאן לתענית צבור שצריך שלשה. מכאן נראה לרבינו תם **סעד**
לתענית אסתר שאנו עושין כמו שעשה בימי מרדכי ואסתר כשנקהלו
היהודים לעמוד על נפשם. ולא מצינו לו סמך בשום מקום אלא בכאן..."

*"Rabbenu Tam explained the statement 'they all gathered' to
mean that all gathered to observe the Fast of Esther, and those*

who lived in the villages came to town to say Selichos [the Penitential prayers) and to present petitions. For it was on this day, the thirteenth of Adar, that the Jews of Esther's time gathered to defend their lives, and they were in need of Heaven's mercy. Similarly, we find that when Moshe engaged Amalek in battle, he and Bnai Yisrael also fasted.

Thus it seems to Rabbenu Tam that the Gemara here, being interpreted in this way can be cited to support the practice of Ta'anis Esther which Jews observe today, just as they did in those days when they had to defend themselves. And indeed, we do not find any other source for the Fast of Esther except from here..."

Thus it becomes clear that the observance of *Ta'anis Esther* does not commemorate the three days on which Esther and her maidens as well as all the Jews of Shushan fasted, but rather it marks the fast day that took place the day before the fourteenth of Adar. This explains why we observe only one day of fasting and not three. Yet, several troubling questions still remain.

1) If this fast commemorates the fast which took place prior to the fourteenth of Adar, why refer to it as the Fast of Esther, *Ta'anis Esther*, since it had nothing to do with Esther?

2) If indeed this is the source for *Ta'anis Esther*, that prior to going out to battle it was customary for the people to fast, then why are we called upon to fast today, when we are not engaged in battle or any special undertaking that requires penitential prayers and fasting.

III

WHEN WAS TA'ANIS ESTHER ESTABLISHED?

It would seem from the above quoted שאילתות and Rabbenu Tam that the Fast of Esther was already being observed as a fast day as far back as the time of Mordechai and Esther. The Ra'avad seems to concur with his opinion in a statement quoted by the Ran in his introduction to *Mesechtas Ta'anis*:

"אלא שהוא [הראב"ד] ז"ל כתב די"ג אינו דומה לשאר תעניות דלזכרון
הוא לנס שנעשה בו. ועוד שיש לנו סמך בכתוב שאמר: וכאשר קימו על
נפשם דברי הצומות, לומר שכשם שקבלו עליהם לעשות יום טוב כן קבלו
עליהם דברי הצומות וזעקתם, כלומר לעשות תענית בכל שנה ושנה..."

"The source for the fast is in the words of the Megillah, 'as they had undertaken for themselves and their descendants the matter of fasting and supplication.' As they accepted upon themselves to observe the holiday [of Purim], so they undertook the matters of fasting and supplication, which means to observe a holiday of fasting each year at this time."

From here we see that according to the Ra'avad, the Fast of Esther was already established in the days of Mordechai and Esther. However, some commentators would not include Rabbenu Tam among those giving sanction to this view. For example, the Ritba in *Mesechtas Megillah* 2a, writes in the name of Rabbenu Tam:

"ופי' רבינו תם ז"ל שיום י"ג נקהלו עם מרדכי ואסתר להתענות לפי שהם
עומדים במלחמה."

"On the thirteenth of Adar, in the time of Mordechai and Esther, the Jews gathered to fast, for they found themselves in the midst of a battle."

We can conclude from this quotation, cited in the name of Rabbenu Tam, that he was not giving a source for our observation regarding *Ta'anis Esther*. Rather, he was explaining the statement made in the Gemara that the thirteenth of Adar does not require a separate verse in order to be included among the days on which one may read the *Megillah*. This explanation was that since people were accustomed to fast on that day, it was therefore an appropriate day for reading the *Megillah*, for it is a day with a special status and significance. However, we are in no way to interpret the statement of Rabbenu Tam as giving an authoritative source for the practice of *Ta'anis Esther* on this day.

Consequently, if we accept this view of Rabbenu Tam, we can conclude that the thirteenth of Adar was instituted as a fast day at a much later date and for an entirely different reason, which we will discuss further. And so, even though this is not the source for establishing this day as *Ta'anis Esther*; yet those who later did establish it as a fast day find support, סעד, from the fact that even during the time of Mordechai and Esther, this day was observed as a fast day.

In support of this view, the Avudraham writes:

"ואינו מפורש בכתוב ולא בתלמוד, אלא החכמים האחרונים תקנוהו
אחר חתימת התלמוד".

> *"Nowhere is the Fast of Esther mentioned in the Scriptures or the Talmud; rather it was the Sages of a later period, after the conclusion of the writing of the Talmud, who established this fast day."*

IV

FASTING THE DAY BEFORE A HOLIDAY IS USUALLY FORBIDDEN

The Rishonim raise several important questions regarding the issue of fasting before a holiday from the Mishna in *Mesechtas Ta'anis* 15b:

"כל הכתוב במגילת תענית 'דלא למספד'. לפניו אסור לאחריו מותר.
רבי יוסי אומר לפניו אסור לאחריו מותר".

> *"For every minor festival recorded in Megillas Ta'anis [a chronicle enumerating all the eventful days in the history of the Jewish people on which mourning and fasting are forbidden] there exists the restriction "not to eulogize" on that day. It is forbidden the day before as well, but it is permitted the day after. R' Yose says: It is forbidden before the festival, but it is permitted the day after it."*

Among the holidays recorded in the *Megillas Ta'anis* are Purim and Chanukah. Although Purim was already established by the *Megillah* as a holiday, it was also recorded in the *Megillas Ta'anis* to forbid fasting on both days of Purim and Shushan Purim, the fourteenth and the fifteenth of Adar. This leads us to ask how we were able to establish the thirteenth of Adar as a fast day, *Ta'anis Esther*, since this is the day before the fourteenth, which is Purim. For the halacha clearly states that fasting is forbidden on the day before a holiday.

However, if we accept that the fast of the thirteenth of Adar was established, together with the holiday of Purim, at the time of Mordechai and Esther, then this means that this fast was already in existence before the *Megillas Ta'anis* was written. Consequently, the law which stipulates "לפניו" will no longer apply to this particular fast.

The truth is that we really do not have a problem regarding the law of "לפניו" even if we were to say that the Fast of Esther was established much later, because that law itself was instituted at the time of the Gaonim, חתימת התלמוד. This means that the halacha follows the opinion that all the fast days and holidays recorded in the *Megillas Ta'anis* are no longer celebrated after the Destruction of the Temple, "בטלה מגילת תענית".

And even though the halacha states that the holiday of Purim was never nullified, but rather remained in existence even after the *Megillas Ta'anis* was nullified, the prohibition against holding a fast day before the holiday was no longer in effect and thus the Fast of Esther was allowed on the thirteenth of Adar.

Furthermore, the Netziv (in his classic commentary to the שאילתות דרב אחאי גאון), contends that even if the fast of the thirteenth of Adar had been established at the time when the *Megillas Ta'anis* was written, yet the halacha of forbidding a fast before a holiday, "לפניו", is not an issue here because all commentators agree that this fast need not be observed on that particular day. Prior to the writing of the *Megillas Ta'anis*, the Fast of Esther may have been observed on the most appropriate day, that is, the thirteenth of Adar; but after the *Megillas Ta'anis* was written this fast day was changed to the eleventh of Adar (even though the twelfth of

Adar, according to the *Megillas Ta'anis*, was also considered a holiday
— יום טורייננס, and thus fasting was forbidden). Thus, once again we
encounter the problem of לפניו.

V

THE RAMBAM: TWO POSSIBLE VIEWS

The Rambam's position regarding this issue depends on how we read
the text of the *Hilchos Ta'anis* 5:4, where we appear to have two different
readings. The Rambam writes as follows:

"וארבעת ימי הצומות האלו הרי הן מפורשין בקבלה, צום הרביעי וצום
החמישי וצום השביעי וצום העשירי. הרביעי, זה שבעה עשר בתמוז.
שהוא בחדש הרביעי. וצום החמישי זה תשעה באב שהוא בחדש החמישי.
וצום השביעי זה שלשה בתשרי שהוא בחדש השביעי. וצום העשירי זה
עשרה בטבת שהוא בחדש העשירי."

*"These four fasts are explicitly mentioned in the prophetic
tradition [Zechariah 8:19], 'the fast of the fourth [month];
the fast of the fifth [month]; the fast of the seventh [month]
and the fast of the tenth[month].'*

*'The fast of the fourth' refers to the fast of the seventeenth of
Tammuz, which falls in the fourth month. 'The fast of the fifth'
alludes to the fast of Tisha B'Av, in the fifth month [Av]. 'The
fast of the seventh' refers to the fast of the third of Tishrei
[צום גדליה] which occurs in the seventh month [Tishrei]. And
'the fast of the tenth' alludes to the fast of the tenth of Teves,
which occurs in the tenth month of the calendar year."*

In the next halacha, הלכה ד', the Rambam writes:

"ונהגו כל ישראל בזמנים אלו להתענות, ובשלשה עשר באדר, זכר
לתענית שהתענו בימי המן שנאמר דברי הצומות וזעקתם."

*"And the entire Jewish people follow the custom of fasting at
these times and on the thirteenth of Adar, in commemoration
of the fasts that the people took upon themselves in the time
of Haman, as mentioned in Esther (9:31) 'the matters of the
fast and the supplications...' "*

According to the reading of this text it would seem that the Rambam
here is continuing his statement from הלכה ד', which is:

1) The other fasts have the authority of received tradition, מדברי קבלה,
   and he finds their sources in verses from the books of the Prophets.
   Thus, in addition to these four fasts, there is also the Fast of Esther,
   which finds its source in the words from the *Megillas Esther* (9:31):
   "דברי הצומות וזעקתם"— *"the matters of fasting and supplication"*.

2) The Fast of Esther was already being observed in the days of
   Mordechai and Esther, and thus it was not a later innovation.

This approach raises the following difficulties, though:

1) HaRav Yosef Dov Soloveitchik made an interesting deduction from
   the Rambam's statement that *Ta'anis Esther* commemorates the fast
   "the Jews fasted in the days of Haman". Since Haman was executed
   in the month of Nissan, eleven months prior to the battle which was
   fought in Adar, Rav Soloveitchik concludes that this reference of the
   Rambam's must allude to the fast which Esther observed in *Nissan*
   before she entered the throne room of the king to make her request.
   Consequently, he concludes that *Ta'anis Esther* commemorates the
   three day fast which Esther embarked on in Nissan.

2) Furthermore, if we accept that the source for this fast is the verse,
   "דברי הצומות וזעקתם", why does the Rambam say that this is only
   "customary" among the Jewish people, "ונהגו", for surely it should
   be considered not a custom but rather an obligation, since the Jews
   at that time took the fast upon themselves from that time onwards, as
   we know from the words of the *Megillas Esther*?

Based on the Rambam's authoritative manuscripts, we find another possible version of his position: According to another text, the connecting vav (ו' החיבור) is not found before the word "בי"ג" — "*on the thirteenth*"; and so now the text reads as follows:

"*Nowadays Jews customarily fast on the thirteenth of Adar.*" This means that the halacha regarding the thirteenth of Adar is limited only to the Fast of Esther and does not apply to the other four fast days. Thus we might conclude that *Ta'anis Esther* is only a "*minhag*", a custom, rather than an obligation, and this is indeed the contention of the Rabbenu Tam and the other Rishonim.

However, this version of the text is not without its problems, for if according to the Rambam, *Ta'anis Esther* is viewed only as a custom, why did the Rambam conclude its discussion by quoting the *pasuk* of "מדברי הצומות וזעקתם"?

Wouldn't this indicate that this fast day is established by received tradition, מדברי קבלה, and it finds its source in the prophetic writings. Wouldn't it have been more appropriate, then, for the Rambam to have concluded his argument by quoting the *pasuk* of "וצום עלי שלשת ימים", which also alludes to the fast of Esther which took place at the time of Mordechai and Esther, but was purely voluntary (See ספר נוראות הרב, חלק שלישי, עמ' 12-15).

VI

THE FAST COMMEMORATES GOD'S PROVIDENCE

Purim is not a holiday which commemorates our being saved from catastrophe, but rather it affirms the promise given us by Hashem Himself that when we petition Him and cry out for help He will listen to our cries and save us from all danger. HaRav Turtzin expresses this view in his sefer "קונטרס חנוכה-פורים", based on the views of the previously mentioned commentators. He quotes, for instance, the Rambam, who writes as follows in his introduction to למנין המצוות:

"ויש מצות אחרות שנתחדשו אחר מתן תורה. וקבעו אותם נביאים
וחכמים ופשטו בכל ישראל כגון מקרא מגילה וכו' אלא כך אנו אומרים
שהנביאים עם ב"ד תקנום וצוה לקרות המגילה בעותה כדי להזכיר
שבחיו של הקב"ה ותשועות שעשה לנו והי' קרוב לשועתנו כדי לברכו
ולהללו וכדי להודיע לדורות הבאים שאמת מה שהבטיחנו בתורה ומי גוי
גדול אשר לו ה' קרובים אליו וגו'."

Here the Rambam explains that after the Giving of the Torah on
Mount Sinai the Sages and Prophets of Yisrael instituted several
additional mitzvos, such as the reading of the *Megilla*h on Purim, to
express our appreciation for Hashem's abiding concern for us as a
nation and to acknowledge that He has always saved us when we
cried out to Him.

This is also true in relation to the Fast of Esther. That fast reinforces
this concept that Hashem is near whenever we call out to Him. Proof
of this approach is the halacha, cited in the שאילתות דרב אחאי גאון,
פרשת ויקהל, where we read:

"ובזמן שחל י"ג באדר להיות בערב שבת או בשבת מקדימין ומתעניין
בחמישי בשבת מפני שהוא נס, ונס מקדימין ולא מאחרין. אבל ט' באב
בזמן שחל להיות בשבת מאחרין ומתעניין לאחר השבת מפני שהי' בו
פורענות ופורענות מאחרין ולא מקדימין."

"If the thirteenth of Adar falls on Friday or Shabbos, then we
push the fast day forward to the preceding Thursday, since a
miracle transpired then, and regarding a miracle we precede
rather than delay. On the other hand, if the Ninth of Av, for
instance, should fall on a Shabbos, we rather delay the fast
day and observe it the following day, for it commemorates a
punishment, and in such cases we are to push off the fast day
to Sunday, and so delay it rather than precede it."

This halacha and the reason for it is spelled out even more clearly in
the sefer "ארחות חיים" where we are told:

"דמה שנהגו להתענות בי"ג שהוא יום שלפניהם, לפי שלא נאסר אלא
תענית צער אבל התענית שאנו עושין אינו אלא זכר לתענית אסתר
ושיזכור כל אדם שהבורא ית' רואה ושומע כל איש בעת צרתו כאשר יתענה
אליו וישוב אליו בכל לבבו כאשר עשה לאבותינו בימים ההם בזמן הזה."

*"We fast on the thirteenth, although it is a day before Purim
and should therefore be forbidden (based on the halacha
that all days which precede a holiday mentioned in the
Megillas Ta'anis are forbidden). But the reason we fast
nevertheless is that only for a fast that commemorates an
ominous occasion is it forbidden to hold a fast day prior
to the holiday. However, the Fast of Esther reinforces the
fact that the Holy One, Blessed be He, is ever present,
listening and He offers salvation to those who petition Him,
as He did to our forefathers and as He did in those days at
this time."*

VII

PUTTING IT ALL TOGETHER

To summarize our discussion, we might say that *Ta'anis Esther*
was initially observed as a memorial to the three-day fast of Esther
that took place in the month of Nissan. Subsequently, however, the
fast was transferred to the month of Adar, because of the consideration
stated in *Mesechtas Sofrim,* that in the month of Nissan we do not
fast, to honor the fact that the dedication of the Mishkan took place in
this month.

As time went on and people were no longer physically able to
observe a three-day fast, only a single day was observed (See the
commentary of the Bais Yosef here). The thirteenth of Adar was chosen
as the fast day, since this day and its fast remind us that Hashem is
close to all who call out to Him. For it was on this very day, the
thirteenth of Adar, at the time of Mordechai and Esther, that the Jewish

people went out to war against their enemies, and they placed their trust in God's promise that He would help them in their time of need. And so, too, when Esther fasted, she had full confidence that the King of kings would hear her plea and help her people. This, then, is how we are to understand the statement of Rabbenu Tam.

Rabbenu Tam explains why it is fitting to read the *Megillah* on this day, based on the verse which tells us: "י"ג זמן קהלה לכל היא". Since at the time of Mordechai and Esther they defended themselves and fasted, therefore this is a suitable day on which to read the *Megillah*, for on that day the Jewish people fasted and both of these events allude to the same concept, that Hashem listens to His people whenever they call upon Him. And this should reaffirm the assurance given by Hashem Himself that He will help whenever He is petitioned.

Consequently, we fast on the thirteenth of Adar, not to commemorate the events that took place on that day, but rather as a substitute day for the original fast of Esther, that three-day fast. And therefore, Rabbenu Tam points out that the fast at the time the Jews of Persia went out to battle on the thirteenth of Adar in Mordechai and Esther's day is a support, "סעד", for the logical reason why this particular day was chosen as a day to substitute for the original fast days of Esther. However, in no way does Rabbenu Tam believe that the fast we observe as *Ta'anis Esther* is due to the events of the thirteenth of Adar in Esther's day.

Once these points have been established, we can now answer our previous questions.

1) It is justified to call this day "*Ta'anis Esther*", for, as we have explained, this day served as a substitute for the original Fast of Esther.

2) Nowadays, we do not fast for three days as Esther did, because times have changed and we are not able to maintain such a rigorous fast. However, we fast for at least a single day.

VIII

THE REMAH'S DECISION

This explains the position of the Remah in regard to the following halacha. In סימן רפ"ו סעיף ב', the *Shulchan Aruch* informs us that we are required to fast on the thirteenth of Adar. However, the Remah adds this amendment:

"ותענית זה אינו חובה לכן יש להקל בו לעת הצורך כגון מעוברת או מניקת וכו'."

"Because this fast is not such an obligatory one, we are therefore lenient when it is necessary; for example, in the instance of a pregnant woman or a nursing mother, that they need not fast."

The question is raised: Why did the Remah have to point out that we are lenient in certain instances regarding this fast, based on the fact that this fast is not an obligatory one. For isn't it the case that even on regular fast days which are obligatory, we are always lenient regarding pregnant women and nursing mothers, and they need not fast?

The answer may be that other fast days commemorate tragic events which befell the Jewish people throughout history; whereas the Fast of Esther is celebrated for an entirely different reason. It commemorates that Hashem came to our aid when we called upon him in our time of need. And thus it demonstrates our commitment to and belief that He is ever present and that He gives us the Divine assurance that He will always respond to our distress and bring us salvation.

Such a momentous reason for a fast might lead us to believe that even a pregnant or nursing woman should fast on such a day. But the Remah specifically addressed this issue in order to emphasize that this is not the case, and in fact we are lenient in this situation (See the sefer "דברי שירה" by Rav Eliyahu Levin, Purim, סימן ד').

Our Heavenly Father

When Queen Esther was informed that Klal Yisrael was in imminent danger, she ordered Mordechai to *"Go and assemble all the Jews to be found in Shushan"* — "לך כנוס את כל היהודים הנמצאים בשושן וגו'" (*Esther* 4:16).

The classic interpretation of her words is that by demanding that all the Jews assemble, Esther was contradicting Haman's slander that the Jews were *"a people scattered and dispersed"* (*Esther* 3:8). In this way she unified the Jewish people both in body and spirit.

Similarly, on Mondays and Thursdays after the completion of the Torah reading the *chazzan,* the prayer leader, adds four petitions which all begin with the words: "יהי רצון מלפני אבינו שבשמים" — *"May it be Your will, our Father in Heaven."*

A fifth petition is then added, as the congregation says in unison: "אחינו כל בית ישראל הנתונים בצרה וכו'" — This is a plea for Hashem's mercy on behalf of our fellow Jews, wherever they might be, who find themselves in situations of danger.

The Belzer Rebbe asks why in the first four petitions we preface the prayer with the words: "יהי רצון מלפני אבינו שבשמים", whereas in the fifth and final petition we omit the words "יהי רצון" ?

The answer he suggests is that when Jews are united and concerned for one another, this is an "עת רצון", a time when the Almighty looks favorably upon our petitions, and we bring His good will upon ourselves.

This was the purpose behind Esther's command to Mordechai to unite all the Jews for the common purpose of praying that they be delivered from Haman's evil decrees. For even though it was a time of הסתר פנים, when the Divine Countenance was hidden from human view, Esther realized that if she could unite all the Jews in a common spiritual purpose, it might succeed in dispelling the Divine Concealment. This would create a moment of Divine good will, עת רצון, during which the Almighty would hear their petition and answer their common prayer by bringing about their salvation.

CHAPTER FOUR

The Inclusion of Megillas Esther in the Kisvei HaKodesh

I

The Book of Esther: for all generations

The Rambam, in *Hilchos Megillah* 2:8 tells us:

"כל ספרי הנביאים וכל הכתובים עתידין ליבטל לימות המשיח, חוץ
ממגילת אסתר, והרי היא קיימת כחמשה חמשי תורה וכהלכות של תורה
שבעל פה, שאינן בטלין לעולם."

*"All the books of the Prophets and all the Holy Writings will
be nullified in the Messianic era, with the exception of the
Book of Esther. It will continue to exist, as will the five books
of the Torah and the halachos of the Oral law, which will
never be nullified."*

This raises an obvious question: why is the Book of Esther different
from the other books of the Kisvei HaKodesh? Why will it alone not be
nullified? The Alshich answers by citing the Gemara in *Mesechtas
Megillah* 7:1, where we are told:

"שלחה להם אסתר לחכמים, 'כתבוני לדורות.' שלחו לה: הלא כתבתי
לך שלישים. שלישים ולא רבעים. עד שמצאו לו מקרא כתוב בתורה,
'כתוב זאת זכרון בספר.' 'כתוב זאת' מה שכתוב כאן ובמשנה תורה...
'זכרון' מה שכתוב בנביאים. 'בספר' מה שכתוב במגילה."

*"Esther submitted the following request to the Sages:
'Write me [the story of the miracle of Purim] for all
generations [she asked that the Book of Esther be
incorporated in the Tanach, in the Kisvei HaKodesh]. They
sent her the following reply: It is written: 'Have I not
written for you three times? (Mishle 22); three times and
not four.' "*

Rashi explains that the prophet here taught that the story of Amalek
may be mentioned only three times and no more. Based on this concept
the Sages were opposed to the thought of including the *Book of Esther* in
the *Kisvei HaKodesh,* until they found a verse in the Torah which provided

for it to be written (*Shemos* 17:14): "כתוב זאת זכרון בספר" — *"Write this as a memorial in a book."*

"Write this," refers to the passages about Amalek, the ones written here (ibid., verses 8-16) and in *Devarim* 25:17-19. *"For a memorial,"* refers to the passage written about Amalek in the Prophets. *"In a book,"* refers to what is written in the *Megillah*.

The Alshich contends that since it is the Torah itself that called for the *Megillah* to be written, just as the Torah will never be nullified, so too, that which the Torah called for — the writing of the *Megillah* — also will never be nullified.

This leads the "מראה פנים", in his commentary to the Yerushalmi, to raise the following question. According to the Alshich's explanation, why will the Book of Shmuel, which also includes the story of Amalek, be nullified in the Messianic era, for doesn't it too find its source in the Torah? When the Torah wrote "זכרון" — *"for a memorial"*, it alluded to the Prophets, including the Book of Shmuel. Therefore one might expect that this book would not be nullified.

To resolve this difficulty, we might suggest that there is an important difference in having the story of Amalek included in the Writings (כתובים) rather than in the Prophets (נביאים). What the Alshich meant when he used the key word "בספר" was not that the Torah was dictating that Amalek be included in the Writings, but rather that a separate book dealing with the issue of Amalek should be written. The word "בספר" — *"in a book"*, indicates this and since this directive was ordered by the Torah itself, it can never be nullified, just as the Torah itself will never be nullified. However, committing to writing prophecy and holy writings is only justified when they are part of either the Prophets or the Holy Writings.

This explains why we place the Book of Esther in the category of Holy Writings. However, regarding the inclusion of the story of Amalek in the Book of Shmuel, the Torah never commanded us to write a separate book and call it "Prophets". Rather, what the Torah meant was that we should not forget to include the story of Amalek. This means that in the future, when all the books of the Prophets will be nullified, the story of Amalek will be nullified as well, for we will no longer need a reminder of it. A similar approach is taken by HaRav Chaim Zimmerman, my rebbe, of blessed memory, in his classic sefer, "בנין הלכה" (ע' יא).

We can now suggest an answer to the question why the Gemara here, based on the key word "בספר", states: "What is written in the *Megillah*," when it should have rather said: "What is written in the Holy Writings." In light of our explanation of the Alshich — that the Torah never commanded us to write a book of Holy Writings and call it the Book of Esther — we can say that on the contrary, a separate book was commanded, namely the *Megillah*, which incidentally belongs to the category of Holy Writings. Therefore the Gemara here mentions "מגילה" and not "כתובים".

II

WRITING PROPHECY

Our justification for including *Megillas Esther* in the *Kisvei HaKodesh* is based on the verse, "כתוב זאת זכרון בספר" — *"Write this as a remembrance in a book"*. "כתוב זאת" alludes to what is written in the Torah; whereas "זכרון" alludes to what is written in the Prophets. And "בספר" alludes to the *Megillas Esther*.

The Maharsha here goes into detail to explain each of these phrases and their accompanying allusions. "כתוב זאת" alludes to the Torah, based on the key word here, "זאת", which we find in *Devarim* 4:44. "וזאת התורה אשר שם משה" — *"This is the Torah which Moshe placed before Bnai Yisrael."*

"זכרון" alludes to the Prophets, based on the verse at the end of the Book of Malachi (3:16): "ויכתוב ספר זכרון לפניו" — *"And a book of remembrance was written before Him."*

"בספר" refers to the *Megillah* and *Kesuvim*, the Holy Writings, as stated in the *Megillah* itself (Esther 9:32). "ונכתב בספר וגו' אסתר ומאמר" — *"Esther's ordinance...was recorded in the book."*

We can shed light on this schematization by examining an insight of Rav Chaim Brisker, recorded by his son, Rav Velvel, in the sefer "הגר"ח והגרי"ז על הש"ס" (חלק ג', בסוגיה של ח' פסוקים). The difference between the Prophets and the Writings is that in the books of the Prophets, the divine communication received by the prophet was first *spoken* by him and only later *committed to writing*. In the Writings, on the other hand, the prophecies were first *written* in a scroll and only later *read* from their manuscripts. (For a fuller discussion of this matter, see *The Commentators' Gift of Torah*, pp. 89-93.)

With this in mind, we can now explain the above discussion regarding the phrases and their allusions. "זאת" alludes to the Torah, and Chazal point out that Moshe used both phrases: "**כה** אמר ה'" and "**זה** הדבר", whereas all the other prophets only said "כה אמר".

משה נתנבא ב'**כה אמר ה**'' והנביאים נתנבאו ב'**כה אמר ה**'' מוסיף עליהם משה שנתנבא בלשון 'זה **הדבר**'.''

"זה" alludes to Torah, which was written and prophesied by Moshe alone. "זה" suggests it is as if the prophet was pointing to something he saw clearly. This refers to the highest level of prophecy, which was attained by Moshe Rabbenu alone among all the other prophets. This clear prophetic vision is called "אספקלריה המאירה", and is contrasted with the unclear, refracted revelation, "אספקלריה שאינה מאירה", which was the most any other prophet ever attained.

"זכרון" refers to the books of the Prophets, for they needed to commit their prophetic visions to memory, since, as we have pointed out, the prophets first communicated their revelations orally and only later did they write them down.

"בספר" alludes to the Holy Writings, *Kesuvim*, which requires the prophetic revelation to be first written down. Therefore, the Torah uses the word "בספר" to signify these Writings.

III

Writing about Amalek: only three times

The classic commentators explain why the Gemara here is difficult to understand. For we are faced with the restriction of "שלישים ולא רבעים", the legal stipulation that the story of Amalek can be written only three times, but not four. If the Torah (in *Beshallah*) and the Mishna Torah (in *Ki Tetze*) are counted together as "one time", we have no problem with this. However, if each of these are to be counted separately, then we certainly have a problem. The Sages initially approached this matter by considering each of them separately. But how does the verse of "כתוב זאת" give us the impression that we are to view them as separate entities? This question was addressed by the פני יהושע, who writes as follows:

"ושמעתי מקשין ממה נפשך, מעיקרא מאי קסברי ולבסוף מאי קסברי?
אי פשיטא להן דתורה ומשנה תורה חשבי חדא, מאי שלחה מעיקרא
'שלישים ולא רבעים', ותיפוק לי' שעדיין לא נכתב כי אם שני פעמים? ואי
ס"ל תורה ומשנה תורה חשבי תרתי, אם כן מאי 'עד שמצאו מקרא
כתוב' דקאמרי, אדרבה מהאי קרא נמי משמע שאין לכתוב יותר
במגילה..."

The answer of the פני יהושע

The פני יהושע answers that this verse from *Mishle*: "שלישים ולא רבעים" is not concerned exclusively with the story of Amalek. The real point of this verse is to emphasize that we are not to add anything to Tanach — the books of the Torah, Prophets and Writings. For the five books of the Torah were written by Moshe Rabbenu and the prophetic books by the prophets. Thus no other book is to be added, and all other issues and subsequent laws are to be viewed as part of the Oral Torah, תורה שבעל פה, and these are forbidden to be committed to writing, based on the halacha which states: "דברים שבעל פה אי אתה רשאי לומר בכתב". Thus before the Gemara assumed that the Book of Esther was written with רוח הקודש, *divine inspiration*, the division of the verses which relate the story of Amalek was: 1) בשלח, 2) כי תצא, and 3) שמואל א'.

However, the Gemara's answer makes us aware that the Book of Esther was indeed written with divine inspiration, רוח הקודש. This means that we now have a new division: 1) Torah: which combines כי תצא and בשלח, and counts them as one, 2) Prophets: שמואל א', and 3) Kesuvim: מגילת אסתר

THE APPROACH OF THE טורי אבן

The טורי אבן also addresses this question, and the answer he suggests is that the verse could have been written simply as: "כתוב זכרון בספר". This would mean that the word "זאת" is really superfluous, even though it is this word, "זאת", which is decisive in the thinking of the Sages. For both "זאת" and "כתוב" are written in the singular, which indicates that each of these words refers to one source — the Torah, and thus we now have room for two more sources, namely the Prophets and the Writings.

THE OPINION OF THE שפת אמת

The שפת אמת is also troubled by this question of what was initially assumed about the inspiration behind the Book of Esther. He suggests that the *pasuk* of "שלישים ולא רבעים" is not concerned exclusively with the issue of Amalek, and therefore the new division should be the following: 1) בספר (4) זכרון (3), זאת (2), כתוב.

He is convinced that as far as the matter of Amalek is concerned here, there can be no objection to writing it a fourth time. This mitzva is indeed unique and the Torah itself sanctioned that this story may be written more than three times.

A beautiful insight is offered by the gaon Shem Yaakov, הג'ר'יעקב פופרש, as cited in the Torah journal (חלק י"א, לפורים) "אורייתא". There we read that the permission denied for the *Megillah* to be incorporated into the *Kisvei HaKodesh* was based on the simple translation of the verse: "הלא כתבתי שלישים וגו'" — *"Behold, I have already written, etc."*

From this we are to understand that only the books that were already written are to be counted. However, after introducing the verse, "כתוב זאת זכרון בספר", and thereby becoming aware that the Torah itself sanctioned the writing of *Megillas Esther*, the verse "הלא כתבתי וגו'" — *"I have already written,"* no longer rules out the writing of the *Megillah,* for we now view the *Megillah* as having already been written. This means that the manner of counting changes and we combine בשלח and כי תצא into one, leaving room for the *Megillas Esther.*

The Admor from Lubavitch, of blessed memory (see קובץ שערי ציון, תשמ"ד עמ' י"ד ואילך) resolves this difficulty in the following manner. The initial approach was that the Gemara views the "three" mentioned in *Mishle* as the three levels of prophecy represented by Torah, Prophets and Writings — תנ"ך. As we have explained, Torah contains the highest level of prophetic vision. However, that highest level of prophecy represented by the Torah is divided into two. The highest level, as represented in the first four books of the Bible, was transmitted "מפי גרונו של משה" by Hashem projecting His voice through Moshe Rabbenu's throat.

The second level is to be found in *Devarim,* where Moshe taught the Torah in his own voice by means of "משה מפי עצמו אמרה", clear prophetic vision: אספקלריה המאירה. These two levels can be summarized as follows: 1) Torah and 2) Mishna Torah.

The third level of prophecy is represented by the other prophets, whose divine vision was received in a manner less clear than the prophetic vision Moshe received. Theirs was characterized as אספקלריה שאינה מאחרה, as if seen through an opaque glass. An example of this is to be found in the Book of Shmuel.

The Sages subsequently redefined their criteria for determining the level of prophecy for the books of the Torah. Now, instead of focusing on how the prophecy was *revealed,* they considered how it was *written.* In this regard both the Torah and the Mishna Torah were written on the same level — אספקלריה המאירה. And this means that both these sections are to be counted as one; leaving room for the other two levels — Prophecy and Divine inspiration, רוח הקודש, with which the Megillah was written.

IV

THE RAMBAM AND THE RAVA'AD

Although the Rambam believes that all of *Kisvei HaKodesh,* except for *Megillas Esther,* will be nullified in the Messianic era, the Rava'ad is of the opinion that all of *Kisvei HaKodesh* will continue to exist, for it contains words of Torah whose study fulfills the mitzva of Talmud Torah. However, it is only the *Megillas Esther* which will continue to be read publicly in Messianic times.

> "וז"ל הראב"ד שם:
> א"א לא יבטל דבר מכל הספרים שאין ספר שאין בו לימוד. אבל כך אמרו אפילו יבטלו שאר ספרים מלקראות בהם מגילה לא תבטל מלקרות בצבור."

The מגיה to the מגיד משנה (*ibid.*) maintains that there is indeed no argument here between the Rambam and the Rava'ad, for the Rambam also agrees that the only difference between the *Megillas Esther* and the other *Kisvei HaKodesh* is that only the *Megillas Esther* will continue to be read publicly in Messianic times.

> "אבל נוכל ליישב שכוונת הרב על קריאתן, שלא יהי' על דרך החיוב רק קריאת המגילה."

The majority opinion among the commentators, though, is that the Rambam here does indeed disagree with the Rava'ad, and the simple reading here seems to indicate and support this view. Added proof is that the Rambam writes here that the *Megillah*, "as well as the Oral Torah", will never be nullified. Therefore, if the issue here relates only to the mitzva of reading, why bring proof from the Oral Torah, which has no mitzva of recitation, קריאה? The proof from the Oral Torah must be rather that just as the Oral law retains its sanctity forever, so does the *Megillas Esther*.

The comparison to the Oral Torah mentioned here which will never be nullified is explained in the sefer (מהרב יהודה גרשוני) "תורת גרשון". This commentator poses the question as to what the Rambam actually meant when he wrote that the *Megillah* will remain intact forever. Did he mean that apart from our continuing to read from the *Megillah* on Purim day, it will also continue to remain an integral part of *Kisvei HaKodesh*? Or perhaps, since all of *Kisvei HaKodesh* will be nullified, the *Megillah* also will lose its status as part of *Kisvei HaKodesh*, yet it will remain intact by retaining its status in relation to the mitzva of continuing to read from it.

The *Megillah* now will perhaps revert to the status it once held when it was first written by Mordechai and Esther. At that time it was not yet part of *Kisvei HaKodesh,* and its being committed to writing was solely for the purpose of reading from it on Purim day. In addition, whereas previously one who read from the *Megillah* also fulfilled the mitzva of Talmud Torah, in the Messianic period the *Megillas Esther* will revert to its original status, as we have explained.

The Rambam concludes here as follows:

"הרי היא קיימת כחמשה חומשי תורה וכהלכות של תורה שבעל פה שאינן בטלין לעולם."

"[The Megillah] will continue to exist as will the five books of the Torah and also the halachos of the Oral Torah, which will never be nullified."

The Rambam here means to tell us that the Torah laws contained in the *Megillah* will never be nullified, and this proves that the

Megillah, even in the Messianic age, will retain its status as part of *Kisvei HaKodesh*.

V

SUPPORT FOR THE RAMBAM'S OPINION

There are other sources suggested by the commentators which support this position of the Rambam that the *Megillah* will never be nullified.

The הגהות מיימוניות cites the Yerushalmi Megillah, Chapter 1, Halacha 5 as being the source for the Rambam.

"ר' יוחנן וריש לקיש, ר' יוחנן אמר: הנביאים והכתובים עתידים ליבטל, וה' ספרי תורה אינן עתידין ליבטל, ומאי טעמא 'קול גדול ולא יסף.' ריש לקיש אמר: אף מגילת אסתר והלכות אין עתידין ליבטל. נאמר כאן, 'קול גדול ולא יסף' ונאמר להלן, 'וזכרם לא יסוף וגו'' "

"Rav Yochanan is of the opinion that the five books of the Bible will never cease, as indicated by the verse cited in Devarim, 5:19: 'the voice of Matan Torah never ceased.' Resh Lakish adds the Megillas Esther to this formulation, for this expression, 'never ceased,' is used also in relation to the Megillah. Just as the Torah will never cease, so will the Megillah never cease."

Based on this, *Habukuk* 3:6 declared: "the ways of the world are His." The words *"the ways of the world"* ("הליכות עולם") can be interpreted as *"eternal laws"* — "הלכות עולם". Thus the Rambam adopts the interpretation of Resh Lakish, that both the *Megillah* and the Oral Torah are eternal.

All the books of the Prophets will be nullified, because in the Messianic age there will no longer be a need for them. This approach is based on a statement in *Mesechtas Ta'anis* 9a:

"מי איכא מידי דכתיב בכתובי דלא רמיזי באורייתא."

"Is there anything written in the Prophets that is not already alluded to in the Torah?"

Rashi explains this statement by pointing out that the Chumash (the five books of the Torah) is the foundation of the Prophets and the Writings, and everything found in them traces its source to what was already written in the Torah. However, as Bnai Yisrael descended into sin, the lessons once derived directly from the Torah became obscured to them, and therefore the books of the Prophets and the Writings, נ״ך, had to be written, for the lessons needed to be explicitly spelled out once again. *Nach* now became the vehicle for expressing the will of Hashem to Klal Yisrael. Thus we can say that it was an act of divine chesed to provide Klal Yisrael with the Prophets and the Writings.

However, in the future Messianic era, when the world *"will be filled with the knowledge of Hashem"* — "ומלאה הארץ דעה", Yisrael once again will attain its lofty heights of spiritual understanding. At that time, the people will be able to derive all the guidance they require from the Torah itself, and they will be capable of learning on their own the lessons which were spelled out explicitly in נ״ך. Thus there will no longer be any need for the Prophets and the Writings.

In light of this, HaRav Yehoshua Turtzen, ז״ל, in his sefer "קונטרס חנוכה-פורים", explains the basis of the disagreement between the Rambam and the Rava'ad as to whether or not the entire corpus of נ״ך will be nullified in the future, or whether they will be nullified only in the sense of not being required to be read publicly, though the books of the Prophets and the Writings will remain intact.

There is a general principle regarding the concept of committing prophecy to writing. There were many prophecies which were never written down, since only a prophecy that was relevant for all future generations was committed to writing: "נבואה שהוצרכה לדורות נכתבה". On the other hand, those prophecies which had only immediate relevance to a particular time or situation and did not relate to future generations were not recorded. Therefore, the Rambam believes that "הוצרכה לדורות" is an ongoing condition. Thus, even a prophecy that had been committed to writing, because it was considered a prophecy for all times, נבואה שהוצרכה לדורות, could later lose this status if it was no longer relevant to the generations to come. Thus, the Rambam's position is that in the Messianic age, all of נ"ך will no longer be needed, and thus it will lose its entitlement to be committed to writing. And the law of "דברים שבעל פה אי אתה רשאי לומר בכתב" will be applied here.

The Rava'ad, on the other hand, maintains that if a book was committed to writing because at one time it was viewed as necessary for the future, "הוצרכה לדורות", this would be sufficient reason to preserve that book even in the Messianic era, even though its explicit message would no longer be necessary. In addition, since the mitzva of Talmud Torah will be fulfilled by reading these chapters, this in itself justifies preserving these books.

What is so unique about the *Megillas Esther* to warrant its survival after all the other books of *Kisvei HaKodesh* will have ceased to exist? This question is asked by HaRav Dovid Milanovsky, ז"ל, in his sefer "אמרי דוד", חלק ב', (See the Preface to *The Commentators' Shabbos*).

We are well aware that Amalek wanted to destroy Yisrael by making them deny the miracles of Hashem which they saw with their own eyes. Amalek realized that outright denial was not possible, and therefore he planned to begin by cooling the intensity of Yisrael's belief in these miracles. This is the meaning of the statement in *Parashas Zachor*: "אשר קרך בדרך". Amalek sought to destroy their faith in Hashem and His miracles by focusing on a particular situation and showing that the miracle could be explained away rationally. By this he hoped to prove that what had happened was in accordance with the laws of nature. In this way he hoped to sow the seeds of doubt in the hearts and minds of Bnai Yisrael regarding all the other miracles as well.

The Book of Esther, our commentators tell us, shows Hashem's way of working *within* the laws of nature, דרך הטבע. Therefore, this book will be relevant forever, because it strengthens our belief in those miracles beyond the laws of nature, חוץ מדרך הטבע, as depicted in the Torah.

VI

WHY DID ESTHER NEED PERMISSION FROM THE SAGES?

Queen Esther sent a message to the Sages requesting that the *Megillah* be committed to writing and included in the *Kisvei HaKodesh*. A question should be asked here: Since we say "אסתר ברוח הקודש נאמרה", that this book was dictated by the Holy Spirit, why was it necessary to get the permission of the Sages to include it in the *Kisvei HaKodesh*? It should have been included by virtue of the divine inspiration which dictated the composition of this book.

The answer suggested to this question is based on Rashi's position, as set forth in *Mesechtas Baba Basra* 15a. There the Gemara states that it was the Men of the Great Assembly who wrote the books of Ezekiel, Daniel and the Scroll of Esther, in addition to the other books of the *Kisvei HaKodesh*. Rashi asks why it was necessary for the Men of the Great Assembly — Haggai, Zecharia and Malachi — to write these books after Klal Yisrael returned to Eretz Yisrael. Why didn't these prophets, Daniel, Ezekiel, etc., write their own prophetic books? Rashi replies that prophecy can not be written in the diaspora: "שלא נתנה נבואה ליכתב בחוץ לארץ". Therefore, only when Klal Yisrael returned to Eretz Yisrael were Haggai, Zecharia and Malachi able to commit these books to writing.

Yet this answer does not seem justified, for the truth is that these two *sugyos* — the Gemara in *Mesechtas Megillah* and the Gemara in *Baba Basra* — touch upon two separate issues. The Gemara in *Megillah* concerns itself with the issue of the permission (היתר) granted to include *Megillas Esther* in the category of *Kisvei HaKodesh*. The issue, however, in *Baba Basra* is that even after permission has been granted to commit this book to writing as part of *Kisvei HaKodesh*, the actual writing of this book cannot take place in the diaspora. Thus again we are confronted with the question of why a היתר was needed at all, after divine inspiration, רוח הקודש, itself dictated its writing.

We might answer this by suggesting that a prophet cannot go against an established law even for the sake of prophecy. Here we are confronted with the *pasuk* of "שלישים ולא רבעים" — the law that the story of Amalek cannot be written down more than three times. We are not permitted to apply here the sanction of the Holy Spirit, רוח הקודש, to justify the writing of the *Megillah*. Rather what is needed here is the sanction of the Sages, who must find a solution to this restriction of "שלישים ולא רבעים". Only after a solution was found by the Sages was Esther granted permission to commit her story to writing.

The Best Answer

O On Purim day it was customary for HaRav Yechezkel Abramsky, the eminent gaon, to relate the following episode about the Gra, the Gaon of Vilna.

A descendant of the Gra, who lived in Warsaw, was once approached by an outstanding local rabbi, who asked him the following question. "Please explain to me what was so unique about your grandfather, that enabled him to enjoy a reputation so great that it reached every corner of the world?"

The Gra's grandson replied, "When my grandfather was only a child he was asked the following question. From his reply you will be able to understand what constituted his greatness. He was asked: In the first Mishna in *Mesechtas Megillah* is it taught: "The Megillah can be read on the eleventh, twelfth, thirteenth, fourteenth and fifteenth days of Adar, *never earlier or later.*" — "לא פחות ולא יותר". And yet, in the Mishna of *Mesechtas Shabbos*, at the end of the chapter entitled, "ר' אליעזר דמילה", we learn that "an infant may be circumcised either on the eighth, ninth, tenth, eleventh, or twelfth [day], yet here it does not say *"but never earlier or later."* The Gaon's answer shows his greatness.

The Rabbi from Warsaw interrupted and said: "Don't tell me his answer; wait until I tell you how I would have answered that question."

For the next hour the rabbi "created" a possible solution to this question which dazzled the Gaon's grandson. He remarked: "Your lecture was very beautiful and the way you answered the question was most impressive, yet the Gaon, my grandfather, gave a better answer."

The rabbi begged for more time to give another answer, one which might match the answer the Gaon offered. Three days later the rabbi returned and delivered a lengthy discourse, lasting several hours, and once more, the Gra's grandson was dazzled. However, he once again told the rabbi: "The Gaon gave a better answer even than this."

Exasperated, the rabbi said: "I give up. I can't do any better than I have already done, though I have certainly tried my best. Please tell me your grandfather's answer."

The grandson answered gently, "My grandfather answered simply that in the Mishna in Shabbos it does say, *"not earlier or later"* — "לא פחות ולא יותר".

The Gaon's greatness was that not only did he know the entire Torah, but he had it all at his fingertips; and he knew it all just as an ordinary Jew knows the *"Ashrei" (See The Commentators' Shabbos*, pp. 143-146). He did not need to force clever answers that were not required.

Perhaps we can learn an important lesson from this story: There are people who spend their entire lives constantly worried, concerned with seeking solutions to problems — which do not exist.

CHAPTER FIVE

The two writings
of the Megillah

I

One for Kisvei Hakodesh and one to be read on Purim

Chazal tell us in *Bava Basra* 15a:

"אנשי כנסת הגדולה כתבו יחזקאל ושנים עשר דניאל ומגילת אסתר."

"The Men of the Great Assembly wrote the books of Ezekiel, the Twelve Prophets, Daniel and the Scroll of Esther."

According to Rashi, the Men of the Great Assembly were Haggai, Zecharia, and Malachai. Rashi then asks why Ezekiel and some of the other prophets did not transcribe their own prophecies. He answers that prophecies can only be committed to writing in Eretz Yisrael. Since Ezekiel, Esther and other prophets lived in the Diaspora, it was left to those who lived in the land of Yisrael — Hagai, Zecharia, and Malachai, to write down the prophecies of the others. These three prophets saw that the era of prophecy was coming to an end, and therefore they took it upon themselves to transcribe these books of holy writings.

Thus it would seem that Haggai, Zecharia, and Malachai were the authors of the book of Esther. But the Brisker Rav, Rav Velvel, points out that this contradicts the statement in (פרק כ"ט) "סדר עולם" that, based on the verse in *Megillas Esther*, "ותכתוב אסתר המלכה", the following year after the Purim miracle Esther wrote the story of the *Megillah*. And so Rashi himself comments, based on what is said in *Mesechtas Megillah 19a:* that the verse in *Esther* (9:20): "ויכתוב מרדכי את הדברים האלה" — *"Mordechai recorded these events,"* refers to the *Megillah* that Esther wrote and sent out to her people — "מגילה זו שהיא שלח להם".

But if it was Esther who wrote the *Megillah*, how does Rashi come to attribute it to the prophets Haggai, Zecharia, and Malachai?

The Brisker Rav, in his sefer "חידושי מרן רי"ז הלוי", explains that there are two separate laws that pertain to the writing of a *Megillah*.

There is the *Megillah* written solely for the purpose of fulfilling the mitzva of reading the *Megillah* on Purim day. This mitzva calls for the story of the Purim miracle to be read aloud from a written scroll. According to the halacha, simply an oral recitation is not enough. "הקורא את המגילה על פה לא יצא ידי חובתו" — *"A person who reads the Megillah by heart does not fulfill his obligation."*

This type of *Megillah* is not an integral part of the *Kisvei HaKodesh*, in the sense that those halachos which pertain to the books of the Holy Writings do not apply to this kind of *Megillah*.

Shmuel contends that this is the only kind of *Megillah* that is to be written, contrary to most opinions that there is yet another category of *Megillah*, as we shall presently discuss.

The Ritba explains the position of Shmuel as follows (מגילה ז, א):

"שלא ניתנה ליכתב בכלל ספרי הקדש עד שתהא כמותם לטמא את הידים, אבל מכל מקום ניתנה ליכתב, שלא תהא בעל פה, והקורא על פה לא יצא."

"The message of the Divine Spirit merely precluded the incorporation of the megillah into the Holy Scriptures. However, it is to be written down in order that its recitation be oraly."

There is also a type of *Megillah* which is an integral part of the Holy Writings, *Kisvei HaKodesh.*

Thus, in relation to writing the *Megillah* for the sole purpose of being able to read from it, that was done by Mordechai and Esther, at the time of the miracle, when they were still in Persia. As Rashi explains, since they were not at that time in the land of Yisrael, they had to wait until Klal Yisrael returned to Eretz Yisrael. Only then was the *Megillas Esther* written by Haggai, Zecharia, and Malachai, for the purpose of being included in the Holy Writings, *Kisvei HaKodesh.*

II

Why the Rambam omitted two important halachos

Based on this approach, the Griz HaLevi explains why the Rambam did not mention two important halachos pertaining to the makeup of the *Megillas Esther*. Though both are mentioned in the Gemara, the Rambam did not include these halachos in *Hilchos Megillah*.

The Gemara in *Megillah* 16b states:

"אמר ר' יוחנן ויו דויזתא צריך למימתחא בזקיפא."

"Rav Yochanan said: The letter vav mentioned in the name of ויזתא *must be written larger than normal."*

The Gemara explains that this long *vav* "alludes to the pole used by boatmen in the River Libros". This signifies that the ten sons of Haman were all hanged on *one long pole*, one above the other, and they all died.

The Gemara (*ibid.*) also states:

"אמר רבי חנינא בר פפא: דרש ר' שילא איש כפר תמרתא, כל השירות
כולן נכתבות אריח על גבי לבינה ולבינה על גבי אריח חוץ משירה
זו [של אסתר] ומלכי כנען, שאריח על גבי אריח, ולבינה על גבי לבינה."

All the songs of praise cited in the Scriptures are written in the form of *"a half brick above a whole brick"* and *"a whole brick above a half brick"*; except the *Megillas Esther* and the song of praise listing the names of the kings of Canaan who were defeated by Yehoshua (see the Book of Yehoshua 12:9-24).

The Gemara explains the reason why this format was followed, so that "there never be a recovery from this downfall." And Rashi explains the meaning of this by saying, "for if there would be here bricks on either side below, then the wicked men would find a firm foothold to break their fall."

However, in light of the above contention by the Brisker Rav, we can say that these two halachos pertain only in relation to a *Megillah* which was written with the intention of being included in the *Kisvei HaKodesh*. The manner of writing a book to be included in the *Kisvei HaKodesh* is based on a tradition, מסורה, handed down throughout the generations, "איש מפי איש".

This determines the specific characteristics of the structure, style, formation of the letters, what is added and what is left out, etc. When the *Megillah* required these two conditions, it predicated these upon that type of *Megillah* which is written as an inpart of the *Kisvei HaKodesh*, and in which the tradition calls for a particular style of writing.

However, as we have pointed out, there is another type of *Megillah*, written solely for the purpose of fulfilling the mitzva of being read on Purim day. In this type of *Megillah*, these requirements do not apply. Consequently, the Rambam in *Hilchos Megillah* did not mention these two requirements, for they pertain only to a *Megillah* written for the purpose of being included in the *Kisvei HaKodesh*. Thus the Rambam justifiably left out these two halachos in *Hilchos Megillah*, because there he is concerned only with the laws regarding the proper manner in which a *Megillah* scroll is to be read in order to fulfill the mitzva of reading the *Megillah*.

III

THE YERUSHALMI ASKS A QUESTION

The *Yerushalmi Megillah* seems to contradict the position of the *Griz HaLevi* by raising a question in Chapter 3, Halacha 7, regarding the requirement that the verses concerning the ten sons of Haman are to be written in the form of *shirah,* a song of praise. This is indicated by leaving spaces between phrases. The Gemara asks whether or not this requirement is decisive.

"מאי כדין למצוה או לעכב. א'ר לר"ח...לעיכוב"

If we accept the position of the *Griz HaLevi* here, we might ask why it is decisive. For if one were to fail to write these verses as a song of praise, then the Megillah could not be considered a part of the *Kisvei HaKodesh*; yet it would still be considered to be a kosher Megillah, and one would fulfill the mitzva if he were to read from it on Purim. Therefore we may conclude that the issue here does not relate to the *Kisvei HaKodesh* but rather to the Megillah itself. And since the Yerushalmi determines that it is decisive, and a Megillah which is not written in this form is not valid, this then refutes the position of the *Griz HaLevi*.

This leaves us once again to confront the question why the Rambam omitted these important halachos which pertain to the writing of the Megillah.

We might suggest a possible answer to this question based on a previous discussion (see *The Commentators' Siddur*, pp. 193-4). There is a difference of opinion among the classic commentators as to whether or not the verse: "כי בא סוס פרעה ברכבו ובפרשיו בים וגו'" is an integral part of the *Shiras HaYam*. The Rema, in "יורה דעה" (סימן ער"ה סעיף ו') writes that all of the *Shiras HaYam,* including the verse of "כי בא סוס פרעה וגו'" must be written in a Sefer Torah in the unique style required when writing *shirah*. This style is defined as: "אריח על גבי לבינה ולבינה על גבי אריח" — spaces left between phrases. The regular manner of writing begins again only with the verse "ותקח מרים". We can conclude from this requirement to write the verse in this manner, that it is indeed part of the *Shiras HaYam*.

Things are not so clear-cut, however, for the Rema also requires that the verse before "כי בא סוס פרעה וגו'", that of "ה' ימלך לעולם ועד" should be written twice. The Avudraham gives the reason for this, which is that it emphasizes that the *shirah* ends with this verse. Thus, if the Rema requires this verse to be written twice, it would seem that he too shares this opinion that the verse of "כי בא סוס פרעה וגו'" is not an integral part of the *shirah*.

But wouldn't this contradict what the Rema himself said previously, which was that this verse of "כי בא סוס פרעה וגו'" must be written in the specified format of *shirah*, which indicates that it is indeed an integral part of the *shirah*?

To answer this apparent contradiction, we might suggest that we write the verse "כי בא סוס פרעה וגו'" in the form required of *shirah*, not because it is part of the *Shiras HaYam*, but rather because of other considerations. Chazal tell us in *Mesechtas Megillah 16b* that the verses which describe the capture of the Canaanite kings in the Book of Yehoshua and the list of the ten sons of Haman who were hanged and their names, listed in the Megillah, must be written in a unique style, consisting of *"blank space over blank space and print over print"* — "אריח על גבי אריח ולבינה על גבי לבינה".

This is similar to the fashion in which *shirah* is written. The rationale behind writing in this manner is based on a verse which states: "באבוד רשעים רנה" that the defeat of the enemies of Hashem and Yisrael is a cause for rejoicing. This then calls for a style of writing which resembles that of *shirah* — songs of praise to the Almighty.

Thus we may say that even though the *pasuk* of "כי בא סוס פרעה וגו'" is not really an integral part of *Shiras HaYam*, nevertheless these verses must be written in the manner required by shirah. For as we have explained, the fall of the Canaanite kings and the hanging of the ten sons of Haman must be written in the same manner as *shirah*, which consists of *"blank space over blank space and writing over writing"*. And if we were to ask whether the verse of "כי בא סוס פרעה וגו'" must also be written in this same unique style of *shirah* which we use when the enemies of Yisrael are defeated, we can ask why it is in fact written in a different manner?

The answer is given by the Ran, in his commentary at the end of the second chapter of *Mesechtas Megillah*. There he states that "blank space over blank space" alludes to our prayer that our enemies be completely destroyed and never rise again. Consequently, we might say that that in the case of the destruction of the army of Pharaoh, their downfall came about as a result of Divine intervention, "כי בא סוס פרעה וגו'" and therefore it is evident that they would never rise again. For this reason there is no need for us to indicate that we hope for this by our allusion to it in the use of *"blank space upon blank space."*

Thus in our prayers, when we are required to sing Hashem's praises, we include the verse of "כי בא סוס פרעה וגו'" in the manner of *shirah* to indicate that we rejoice in Hashem, who caused the downfall of our enemies. At the same time, however, by repeating this final verse, we thereby indicate that the *Shiras HaYam* ends here with the phrase of "ה' ימלך לעולם ועד".

This succeeds in resolving the apparent contradiction of the Rema. Thus we can now say that, as the tradition dictates, only *Kisvei HaKodesh* requires to be written in the manner of *shirah*. However, the hanging of Haman's ten sons also calls for rejoicing in the form of *shirah*, because it signified the vanquishing of our enemies and the enemies of Hashem. In order to emphasize this we write the names of Haman's ten sons, as well as the story of the capture of the Canaanite kings, in the same form as we write *shirah*, "אריח על גבי אריח וכו'".

This is the reason the *Megillas Esther* is also written in the form of *shirah*, "באבוד רשעים רנה" to indicate that when our enemies are vanquished by the hand of Hashem we rejoice. The Yerushalmi then asks, isn't this manner of writing decisive?

The Rambam answers that since the Bavli never touched upon this issue, we can assume that this manner of writing is *not decisive*, but rather only *preferable*, and this is why the Rambam himself omits this halacha from the *Hilchos Megillah*, for this manner of writing is not unique to the *Megillah* but rather represents the general concept that we rejoice in the downfall of our enemies.

IV

Is a Megillah written by a woman valid?

Halachically, a sefer Torah written by a woman is not valid. But what about a *Megillah*? This is a relevant question, since we find it mentioned in the *Megillah* that it was a woman, Esther herself, who wrote the first

Megillah. We read there, in 9:29: "ותכתב אסתר המלכה וגו" — *"And Queen Esther wrote."* This seems to imply that a woman is eligible to write a *Megillah.* So why raise this issue at all?

The answer given is that what the *Megillah* means here is not that Esther actually wrote the *Megillah* herself, but rather that she was the one who caused the *Megillah* to be written. Therefore, since she was instrumental in having the *Megillah* written, we attribute it to her as if she was the one who wrote it. A similar situation is found in relation to the mitzva of circumcision. A woman is not allowed to circumcise a Jewish boy. But in the Torah we find it stated that Tzippora, the wife of Moshe Rabbenu, circumcised her son, as the verse tells us: "ותקח צפורה צור ותכרות את ערלת בנה".

The Gemara explains, in *Avodah Zarah 23a,* that it was someone else, a male, who actually circumcised her son, yet the Torah credits her with this meritorious act, as if she herself actually performed it, for it only came about as a result of her efforts (See מקראי קדש, מהרב פרנק, פורים, סימן ל"ג). The question of whether or not a woman is qualified to write a *Megillah* can be asked in light of the contention of the Brisker Rav that there are two types of *Megillah:* one for reading and the other as part of *Kisvei HaKodesh.*

It is clear that a woman can not write a Sefer Torah, which is part of *Kisvei HaKodesh* and therefore it can only be written by a man. This applies to the second type of *Megillah.* However, in relation to the first type of *Megillah,* that written for the purpose of fulfilling the mitzva of being read on Purim day, perhaps a woman would be allowed to write this kind of *Megillah.*

Based on this idea, HaRav Avraham Gurvitz explains the prayer quoted in the *Selichos* recited on the fast day of Esther, *Ta'anis Esther* (ד"ה אדם בקום עלינו):

"ותכתב אסתר תקף לקרא כבהלל מהודים".

"Esther recorded the mighty miracle to be read by the grateful like Hallel."

Thus we can say that initially the *Megillah* was written by Esther for the purpose of fulfilling the obligation of reciting Hallel, for we say that reading the *Megillah* is akin to reciting Hallel: "קרייתא זו הלילא".

This type of *Megillah* is permitted to be written by a woman. Later, however, when the *Megillah* became an integral part of the *Kisvei HaKodesh*, a woman was not allowed to write such a *Megillah*. Thus we can interpret the Selichos prayer on *Ta'anis Esther* to mean that Esther wrote that *Megillah* from which we recite Hallel, but not the *Megillah* which is an integral part of the *Kisvei HaKodesh*.

From this it becomes clear that when the *Megillah* states that Esther wrote this book, this statement refers to the original *Megillah*, which was written for the purpose of Hallel. Later, as we have explained, when the *Megillah* took on the status of *Kisvei HaKodesh*, women were now prohibited from writing such a *Megillah*.

A Torah of thirds

At the end of *Hilchos Megillah* 2:18, the Rambam states:

‏"כל ספרי הנביאים וכל הכתובים עתידין לבטל לימות המשיח..."

"All the books of the Prophets and all of the Holy Writings will be nullified in the Messianic era..."

But this seems to contradict what we learn in another Gemara, *Mesechtas Shabbos 88a*, where we find:

‏"דרש ההוא גלילאה עליה דרב חסדא: בריך רחמנא דיהיב אוריאן תליתאי לעם תליתאי."

"A certain Galilean lectured in the presence of Rav Chisda and said: 'Blessed is the merciful One, Who gave us a Torah of thirds'."

By this he meant: a Torah which is comprised of three parts, namely, the Pentateuch, the Prophets and the Writings. And according to the commentary of the Ritba here, all three parts were alluded to at Sinai.

But if we are so grateful to Hashem for giving us this gift of the books of the Prophets and the Writings — to the extent that we view this gift as an integral part of the Torah which was given to us at Sinai — how can the Rambam claim that in Messianic times this Divine gift will be nullified?

The Gemara in *Shabbos 88a* addresses this issue in relation to what is stated in the Gemara in Nedarim 22b:

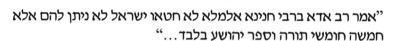

"אמר רב אדא ברבי חנינא אלמלא לא חטאו ישראל לא ניתן להם אלא
חמשה חומשי תורה וספר יהושע בלבד..."

*"R' Adda, the son of R' Chanina, said: 'Had not Yisrael
sinned, only the Pentateuch and the Book of Yehoshua would
have been given to them.' "*

This seems to imply that it was only because Yisrael sinned [with
the Golden Calf] that they were given the books of the Prophets
and the Holy Writings. And had they not sinned, they would
have been given only the five Books of Moses. This statement
of Chazal seems to contradict our appreciation of the Prophets
and the Writings. But then again, if we are to view them as
"gifts", does this mean that those who sinned are to be rewarded
with Divine gifts — "וכי החוטא נשכר"?

The Gemara in *Shabbos 88a* suggest a possible answer, when
it states:

"דרש ההוא גלילאה עליה דרב חסדא: בריך רחמנא דיהיב אוריאן
תליתאי, לעם תליתאי, על ידי תליתאי ביום תליתאי, בירחא תליתאי..."

*"A certain Galilean lectured before Rav Chisda, saying: 'Blessed
be He the merciful One, Who gave us a Torah of thirds: Torah,
Prophets and Writings, to a people of thirds: Kohanim, Levi'im,
and Yisraelim. Through a person born third to his mother:
Miriam, Aharon, and Moshe. On the third day of Abstinence,
during the third month of the year: Nissan, Iyar, and Sivan."*

The sefer תשובה מאהבה", "מהג' ר' אלעזר פלעקלס", raises a number of
questions regarding this statement of the "Galilean" (See there in the
פתיחה, עמ' 8, and also at the end of the sefer "שלמי תודה"). Several of
these questions pertain to what we are discussing here.

1) If indeed the Galilean was fascinated by thirds, he could have added many more examples, such as: a nation which celebrates three pilgrimage holidays (Pesach, Shavuos and Succos); and a people who observe three prayers (Shacharis, Mincha and Ma'ariv); and who possess three temples: (The first and second Bais Hamikdash and the third, which will be rebuilt in the future).

2) The threes here do not seem to be balanced. For example, in the first two sequences of three (the Torah, Prophets and Writings, and the Kohanim, Levi'im and Yisraelim) all three are included in the "gift". He gave all three to a nation made up of three parts. However, in the other examples only the third item is emphasized. For example, to a third born child, the first and the second born siblings are of no consequence. And similarly, it is the third month which is ocused upon, and thus the first and second are of no consequence in this context.

Therefore, we must say that the Galilean here, when he comes to enumerate sets of three, meant to tell us that in truth only one should have been chosen, however, because man has free will, any one of the three could have been chosen.

For example, regarding the Kohanim, Levi'im and Yisraelim, it would seem that originally the Kohanim should not have been the only ones chosen, for all of Yisrael had the potential to be "priests", as the verse tells us: "ואתם תהיו לי ממלכת כהנים" — *"And you will be for Me a kingdom of priests."*

For all of Yisrael were fit to be priests, and it was because of the sins of Bnai Yisrael that only the kohanim were chosen to serve in the Mishkan and in the Bais HaMikdash.

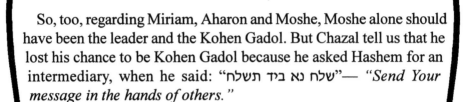

So, too, regarding Miriam, Aharon and Moshe, Moshe alone should have been the leader and the Kohen Gadol. But Chazal tell us that he lost his chance to be Kohen Gadol because he asked Hashem for an intermediary, when he said: "שלח נא ביד תשלח"— *"Send Your message in the hands of others."*

Regarding *"the third month"*, had the Jews not sinned by complaining against Hashem, for lack of meat and for lack of water, the Torah would have been given immediately in the month of Nissan. But because of their complaints they had to wait until Sivan, the third month.

The question remains, how are we to understand this concept in relation to the three aspects of Torah, Prophets and Writings? We are told that had the Bnai Yisrael not sinned we would have been given only the Torah, for we would have retained the sensitivity to be able to understand the words of Hashem directly through the Written Torah alone, without the necessity for the Oral Torah. However, because we did not remain at that high spiritual level, we needed the Prophets to elucidate the words of the Torah for us and the Holy Writings to spell out that message in ways we could comprehend. Thus the statement of the Galilean in the Gemara shows us the results of our actions.

This is the reason we say that in future Messianic times, we will have refined our souls to the extent that we will no longer need the books of the Prophets and the Writings to understand the word of Hashem. The Written Torah alone will suffice.

CHAPTER SIX

Who ordained the Megillah Reading: The Prophets or Bais Din?

I

The Gemara's view

The Rambam in Hilchos *Megillah*, Chapter 1, Halacha 1, writes:

"קריאת המגילה בזמנה מצות עשה מדברי סופרים. והדברים ידועים
שהיא תקנת הנביאים."

*"The reading of the Megillah at its appointed time is a positive
mitzva ordained by the Rabbis. It is well known that this was
ordained by the Prophets."*

The source of this halacha is traced to the Gemara *Megillah* 14a:

"תנו רבנן: ארבעים ושמונה נביאים ושבע נביאות נתנבאו להם לישראל
ולא פחתו ולא הותירו על מה שכתוב בתורה חוץ ממקרא מגילה."

*"The Rabbis taught in a Baraisa: Forty-eight prophets and
seven prophetesses prophesied to Yisrael, and they did not
detract or add to that which is written in the Torah, except
for instituting the reading of the Megillah every Purim."*

The Gemara then explains the rationale of the Prophets:

"מאי דרוש? אמר רבי חייא בר אבין אמר רבי יהושע בן קרחה: קל
וחומר, ומה מעבדות לחירות אמרי' שירה ממיתה לחיים לא כל שכן."

*"What did the Prophets interpret that led them to create the
reading of the Megillah? They advanced a kal v'chomer —
namely, if the Jews, when delivered from slavery in Egypt to
freedom, sang a song of praise to Hashem, how much more
so should we commemorate our deliverance from death at
the hands of Ahashveros and Haman, with a public reading
of the Megillah."*

From this it would seem that the mitzva of reading the *Megillah* was
instituted by the Prophets, and indeed, the טורי אבן, in his Commentary to
Mesechtas Megillah (י"ט, ב', ד"ה ר' יהודה מכשיר), maintains that since we

say "אסתר ברוח הקודש נאמרה", that the Book of Esther was composed with divine inspiration, therefore we consider this mitzva to have come from "דברי קבלה".

Consequently, both the *Griz HaLevi*, cited in קונטרס המועדים–תורת בריסק (עמוד מ"ד), and הג' ר' שמואל רוזובסקי ז"ל raise the same question, the latter in sefer זכרון שמואל (עמ' קט"ו או"ק ח'). The Gemara in 2a states: All the dates listed in the Mishna (the 11th, 12th, 13th, 14th and 15th of Adar) must have originally been established by the *Men of the Great Assembly*, אנשי כנסת הגדולה. Because if you think that they established only the 14th and 15th of Adar as the dates for reading the *Megillah*, then wouldn't they thereby abrogate an enactment by the *Men of the Great Assembly* if they were to read the *Megillah* earlier? For we have learned in the Mishna (*Eduyoth* 1:5) that one court can not overturn the ruling of another, unless it is superior to the other court in wisdom and in numbers.

Now, if the *Megillah* reading was ordained by the Prophets, then even if a subsequent rabbinical court was greater, both in scholarship and in numbers, they still could not overturn what was established by the Prophets. Therefore, we must conclude, since the Gemara indeed touches upon the issue of overturning the dates of the 14th and the 15th of Adar, that we do not view this mitzva as being established by the Prophets. And as for the Gemara's statement in 7a: "אסתר ברוח הקודש נאמרה", this is not to be understood to mean that it was *divine inspiration*, רוח הקודש, which dictated this mitzva of reading the *Megillah*, but rather that Esther called for this matter to be instituted by the Rabbis and the Bais Din. (However, see פני יהושע here ד"ה אין בי"ד יכול לבטל, who contends that the question raised here of אין בית דין יכול לבטל is geared *only* if we hold that Esther was not written ברוח הקדש.)

In defense of the טורי אבן, who maintains that indeed it was רוח הקודש which dictated that this mitzva be created, we would answer this question posed by הג' ר' שמואל רוזובסקי ז"ל based on the following insight of the פחד יצחק (חנוכה-מאמר י"ד או"ק ב'):

"רצוננו לחזור בכאן על חידושו של אחד מגדולי הדור שלפני פנינו בענין
שייכותה של נבואה לכח התורה. אף על פי שהלכה רווחת היא שאין

לנבואה מבוא בהוראה, מכל מקום בהערכת סנהדרין מול סנהדרין,
כשאנו צריכים לדעת איזו מהן נחשבת גדולה בחכמה לגבי חברתה,
בזה שפיר תפסינן דסנהדרין כזו שבין חבריה נמצאו גם נביאים הרי
היא גדולה בחכמה מן הסנהדרין שלא היה בה נביאים. דמהני ישיבת
נביאים בסנהדרין לעשותה גדולה בחכמה אף לענין ההכרעה בהוראה."

*"Although a prophet by means of prophecy cannot legislate
a law, yet the mere presence of a prophet seated as a member
of a Sanhedrin elevates the prestige of that Sanhedrin to the
extent that it is viewed as Superior to all subsequent
Rabbinical courts (Batei Dinim) due to the fact that prophets
sat in as members of the Sanhedrin."*

Proof of this theory, contends the Pachad Yitzchak, is that when we
identify those who made up the כנסת הגדולה אנשי, the *Men of the Great
Assembly*, we find that of the 120 elders who made up the membership,
many were prophets. What is the significance of this fact? Surely, when
it comes to decision making, prophecy is of no advantage, and in fact it
is to be rejected as a criterion in making decisions. Yet despite this fact,
the mere presence of a prophet as a member of the Sanhedrin makes it
superior and more authoritative than any subsequent Sanhedrin.

Chazal, at the beginning of *Mesechtas Megillah*, maintain that it was
this Sanhedrin, the Anshei Knesses Hagadolah, which must have ordained
all five days on which it was acceptable to read the Megillah (from the 11th
until the 15th of Adar). Yet subsequently, when the 14th and the 15th became
the days on which the Megillah was actually read, this must reflect the fact
that it was not the subsequent elders of the Mishnaic period — the *Chachamei
HaMishna* — who ordained these five days, for how then could we have
added three additional days to the two which they upheld (the 14th and 15th)?

The principle we apply in such cases is that a bais din, one particular
rabbinical court, cannot create a new ruling which contradicts that of
another bais din, unless it is superior in number and scholarship to that
previous bais din which made a particular ruling. Thus we can assume
that the bais din at the time of the *Anshei Knesses Hagadolah* must have
been superior to any subsequent bais din.

Yet this is not necessarily true. The superiority of the Anshei Knesses Hagadolah resulted from the fact that prophets sat as members of that Sanhedrin. And since the era of the prophets had ended, it is evident that the bais din of that time was superior because of the fact that prophets sat on it. This then is the point the Gemara is trying to make here, to prove that it must have been the Anshei Knesses Hagadolah which ordained all five days for reading the Megillah, for it would have been impossible for another bais din to arise which was superior to them.

With this in mind, we can now answer the question of Rav Shmuel Rozovsky, namely that if it was the prophets who ordained the Megillah reading, how could a subsequent bais din overturn that which the prophets ordained? The Gemara touched on the issue of a superior bais din having greater authority to overturn a law, in order to show us that, as the insight of the Pachad Yitzchak discovered, it was exactly this which the Gemara wished to prove, that since it was the prophets who ordained these days of the 14th and 15th, then it would have been impossible for any other bais din to add other days, for no one had the power or greater authority to overturn an ordinance which had been set down by the prophets.

II

APPLYING THE י"ג מדות TO DERIVE NEW HALACHOS

The טורי אבן understands the statement "אסתר ברוח הקודש נאמרה" to mean that it was the Holy Spirit which dictated the actual writing and the mitzva. Thus, one may well ask, if the 14th and 15th of Adar were explicitly established in the *Megillah* as instituted by the Prophets with divine inspiration, how could the *Men of the Great Assembly*, by focusing on the key word "זמניהם" include the other days mentioned in the Mishna as days on which the *Megillah* may also be read?

To review this point, we see that, based on the verse in *Esther 9:31,* "לקיים את ימי הפורים **בזמניהם**", *Chazal* commented that the word "בזמניהם" is superfluous, and therefore its purpose is to teach us that there are other days besides the 14th and 15th of Adar on which the *Megillah* can be read. A further examination of this word limits the inclusion to two days, similar to the main dates "זמנים", which are the two days of the 14th and the 15th. In addition, the 13th of Adar is automatically included, for this day is *Ta'anis Esther*.

We might suggest a possible way of resolving this discrepancy. The Rambam's well-known position — that the Book of Esther will never be nullified, not even in the Messianic age, although the other books of the *Kisvei HaKodesh* will be — is cited in *Hilchos Megillah* 2:18. Not only will the *Megillah* remain intact, but also all the laws mentioned there, including those halachos which are derived by applying the principle of the Thirteen Attributes: "י"ג מדות שהתורה נדרשת בהם" will be preserved. The rationale here as to why all the other books of *Kisvei HaKodesh* will be nullified in the future is as follows. There is a halacha which dictates that a prophet has no jurisdiction to introduce new laws: "אין הנביא רשאי לחדש דבר מעכשיו".

Therefore, all the laws that appear in נ"ך are to be viewed not as "new" laws, but rather as halachos that already existed because of the concept of הלכה למשה מסיני, laws that were not committed to writing but were given orally to Moshe Rabbenu, and the Prophets only committed them to writing later when they came to write the *Kisvei HaKodesh*. (See my sefer "מחזה עליון" for a discussion of the issue of the Oral Law not allowed to be written, and yet how the prophets were nevertheless able to write it down.)

In the Messianic age, when men will once again be able to see things clearly and "the earth will be filled with knowledge of God", all of נ"ך will be nullified, since its teachings and messages will now be able to be derived from the Torah itself. However, in regard to the *Megillah*, based on the verse of "דברי שלום ואמת" (*Esther 9:31*), *Chazal* say that the words of the *Megillah* are considered to be Torah itself, and thus since the Torah allows new laws to be extracted from its text, by means of the י"ג מדות, so too does the *Megillah* derive new laws from the text in the same way. These laws derived from the *Megillah* will never be nullified, for they are viewed as having the status of Torah.

In light of this we may say that although to the טורי אבן the 14th and 15th of Adar are "מדברי קבלה", based on the concept of "אסתר ברוח הקודש נאמרה" yet we may include the other days, for as we have said, since the *Megillah* is viewed as Torah, we may now apply the י"ג מדות to extract new halachos and in this way include the other days of Purim (namely, the 11th, 12th and 13th of Adar). This is not considered in any way to clash with that divine inspiration, the words of the prophets who introduced the 14th and 15th of Adar.

III

THE RAMBAM'S VIEW

The Rambam in his introduction to *Mishna Torah* writes:

"ויש מצות אחרות שנתחדשו אחר מתן תורה, וקבעו אותם נביאים וחכמים, ופשטו בכל ישראל, כגון: **מקרא מגילה**, ונר חנוכה, ותענית תשעה באב...

כל אלו המצות שנתחדשו, חייבים אנו לקבלם ולשמרם שנא': לא תסור מן הדבר וכו'. ואינם תוספות על מצות התורה. ועל מה הזהירה תורה: לא תוסיף עליו ולא תגרע ממנו? שלא יהא נביא רשאי לחדש דבר ולומר, שהקדוש ברוך הוא צוהו במצוה זו להוסיפה למצות התורה...

אבל אם הוסיפו בית-דין עם נביא שיהי' באותו זמן מצוה דרך תקנה או דרך הוראה או דרך גזרה – אין זו תוספות, שהרי לא אמרו שהקב"ה צוה לעשות עירוב או **לקרות מגלה בעונתה**, ואילו אמרו כן-היו מוסיפין על התורה.

אלא כך אנו אומרים: **שהנביאים עם בית-דין** תקנום וצוו לקרות המגלה בעונתה כדי להזכיר שבחיו של הקב"ה ותשועות שעשה לנו והי' קרוב לשועתינו, כדי לברכו ולהללו, וכדי להודיע לדורות הבאים שאמת מה שהבטיחנו בתורה 'ומי גוי גדול אשר לו אלוקים וגו'. "

"There are also other commandments that were instituted after the giving of the Torah. They were established by the Prophets and Sages and spread throughout Yisrael — for example, the reading of the Megillah, lighting a Chanukah candle, fasting

on Tisha B'Av...We are obligated to accept and observe all of these commandments which were instituted as implied in Devarim 17:11 — 'Do not deviate from this instruction...'

They should not be considered additions to the commandments of the Torah. Then what does the Torah's warning in Devarim 13:11 refer to, when it says: 'Do not add to it or detract from it'? It means that a prophet is not allowed to introduce a new measure and say that the Holy One, Blessed be He, commanded this mitzva to us and that it should be added to the Torah's mitzvos.

However, if a court, together with the prophet of that age, adds a mitzva as an addition, a lesson or a decree, this is not considered an addition. He is not saying that the Holy One, Blessed be He, commanded us to make an eruv or read the Megillah at its appointed time. Were he to say so, he would be adding to the Torah.

Instead, we are saying that the prophets and the courts ordained that the Megillah be read...in order to recall the praise of the Holy One, Blessed be He, the salvation He wrought for us, and His response to our cries; so that we will bless Him, extol Him, and inform future generations of the truth of the Torah's promise (Devarim 4:7) 'What nation is so great that it has Hashem close to it?' "

Thus we clearly see that the Rambam is of the opinion that both the Prophets (Mordechai and Esther) and the Sanhedrin instituted the reading of the *Megillah*. And this is indicated from what we read in *Mesechtas Megillah* 7a:

‏"אמר רב שמואל בר יהודה: שלחה להם אסתר לחכמים 'קבעוני‏
‏לדורות.' ".‏

"Rav Shmuel bar Yehudah said: Esther submitted the following request to the Sages: 'Establish me for all generations.' "

Rashi (*op.cit.*) comments: "Establish an everlasting name for me by mandating a festival of Purim and the reading of the *Megillah*."

Again we see that it was the Sanhedrin that instituted the reading of the *Megillah*. The Maharsha notes that this request here is alluded to in the *Megillah* itself.

Esther's original request for the establishment of Purim is recorded as follows (*Esther 9:20-21*): "And Mordechai wrote...and send letters to all the Jews...charging them to observe the 14th of Adar." The Sages rejected her first request by saying (*Megillah 7a*):

"קנאה את מעוררת עלינו לבין האומות."
"You will incite the wrath of the nations against us."

Thereupon Esther sent a second message: "Then Esther wrote...this second letter of Purim and letters were sent to all the Jews..." There she wrote that we should not be concerned about the danger of inciting the nations against us, for my words are "words of peace and truth". (*Megillah 9:30*). And she pointed out that the events she wished to write down "had already been recorded in the chronicles of the kings of Persia and Medea." (*Megillah 10:2*) This is spelled out clearly in the *Yerushalmi Megillah*, Chapter 1, Halacha 5.

If indeed the *Megillah* reading was ordained by both the Prophets and the Bais Din, why did the Rambam here at the outset state that *"the reading of the Megillah was ordained by the Prophets"* — "שהיא תקנת הנביאים" and he does not mention the Bais Din at all?

To resolve this question, we might suggest that when the Rambam mentions that the *Megillah* was ordained by the Prophets his intention was not to inform us *who* ordained the reading of the *Megillah*, but rather he had something else in mind altogether. He was addressing the issue of *why* this mitzva of reading the *Megillah* was not an infraction of the prohibition against "adding to the mitzvos of the Torah". There are two possible ways in which the Rambam solves this problem.

HaRav Yosef C. Eisenbach, שליט"א, in his sefer "מחנה יוסף – יו"ט ומועדי השנה" (סימן י"ז), offers the following insight. The Rambam writes:

"והדברים ידועים שהיא תקנת הנביאים"

"It is well known that the reading of the Megillah was ordained by the Prophets."

By emphasizing *"it is well known"*, the Rambam alludes to something he states elsewhere, in הלכות ממרים ב:ט. There he details the prohibition against adding to the mitzvos of the Torah. He contends that this can be avoided if the Sages declare that whatever they ordained was only as a preventive measure. A prime example of this is the prohibition against cooking and eating meat and milk together. "Meat" includes the flesh of any domestic animal as well as a wild beast, even though the word "גדי", "goat", is written here. Thus the Rambam includes in this prohibition also chicken and milk. He explains this in the following manner:

"אבל אם אמר: בשר בעוף מותר מן התורה, ואנו נאסור אותו, **ונודע לעם** שהיא גזרה שלא יביא מן הדבר... אין זה מוסיף אלא עושה סייג לתורה..."

"Even though the Bais Din declares that chicken and meat are biblically allowed to be eaten together, yet we Bais Din forbade it as a preventive measure." [For if people could eat chicken and milk because "chicken" is not spelled out in the Torah, then they would also come to eat the meat of a wild beast together with milk, because it, too, was not spelled out in the Torah, even though in truth it is forbidden by the Torah.]

And since *it is well known to the people* that the Bais Din forbade it as a preventive measure, therefore this would not be an infraction of the prohibition against adding to the mitzvos of the Torah.

This then is what the Rambam means here when he writes in Hilchos Megillah: "it is *well known* that this is an ordination of the Prophets" — to alert us to the truth that the prohibition of adding a mitzva has not been transgressed. For everyone knows that this is not a dictate of the Torah but rather one of the Prophets.

HaRav Yosef Soloveitchik also contends that this was the Rambam's intent here — to forewarn that no infraction of "בל תוסיף" adding to the mitzvos of the Torah, is taking place here. He bases this on the following rationale.

Although the obligation — the חיוב — to read the *Megillah* was Rabbinically ordained, yet the fulfillment of this obligation — the קיום — is from the Torah itself. This means that even though the *manner of performing this mitzva* came from the Rabbis, the *actual performance* of this mitzva fulfills an obligation that was already set down in the Torah, which is to express verbally one's gratitude to Hashem for all the miracles He performed for the Jewish people. And if we would ask, how do we know that this is indeed so, we might find the answer in the *Yerushalmi*, which comments on the words "קימו וקבלו" — *"they confirmed and undertook"* (*Esther 9:27*).

The *Yerushalmi* tells us: "קימו למעלה מה שקבלו למטה", that the fulfillment of a mitzva is viewed as a mitzva dictated by the Almighty in His Torah. We were told by the Prophets that this is so. Therefore, the Rambam mentions the Prophets, נביאים, here to allude to this insight and to prove that there was no infraction of the prohibition against adding to the mitzvos of the Torah in this case.

From this we see that the Rambam is not concerned here to pinpoint exactly *who* ordained this mitzva of reading the *Megillah*; and thus we attribute it to both the Prophets and the Bais Din, as the Rambam himself tells us in his commentary to the *Sefer HaMitzvos*.

IV

FORTY-EIGHT PROPHETS

Rashi comments on the following statement:

"ארבעים ושמונה נביאים...נתנבאו...ולא פחתו ולא הותירו על מה
שכתוב בתורה חוץ ממקרא מגילה..."

"Forty-eight prophets...prophesied...and they did not add to or detract from what was written in the Torah, except for instituting the mitzva of reading the Megillah."

Rashi asks:

"ואם תאמר נר חנוכה כבר פסקו הנביאים אבל בימי מרדכי היו חגי זכריה ומלאכי."

Why doesn't the Gemara here also mention the mitzva of kindling the Chanukah lights, for doesn't that too seem to be an addition? The answer is that since that precept [of kindling Chanukah lights] originated in the post-prophetic era, it is not included. The mitzva of Purim, on the other hand, was instituted when the Prophets Haggai, Zecharia and Malachi were still alive. This leads the Maharsha to ask the following question: Later on in this page, 14a, Rashi enumerates the forty-eight prophets and in this list he includes Mordechai. Why, then did Rashi have to mention Haggai, Zecharia and Malachi, when he could have simply mentioned Mordechai alone?

We might suggest the following answer. The Gemara here asks: "ותו ליכא?" — Why say there were only forty-eight prophets, when we know that there were many more? To which the Gemara answers: Only those prophets whose prophecies were recorded are counted here. However, although Yisrael possessed additional prophets — "double the number of those who left Egypt" — yet their prophecies were not recorded. In addition, *Chazal* tell us in *Baba Basra* 14a that the *Men of the Great Assembly* wrote the Book of Esther, to which Rashi comments that it was Haggai, Zecharia and Malachi who actually wrote the *Megillah*. We will continue this discussion in the following chapters.

Consequently, if the Gemara states here that "forty-eight prophets prophesied to Yisrael", this refers to those prophets who wrote *Kisvei HaKodesh*. Thus it was indeed Haggai, Zecharia and Malachi, and not Mordechai, who authored the Book of Esther, for Mordechai never wrote a book of the *Kisvei HaKodesh*. This explains why Rashi mentioned these three prophets here and not Mordechai.

Reading the Megillah means hearing its message

The Mishna (Megillah 17a) states:

"הקורא את המגילה למפרע לא יצא."

"One who reads the Megillah out of sequence has not fulfilled his obligation."

The gaon and tzaddik, Rav Meir Yechiel HaLevi, the Admor of Ostrov explained the meaning of the Mishna here in the following way.

If one were to read the verses of the Megillah which state: "In those days while Mordechai was sitting at the king's gate, Bigsan and Seresh became angry and planned to assassinate the king... It was recorded in the book of chronicles in the king's presence" (*Esther 2:21*), one might wonder why this was mentioned here in the Megillah, right in the middle of the narrative which discusses the respective roles of Vashti and Esther in the Purim story. For we do not immediately understand that the incident involving Bigsan and Seresh is to have a direct and decisive effect on subsequent events. It is only in a later chapter (Chapter 6, verse 1), when "sleep eluded the king" and he called his servants to bring him the book of chronicles, that this forgotten incident surfaces — "בלילה ההוא נדדה שנת המלך".

As the king Ahashveros reads, he learns that "Mordechai the Jew was the one who uncovered the murderous plot and denounced Bigsan and Seresh... who had plotted to lay hands on the king." Only then does the reader understand retroactively that at the time when Mordechai actually

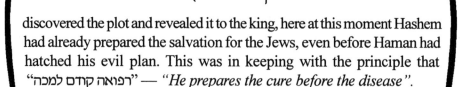

discovered the plot and revealed it to the king, here at this moment Hashem had already prepared the salvation for the Jews, even before Haman had hatched his evil plan. This was in keeping with the principle that "רפואה קודם למכה" — *"He prepares the cure before the disease"*.

If one who hears the story of the Megillah does not realize that Hashem is always ready to protect His people from the evil designs of their enemies, then he has not fulfilled his obligation of "hearing" the true message of the Megillah. For upon reading in Chapter Two the incident of Bigsan and Seresh, the person listening to the Megillah should have been aware that the wheels of salvation were already being set in motion. And if one only realizes it later and only in retrospect, then he has not fulfilled his obligation of reading the Megillah. For in this case he will be "reading the Megillah out of order", in the sense that its deepest message will not be grasped. Thus the Megillah teaches us to be sensitive and to appreciate that even the smallest incident shows us how Hashem guides the destiny of the Jewish people.

Perhaps we can suggest that since the miracle of Purim occurred within the laws of nature, we can only appreciate it if we trace the sequence of events from the beginning to the final resolution and understand the underlying spiritual meaning of it all. If we trace the steps in sequence we can conclude that those steps reveal the imprint of Hashem at every stage. However, if one reads the events of the Purim story out of sequence, then one cannot see or truly appreciate the Divine Hand at work in events here. For miracles must follow a prescribed order, and every detail must fall into place at exactly its appropriate moment. Being aware of the right time and the right place are what makes it possible to detect the miracle. And if one is not in the right place at the right time, he may very well miss out on a miracle. This, then, is the thrust of the statement that one who reads the Megillah out of sequence does not fulfill his obligation.

CHAPTER SEVEN

Reading the Megillah both day and night

I

THE COMMENTATORS DISAGREE

The Gemara in *Megillah* 4a states:

"ואמר ר' יהושע בן לוי: חייב אדם לקרות את המגילה בלילה ולשנותה ביום שנאמר: 'אקרא יומם ולא תענה ולילה ולא דומיה לי'(תהלים כ"ה). סבור מיניה למקרייה בליליא ולמיתנא מתניתין דידה ביממא, אמר להו ר' ירמיה לדידי מיפרשא לי מיניה דרבי חייא בר אבא כגון דאמרי אינשי אעבור פרשתא דא ואתנייה."

"And Rav Yehoshua ben Levi also said: A person is obligated to read the Megillah on the night of Purim and to repeat it on Purim day. It is said: 'O my God, I call out by day and You do not answer; by night and there is silence for me.' The students who heard this ruling understood it to mean that one is obligated to read the Megillah at night and to learn the Mishnayos of Tractate Megillah by day. Rav Yirmiyahu said to them: It has been explained to me personally by Rav Chiya bar Abba that Rav Yehoshua ben Levi meant that one must repeat the Megillah. As people say: I will finish this section and then repeat it."

The Gemara continues:

"אתמר נמי אמר רבי חלבו אמר עולה בירא: חייב אדם לקרות את המגילה בלילה ולשנותה ביום שנאמר: 'למען יזמרך כבוד ולא ידום ה' אלוקי לעולם אודך.'"

"We also learned that this ruling was made by Rav Chelbo in the name of Ulla from Biri: A person is obligated to read the Megillah on the night of Purim and to repeat it on Purim day, as it is said: 'So that my soul might sing to You and not be stilled, Hashem my God, forever will I thank You.'"

The ruling of the Gemara here raises several questions:

1) The Mishna, in 20b states: "The entire day is valid for reading the *Megillah*." The source for this halacha is the verse in Esther 9:28: "**והימים** האלה נזכרים ונעשים" — *"And these days should be remembered and celebrated."* This ruling was cited in the Mishna along with all the other mitzvos which are to be performed by day. Thus we see that the obligation to read the *Megillah* by day was already cited in the Mishna, based on a verse. Why, then, did Rav Yehoshua ben Levi need to remind us about this ruling?

2) Why is it that for all the other mitzvos — both those dictated by the Torah and those rabbinically ordained — we are required to do the mitzva only once, either during the day or at night? For example, the ceremonial eating of matza is only an obligation on the first night of Pesach. Similarly, the esrog and lulav are taken only on the first day of Succos, according to the Torah. Why then, are we obligated to read the *Megillah* twice, once at night and again by day?

3) Why does the Gemara here cite two sources for the nighttime reading? And why indeed does each Amora cite a different source and is not satisfied with the source of the other Amora?

4) There is a difference of opinion between the Ba'alei Tosafos and the Rambam as to whether the beracha of שהחיינו should be recited at both readings of the *Megillah* or only at the first reading at night. Tosafos (in *Megillah* 4a ד"ה חייב אדם) expresses the following opinion:

> "דאע"ג דמברך זמן בלילה חוזר ומברך אותו ביום דעיקר פרסומי ניסא הוי בקריאה דיממא. וקרא נמי משמע כן, דכתיב: 'ולילה ולא דומיה לי.' כלומר אע"פ שקרא ביום, חייב לקרות בלילה, והעיקר הוי ביממא כיון שהזכירו הכתוב תחילה..."

> *"Although the blessing of Shehecheyanu was already recited on the previous evening's reading, one must repeat this beracha during the daytime reading of the Megillah. The rationale for this is that the reading by day is considered to be the main reading, as alluded to in the verse cited in the Gemara, 'And at night...' The point here is to indicate that*

although one should also read at night, yet the main reading
is in the daytime, for it is mentioned first in the verse."

The Rambam, on the other hand, believes that the beracha of
Shehecheyanu should *not be* repeated at the daytime reading. Thus
he writes in *Hilchos Megillah* 1:3, "וביום אינו חוזר ומברך שהחייינו" —
"And by day one does not repeat the beracha of Shehecheyanu".
What is the basis for this disagreement among the commentators?

5) The Ran raises an important issue at the very beginning of this
Mesechta. For those residents of villages who are allowed to read the
Megillah earlier than the 14th of Adar, must they also read the *Megillah*
twice — once at night and again by day — or is the daytime reading
sufficient? What was the Ran perplexed about when he raised
this issue?

II

The practice of Rav Yehoshua ben Levi

Before we attempt to resolve the differing opinions of the
commentators, we must address two further questions:

1) Why did Rav Yehoshua ben Levi state: "One is obligated to read the
Megillah at night and repeat it on Purim day"? Why did he not say
simply: "קורין את המגילה בין ביום בין בלילה." — *"One is obligated to*
read the Megillah both by day and by."

2) Rav Yehoshua ben Levi was an Amora who lived several centuries
after the destruction of the Bais HaMikdash. The reading of the
Megillah was already in practice from the time of Mordechai and
Esther. What then did Rav Yehoshua ben Levi add to our knowledge
when the reading of the *Megillah* both by night and by day was known
for centuries? In this connection, we can examine the responsa of
HaRav Shlomo HaKohen of Vilna, who maintains that the reading of

the *Megillah* was a later innovation. However, this theory is refuted by HaRav Tzvi Pesach Frank in his sefer "שו"ת הר צבי".

To resolve this issue we might suggest that Rav Yehoshua ben Levi did not intend to introduce a "new law", one which was not known previously, for, as we have pointed out, the reading of the *Megillah* by day and by night was well known both by tradition and by its being recorded in the Mishna. Rather, what Rav Yehoshua ben Levi was doing here was attempting to explain the rationale for reading the *Megillah* at night and again during the day; whereas the other mitzvos of Purim, such as eating the festive meal, giving portions of food to friends and neighbors, and giving gifts to the poor, are practiced only during the day. Why, then, is the *Megillah* read also at night?

We find in other places that it was the practice of Rav Yehoshua ben Levi to articulate laws we are already familiar with. His purpose was not to inform us of the law but rather to explain its underlying rationale. For example, in *Pesachim* 114a, Rav Yehoshua ben Levi tells us that women are obligated to drink the four cups of wine at the Pesach seder, for they too were involved in the miracle — "אף הן היו באותו הנס". And the point is made on the very next page of the Gemara , 114b, that there is a *Baraisa* which states:

"אחד אנשים ואחד נשים וכו' חייבים בד' כוסות."

"Both men and women are obligated to drink the four cups, etc."

Thus we have a previous source to teach us that women are obligated in this mitzva. Why, then, was it necessary for Rav Yehoshua ben Levi to make his statement? The answer must be (see *The Commentators' Pesach*, pp. 28-9) that Rav Yehoshua wished to explain *why* women are obligated in this mitzva, even though it is time-bound, and women are normally exempt from time-bound mitzvos. Rav Yehoshua explained this by saying that since women were also involved in the miracle of redemption from Egypt, (see Rashi and Tosafos here) this neutralizes the time-bound element and makes women equally obligated in this mitzva.

To answer these problems we might suggest that the word "לשנותה"

can mean either "to repeat" or "a second time". Thus we are being told here either that we must repeat the *Megillah* reading or we must read it a second time. If we adopt the view that we are called upon to repeat the reading of the Megillah, this implies that the purpose of reading the *Megillah* at night and then repeating it the next day is to give us a deeper understanding and appreciation of the Purim story. Just as in all studies, the more one reviews the lesson already taught, the greater will be the clarity of comprehension.

Thus, since the purpose of reading the *Megillah* is to publicize the mitzva, "פרסומי ניסא", this is accomplished with a second reading, which serves to underline the meaning of the Purim miracle even more strongly. From this we understand that the daytime reading of the *Megillah* is the primary focus of the mitzva, from which we gain that deeper insight. This is how the Netziv explains the intent of the word "ולשנותה". He writes as follows:

"פי' ולשנותה דצריך להיות הקריאה בידיעה של הביאור להבין ולהשכיל
בה, והוי זה כמו שלומד פרשה, דפעם הראשון עובר עליה בלי ניתוח
המאמרים, ובשעה שעובר שנית הוא שם לב להשכיל יותר עליה..."

However, if we are to understand "לשנותה" as meaning *"a second time"*, then the emphasis here is on the performance of the mitzva once at night and then a second time the next day.

This, then, is the rationale behind the decisions made by the Rambam and the *Ba'alei HaTosafos* previously mentioned. The *Ba'alei HaTosafos* are of the opinion that "ולשנותה" means *"to repeat"*, for the purpose of giving deeper insight and thereby gaining new appreciation for the mitzva. The special blessing of *Shehecheyanu* is said at night because it is the *first time* this mitzva is being performed this year. And because we gain a "new insight" the next morning when we read the *Megillah* again, this requires that *Shehecheyanu* be recited the next day as well. And since we derive greater appreciation from the miracle in the daytime, we consider the daytime reading to be the main mitzva, העיקר. This is the reason why Tosafos adopts the verse of "אלוקי אקרא יומם" to stress the daytime reading. And in this context, "ולשנותה" is to be understood to mean *"to repeat"*.

The Rambam, on the other hand, adopts the verse of "למען יזמרך כבוד ולא ידום...**לעולם** אודך" to indicate *constant praise*, beginning at night and continuing into the next day. According to this view, "ולשנותה" is to be understood as *"a second time"*, and it does not require a second recitation of *Shehecheyanu* the next day. For here we do not have a new experience, but rather an ongoing recitation of praise and thanksgiving extending both at night and into the next day.

With this difficulty resolved, we can now answer all the above questions:

1) The Mishna in 21b, which cites the *pasuk* of "והימים האלה נזכרים ונעשים", serves as the *source* for the requirement to read the *Megillah* by day. The verses mentioned in 4a account for the *reason* we repeat the *Megillah* reading.

2) And the reason why all other mitzvos are performed only once, whereas the *Megillah* is read twice, is that the mitzva here must be publicized, פרסומי ניסא, and this enables us to gain a greater appreciation for and understanding of the events which transpired on Purim, as a result of the *Megillah* reading being repeated and re-emphasized yet again.

3) We can now appreciate why we need two different verses to explain why we require a second reading of the Megillah. These verses are: "אלוקי אקרא יומם" and "למען יזמרך וכו'". And, as we have explained, each verse alludes to a different meaning of the word "למען יזמרך וכו'". The word "לשנותה" emphasizes the requirement of doing this mitzva twice, whereas "אלוקי אקרא יומם" calls for a repetition of the *Megillah* reading.

4) We have already explained the basis for the disagreement between the Rambam and the Baalei Tosafos.

5) Based on the above, we can now understand what motivated the Ran

to question the kind of reading required in the villages. For if the purpose of the second reading was to gain a deeper insight and appreciation of the mitzva, then the villagers too should be required to read the *Megillah* at night, in order that the day's reading, by being repeated, should have greater meaning. However, if the purpose of the second reading is merely to do this mitzva twice, then we might say that just as the halacha was lenient towards the villagers, by allowing them to read the *Megillah* on an earlier day, so too was the halacha lenient here regarding the number of times reading the *Megillah* was required.

III

A DEEPER UNDERSTANDING OF THE RAMBAM'S VIEW

The Rambam in *Hilchos Megillah*, Chapter 1, Halacha 3, writes as follows:

"מצוה לקרות את כולה. ומצוה לקראתה בלילה וביום."

"It is a mitzva to read all of the Megillah. And it is a mitzva to read the Megillah both by night and by day."

Although this seems to detail two distinct laws, the common denominator would be the *amount* , "שיעור" required in this mitzva of reading the *Megillah*. This aspect of quantity encompasses (1) all of the *Megillah*, and (2) both by night and by day. However, in light of our above discussion, we might suggest another possible reason for linking these two separate mitzvos.

The Mishna on page 19a states:

"ומהיכן קורין אדם את המגילה ויוצא בה. ר' מאיר אומר: כולה. ר' יהודה אומר: מאיש יהודי. ר' יוסי אומר: מאחר הדברים האלה."

"From which point in the Megillah must one read in order to fulfill one's obligation? Rav Meir says: One must read all of it. Rav Yehuda says: From the verse 'A Jewish man' (Esther

2:5) to the end. Rav Yose says: From the verse 'After these things' (Esther 3:1) to the end."

And the Gemara cites a fourth opinion:

"ר' שמעון בן יוחאי אומר:מבלילה ההוא."

"Rav Shimon ben Yochai says: One must read from 'On that night' (Esther 6:1)."

Rav Yochanan explained the rationale behind each of these opinions.

1) The one who requires the reading of the entire *Megillah* does so because we must speak of the might of Ahashveros.

2) The one who says from "A Jewish man" does so because we must emphasize the role played by Mordechai in these events.

3) The one who says from "After these things" does so to emphasize Haman's power.

4) And the one who requires the reading from "On that night" does so to focus on the importance of the miracle itself (For this *pasuk* marks the turning point in the Purim story and the beginning of the miraculous events hidden within the narrative.)

Thus we might say that if "לשנותה" alludes to *repeating* the reading of the *Megillah* to gain clarity, then we must read all or at least most of the *Megillah* in order to see the entire picture emerging. However, if we are to start from the point where Rav Shimon ben Yochai suggests, near the end of the Purim story, in order to emphasize the power of the miracle, then perhaps we need not review the events which took place, and we need not emphasize the repeating of the *Megillah*. This would confirm the Rambam's view, that since we are required to read the entire *Megillah*, we must read it both at night and in the day, in order to gain greater clarity and deeper insight into the events which revealed the workings of God's intervention. For even though the story appears to have taken place within the laws of nature, yet Hashem's Hand becomes more and more visible as we read the entire *Megillah* — "כל המגילה" — and as we repeat the reading of the story once again — "לקרותה בין ביום ובין בלילה". As to why the Rambam therefore does not require a second beracha of שהחיינו we will soon explain.

IV

THE CUSTOM OF READING THE MEGILLAH ON SATURDAY NIGHT PRIOR TO PURIM

If we adopt this interpretation of "לשנותה", to mean to repeat the reading of the Megillah for the purpose of gaining clarity and deeper appreciation of the Purim miracle, we might perhaps be able to explain the following Mishna in *Mesechtas Sofrim* 14:18:

> "אמר רב לוי: מגילת אסתר צריך לקרותה בלילה ולשנותה ביום שנאמר [תהלים ל'] 'למען יזמרך כבוד' בלילה, 'ולא ידום' ביום (לפיכך נהגו לקרותה במוצאי שבת שתים)."
>
> *"Said Rav Levi: One must read the Megillah at night and repeat it by day, as it is said, 'So my soul may sing to You' — at night; 'and not be stilled'; — by day. (Thus it is a custom to read it at the termination of the Shabbos on two successive weeks.)"*

In the commentary of the נחלת יעקב (*op. cit.*), this custom is explained:

> "שהיה מנהג בימיהם ב' שבתות קודם פורים היו כל הקהל קורין המגילה ביחד בבית הכנסת."
>
> *"There was a custom in those days to assemble and read the Megillah in the synagogue on the two Saturday evenings prior to Purim."*

But what is the source for this practice and what is its purpose? In light of the interpretation of the word "לשנותה" as meaning to repeat for the sake of gaining greater clarity and deeper understanding, perhaps we can understand the reason for this custom. And we can understand the sequence of the Mishna here, which is that since we are required to read the *Megillah* twice, this underlines the fact that we seek clarity and therefore we may extend the reading of the *Megillah* to even before the holiday, in order to "practice" becoming accustomed to the story of Purim.

V

Saying "Shehecheyanu" twice

HaRav Yosef Dov Soloveitchik explains the thinking of Rabbenu Tam, who maintains that the beracha of *Shehecheyanu* is to be recited both at night and again during the day before reading the *Megillah*. For with the reading of the *Megillah* we have two obligations, קיומים, to fulfill the mitzva.

1) An obligation to read the *Megillah* as ordained by the Rabbis, מדברי סופרים.

2) We are obligated to recite Hallel. And although on Purim we do not recite the standard Hallel, but instead we say: "קריתא זו הלילא" — *"the reading of the Megillah is equivalent to reciting Hallel."*

This means that at night, when Hallel is never said (except on Pesach night) the only obligation we have to fulfill the mitzva is the actual reading of the *Megillah*. This reading thus requires the blessing of *Shehecheyanu*. During the day, on the other hand, not only must we fulfill the mitzva of reading the *Megillah*, but we are also obligated to fulfill the mitzva of reciting Hallel.

This "new obligation", קיום, thus requires that we recite another *Shehayanu*. Yet, even though we never make a *"Shehayanu"* when we recite Hallel, this is so only for the standard form of Hallel, consisting of those chapters from the Book of Psalms. Since we read this order of Psalms several times a year, no beracha of *Shehayanu* is required.

However, when the Hallel is given a new form, as it is on Purim when the reading of the *Megillah* replaces the standard form of Hallel, "קרייתא זו הלילא" now we might say that this form of Hallel does indeed require the recitation of *Shehecheyanu*. With this in mind, we might now suggest the following. It is well known that the Meiri believes that if one is unable to read or hear the *Megillah*, for whatever reason, that person may fulfill his obligation of *Megillah* by reciting the standard Hallel instead. The justification for this is "קרייתא זו הלילא".

Thus we might say that if one were to recite the Hallel instead of the *Megillah*, then it should follow that the beracha of *Shehayanu* should not be said. The reason for this, as we have explained, is that our obligation to recite the *Shehecheyanu* upon hearing the *Megillah* applies only in the form of the Megillah reading. And since Hallel is now being recited in its standard format, this does not require a *Shehecheyanu*.

In addition, we might point out that since the justification for reading Hallel is only to make up for the absence of a Megillah, therefore this consideration applies only during the day. This means that if one was not able to hear the reading of the Megillah at night, one could not fulfill the mitzva by substituting the recitation of Hallel, for Hallel is never said at night.

This helps us understand the rationale of the Rambam here. For he maintains that *Shehecheyanu* is not required for the daytime reading of the *Megillah*, even though we now have a new obligation, which is that of Hallel; and we might think that this new obligation would warrant a new recitation of *Shehecheyanu*. There are two possible explanations why a new *Shehecheyanu* is in fact not required.

When we do a mitzva once a year, we are required to recite the blessing of *Shehecheyanu*. But is the reason for the blessing that we are fulfilling a mitzva, קיום מצוה, which we have not fulfilled for an entire year, or is it rather because we have not performed this mitzva since last year, and it is this act of performing the mitzva anew, מעשה מצוה, which requires the beracha? This subtle distinction forms the basis of the disagreement between the Rambam and Rabbenu Tam, as we shall explain.

Rabbenu Tam is of the opinion that the obligation to recite *Shehecheyanu* arises from the קיום מצוה, the fact that we are fulfilling this mitzva after a long time. This is why the *Shehecheyanu* is made *at night*, for that is when we fulfill the mitzva of reading the *Megillah* for the first time since last year. And in the morning, when we read the *Megillah* again, we recite *Shehecheyanu* because we are now fulfilling our obligation of Hallel, praising the Almighty for the Purim miracle.

The Rambam, on the other hand, is of the opinion that *Shehecheyanu* is said because of the actual performance of the mitzva, מעשה מצוה, for the first time after so long. And because this is the reason for the beracha, the fact that we made it at night for the first performance of the mitzva means that we do not have to make the beracha of *Shehecheyanu* again in the morning, since we already performed the mitzva the night before. This is in spite of the fact that in the morning we do have a new קיום, an obligation to fulfill the mitzva of Hallel, which was not required the night before.

There is another way to explain the rationale behind the Rambam's way of thinking. We can see this if we examine the Gemara in ערכין י׳-ב׳, which sets down the formula for when Hallel is to be recited: If the day is referred to as a מועד, a festival day, or if the day requires us to refrain from work, מלאכה.

Thus the Gemara asks why Hallel is said on Chanukah, when neither of these conditions are met. And the Gemara answers: "מטעם הנס", Hallel is recited nevertheless because of the miracle that transpired on Chanukah.

Perhaps, then, we can draw a distinction between Hallel which is said because it is a festival, מועד, and Hallel which is said because of a miracle. Hallel which is said on a festival is required because of the holiness of the day, קדושת היום, which calls for the specified form of *shirah*, praise of Hashem, to be said on this day, הלל דפרקים. The Hallel which is due to a miracle, on the other hand, requires that the miracle be commemorated in a public manner, פרסומי ניסא. And the appropriate form of publicizing a miracle is the recitation of the standard Hallel. This implies that on Purim, both the mitzva of reading the Megillah and the recitation of Hallel is done to publicize the miracle. This is, perhaps, the deeper meaning of the phrase "קרייתא זו הלילא", that the reading of the *Megillah* is equivalent to reciting Hallel, for they are both a fulfillment of the mitzva of פרסומי ניסא, publicizing the miracle. Thus, if at night we already made a *Shehecheyanu* for the reading of the *Megillah*, which is basically a fulfillment of the mitzva of פרסומי ניסא, then we need not make another *Shehecheyanu* for the morning's Hallel, which fulfills the same purpose.

VI

The עיקר and the טפל

In light of the above, we may now try to answer the following questions asked in the sefer "לב שלם". Tosafos is of the opinion that although one offered the beracha of *Shehecheyanu* at night, one must repeat this beracha before reading the *Megillah* again the next day, because the עיקר of the mitzva, its main occurrence, is during the day.

Consequently, we see that if one made a beracha on a טפל, a secondary feature, that beracha does not suffice for the עיקר, the main event of the mitzva. In this case, the טפל is the night time Megillah reading, whereas the עיקר is the reading of the Megillah during the day. This means that we must make the blessing of *Shehecheyanu* not only at night, but the next day as well, for the עיקר requires its own separate beracha.

The "לב שלם" suggests that there is proof from various sources to substantiate that a beracha over a "טפל" does in fact suffice, even for the עיקר. For example, the Gemara tells us in *Mesechtas Pesachim* 115a that according to the opinion of Rav Chisda, if a beracha of "בורא פרי האדמה" was said over a vegetable, the *Karpas*, used for the first of the two "dippings" on Pesach night, this beracha suffices for the vegetable used later on in the Seder, the *Maror*, even though the karpas vegetable is considered to be the טפל and the later maror, the עיקר, which is the main mitzva of the evening involving vegetables. And so here we see that a beracha over the טפל can suffice for the עיקר and an additional beracha is not required.

We can prove this theory in another way as well. The beracha recited over the sounding of the shofar prior to the Amidah prayer on Rosh Hashanah, תקיעות דמיושב, is sufficient for the rest of the service, and we do not have to make another beracha for the next occurrence of shofar blowing, the תקיעה דמעומד, which occurs during the repetition of the Mussaf Amidah prayer. This is so even despite the fact that the beracha of the תקיעות דמיושב is considered to be the טפל, whereas the sounding of the shofar during the repetition of the Mussaf Amidah is considered to be the עיקר.

Yet another proof of this theory is that the beracha of "על אכילת מצה", said at the outset of the seder meal, frees one from the obligation of making a beracha over the Afikomen, which is eaten at the very end of the meal. This is in spite of the fact that the matza eaten at the end of the meal, the Afikomen, is considered to be the main occurrence of the mitzva of eating matzah, the עיקר, and the matzah eaten at the beginning of the meal is considered to be a secondary mitzva, the טפל.

With all these proofs in mind, asks the "לב שלם", why does Tosafos contend here that two berachos must be made over the *Megillah* readings, once at night and a second time during the day, for he is of the opinion that a beracha over the טפל can suffice even for the עיקר?

To resolve these questions we might suggest that there is a great difference between the issues cited here as proof that a טפל can suffice for the עיקר, and the issue of the two readings of the *Megillah*, by night and by day. For in the case of the two instances of eating matzah and pronouncing the blessing of "על אכילת מצה" we have two separate and distinct mitzvos: eating matzah at the beginning of the Pesach Seder meal, and eating matzah at the end of the seder meal to fulfill the mitzva of "מצה" (according to those who maintain that matzah eaten at the end of the meal constitutes the actual mitzva of אכילת מצה, the required eating of matzah).

Similarly, in the instance of the mitzva of maror, we have two separate acts of eating the maror: eating מרור for the karpas, in the event that there is no other vegetable available for that purpose, and eating maror later on in the seder meal, to fulfill the mitzva of "אכילת מרור".

As for the mitzva of shofar, we find that we have two separate mitzvos here as well: sounding the shofar *before* the Amidah prayer, and sounding the shofar *during* the Amidah prayer.

On the other hand, when it comes to the reading of the *Megillah*, it is not that we have two separate mitzvos and one is more important than the other, but rather that one of these is only a preparatory mitzva, whose purpose is to serve the main mitzva. Thus the main function of the nighttime reading is to precede the reading of the next day, and to insure that the daytime reading be the *second* reading. This means that the *Megillah* reading of the night is not viewed as a separate mitzva at all, but rather as a preparation, מכשיר, for the main mitzva, which is the *Megillah* reading of the day. Consequently, a beracha recited over such a mitzva, הכשר מצוה, does not suffice to exempt one from a beracha required for the main mitzva.

The Rambam, on the other hand, does not view the nighttime *Megillah* reading as a מכשיר for the day's reading, but rather as a mitzva in and of itself. Therefore, the beracha said then can exempt one from having to recite the beracha which is called for at the daytime *Megillah* reading.

The following halacha gives further support to the position that if we have two separate mitzvos which cover the same theme, even if both are equally important, one beracha of *Shehecheyanu* suffices for both. This halacha is that on Chanukah each day is viewed as a separate day of the miracle, and yet a single beracha of *Shehecheyanu* is recited only on the first day of the holiday. We could certainly make a case that *Shehecheyanu* should be required every day of Chanukah if we view the miracle as a new miracle every day. Yet the halacha unequivocally states that one beracha of *Shehecheyanu* suffices for all eight days.

In the same vein, although we say that we have two separate and distinct *Megillah* readings, yet a single beracha of *Shehecheyanu* suffices for both of them. The Vilna Gaon, however, seems to indicate that this is not so, and the Rambam is of the opinion that the day's reading does not require a *Shehecheyanu* is based entirely on other considerations.

The Vilna Gaon, in סימן תרצ"ה, writes as follows:

"וביום אינו חוזר ומברך שהחיינו אע"ג דעיקר זמנה ביום מכל מקום
כיון שבירך בלילה יצא, דלא גרע מאם בירך אסוכה ולולב בשעת
עשייתה. וכן לכתחילה יש לברך בלילה ומשבירך בלילה אינו מברך ביום
כמו בסוכה שהחיינו."

*"One need not repeat the beracha of Shehecheyanu during
the day, even though the second day's reading is viewed as
the main reading of Purim. For because one made a beracha
at night, he need not repeat the beracha on the next day. For
this is not considered to be any worse than the situation in
which one made a beracha at the time of creating a succah or
holding a lulav prior to the actual holiday of Succos. And
even if a blessing of Shehecheyanu was made then, one need
not repeat the Shehecheyanu over the succah or the lulav when
it comes time to perform the mitzva."*

The Vilna Gaon compares reading the *Megillah* to the mitzvos of succah
and lulav. Just as in those instances, the preliminary acts of making the succah
and preparing the lulav and the actual performance of the mitzvos of succah
and lulav are viewed as one mitzva. And the beracha recited at the outset of
this mitzva frees one from the obligation of having to recite the beracha
again when one later fulfills the actual mitzva of sitting in the succah and
taking the lulav. We can similarly say that the beracha recited at night before
we begin to fulfill the mitzva of reading the *Megillah* also covers the main
mitzva of the daytime *Megillah* reading and does not have to be repeated.

VII

REPEATING SHEHECHEYANU IN THE MORNING

We might suggest several answers to the question why we need to
repeat the *Shehecheyanu* blessing at the morning Megillah reading. There

is a disagreement among the commentators regarding the halachic status of the nighttime Megillah reading. The Rokeach is of the opinion that the nighttime reading is the more important of the two readings and thus requires a Shehecheyanu blessing. Yet most opinions, such as that of the טורי אבן and the נודע ביהודה, maintain that the nighttime reading is only a Rabbinic ordinance — מדרבנן, whereas the reading of the Megillah by day is directly dictated by received tradition, מדברי קבלה.

Thus we might therefore contend that since the daytime reading contains a higher degree of sanctity, the repetition of *Shehecheyanu* is justified. If we accept this contention that the nighttime reading is only a Rabbinic ordinance, then we can shed light on the following words of the Rambam. In *Hilchos Megillah* 1:11 he writes:

''עיר שהיא ספק ואין ידוע אם היתה מוקפת חומה בימות יהושע בן נון
או אחרי כן הוקפה, קוראין בשני הימים שהן י"ד וט"ו **ובליליהם**...''

"If there is doubt concerning whether a city was already walled at the time of Yehoshua ben Nun or only afterwards, we are to read on both days, the 14th and the 15th, including both nights..."

Why does the Rambam stress that we are to read on *"both nights"* when this should appear to be obvious, since because this might have been a walled city we must read again on the 15th as well as on the 14th. But if we are obligated to read on the 15th, this would naturally also include the night of the 15th. Therefore, why did the Rambam find it necessary to point out that we must also read on the night of the 15th?

The answer suggested (see the journal "מסורה") is that the only reason we read the Megillah at night is to assure that the reading of the day is repeated as the "second reading". Thus, if we have already read the Megillah on the previous night, on the 14th, then there would be no reason to read the Megillah again on the night of the 15th. This is the reason we are specifically told by the Rambam that we are obligated to read on the night of the 15th.

Another reason why we must read *"on both nights"* is that the

Rambam himself maintains that *Shehecheyanu* is said only at the nighttime reading, thus proving that this blessing is recited only at night. Thus we must read on the night of the 15th in order to recite the obligatory Sheheyanu.

However, in light of the view that the nighttime reading is a mitzva מדרבנן, only of rabbinic origin, whereas the daytime reading fulfils a mitzva of received tradition, מדברי קבלה, this means that the daytime reading is more stringent. Thus we can understand why we must read on both days. However, since the nighttime reading is only Rabbinically ordained, we might think that we could be more lenient, and therefore the Rambam reminds us that this is not so, and we must read on *both nights*.

VIII

Two pasukim: Two opinions

As we have mentioned, there are two verses which allude to the requirement of reading the Megillah. They are:

1) "אלוקי אקרא יומם ולא תענה ולילה ולא דומיה לי" — *"My God, I call out by day...by night..."*

2) "למען יזמרך כבוד ולא ידום ה' אלוקי לעלם אודך" — *"So my soul may sing to you and not be stilled, Hashem, my God, forever will I thank You."*

We have already discussed the practical implications concerning these two verses, yet there is another aspect which needs to be explored.

There is a difference of opinion among the commentators regarding the status of the Megillah reading at night. The Rokeach, as we have seen, believes that the nighttime reading is the major reading, whereas the טורי אבן in his commentary to this Mesechta (ד', א' ד"ה חייב אדם) and the נודע ביהודה, in his responsa (שו"ת נוב"ק או"ח סימן מ"א) maintains that only the daytime reading was dictated by רוח הקודש, the Holy Spirit. The nighttime reading, on the other hand, as we have discussed, was a Rabbinic ordinance. HaRav Shlomo HaKohen of Vilna (שו"ת בנין שלמה, ח"א סימן נ"ח) maintains that not only is the nighttime Megillah reading an ordinance of the Rabbis, but was introduced only much later, at the time of Rav Yehoshua ben Levi (שו"ת הר צבי ח"ב סימן ו', מהרב צ.פ. פרנק).

It would appear on the surface that there is a practical difference whether we say the Megillah reading is of Rabbinic origin or was rather dictated by the Prophets, מדברי סופרים, regarding the time period we call *"twilight"* — בין השמשות. This period is not clearly defined and whether it belongs to the day or to the night. Consequently, if we say that the obligation of reading the Megillah is only a Rabbinic ordinance, then we can take a lenient view and say that this period is considered to be night, and thus it is an appropriate period in which to fulfill the mitzva of the nighttime reading of the Megillah. However, if we say that the reading of the Megillah at night is also מדברי קבלה, from received tradition, then we would have to take a stringent view and not regard this period as nighttime.

Indeed, the Pri Megadim, in סימן תר"פ, rules that if one finds that due to circumstances beyond his control, he is compelled to read the Megillah earlier, then he may read at *"twilight"*, even though it remains doubtful whether this period is actually nighttime. The reason for this is that we view the nighttime Megillah reading as only a Rabbinic ordinance and therefore we may be lenient and regard this period as nighttime.

In the sefer "מעגלי צדק" by HaRav Karelinstein, (עמ' ע"ח-ע"ט) the author discusses this decision of the Pri Megadim, based on the insight offered by his rebbe, HaRav Yosef Shlomo Kahanaman, ז"ל, who defines the issue as to what exactly constitutes the time period of twilight, בין השמשות. We are told that we must distinguish between two basic issues here: when nighttime begins, and what is the status of בין השמשות?

Nighttime is determined by the appearance of three stars, at which time was can say that night has commenced. Therefore, all those mitzvos that are to be done only by day can no longer be performed. And those mitzvos which are to be done at night can now be performed after the appearance of these three stars.

However, the issue of "twilight time" does not concern itself with the question of day or night, but the issue here is rather which calendar day does this time period belong to yesterday or tomorrow, the following day?

Based on this premise, it would follow that one certainly could not read the Megillah at בין השמשות, for this period is viewed as still being daytime, and therefore the only relevant question would be what calendar day does this time period belong to? This means that even if the nighttime Megillah reading is only of Rabbinic origin, one could not read it then, at בין השמשות.

This challenges the decision of the Pri Megadim. To resolve this disagreement, the מעגלי צדק concludes that we must say that the mitzva of reading the Megillah twice does not require a reading at night and then one again the next day, but rather one is required to read once at the beginning of Purim, during the first half of Purim, and again on the following morning, during the second half of Purim day. Thus although the time period of בין השמשות is viewed as daytime, yet at the same time it can also be considered to be the beginning of the 14th of Adar, Purim day, in other words, the first half of the day of Purim.

Finally we might suggest that this issue of when we read the Megillah, whether nighttime and daytime or during the first and second halves of Purim is dependent on which of the two verses we adopt. If we adopt the pasuk of "ולילה ולא דומיה לי" as the source of the requirement to read the Megillah, then we could assume that day and night are the dominant consideration.

However, if we adopt the other pasuk, that of "למען יזמרך כבוד ולא ידום" which calls for continually praising Hashem, then we could conclude that this praise of Hashem should remain constant, and extend from the beginning of Purim until its conclusion.

The Power of Jewish Prayer

The Gemara in Megillah 16a records the following incident:

"When Haman came to take Mordechai, he found him engaged in teaching Torah to the Rabbis. After Mordechai had finished his lecture, Haman asked the students what they had been studying. They replied: 'When the Holy Temple stood, a man brought a meal offering. He would take a handful of fine flour (קמיצה) and make atonement with it.'

Said Haman: 'Your handful of fine flour has come and displaced my ten thousand talents of silver [which he gave to Ahashveros for permission to destroy the Jewish people].' "

The אבני נזר asked, how could Haman make such a declaration that his plan of destruction had been frustrated, when in fact the decree issued against the Jews was still in effect? And he answers, that Haman was using a ploy here. He was well aware of the "secret weapon" of the Jews — prayer, and he thought that if he could lead them to believe that the danger to their lives was past, they would be lulled into a false sense of security and would stop praying to Hashem with such heartfelt devotion. Only then, he believed, would his evil plan have a chance of success.

However, Haman's scheme failed. Our holy seforim point out that when we hold the grogger, the noisemaker which we use on Purim when Haman's name is mentioned during the Megillah reading, we find that the handle is on the bottom. On Chanukah, on the other hand, when we spin the dreidel, we hold it from the top. Why is this so?

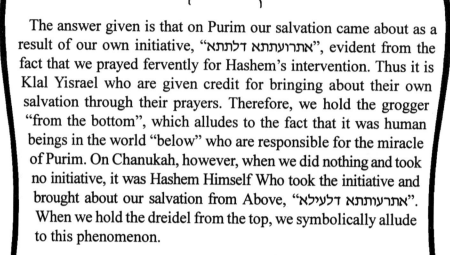

The answer given is that on Purim our salvation came about as a result of our own initiative, "אתרועעתתא דלתתא", evident from the fact that we prayed fervently for Hashem's intervention. Thus it is Klal Yisrael who are given credit for bringing about their own salvation through their prayers. Therefore, we hold the grogger "from the bottom", which alludes to the fact that it was human beings in the world "below" who are responsible for the miracle of Purim. On Chanukah, however, when we did nothing and took no initiative, it was Hashem Himself Who took the initiative and brought about our salvation from Above, "אתרעותתא דלעילא". When we hold the dreidel from the top, we symbolically allude to this phenomenon.

On Purim, it was the power of Jewish prayer which brought about a reversal of events and resulted in our salvation. Haman's ploy failed and he was unable to trap us into ceasing our prayers.

CHAPTER EIGHT

The Berachos after Megillah Reading

I

A MATTER OF CUSTOM

The Mishna in *Mesechtas Megillah* 21a states:

‎"מקום שנהגו לברך יברך, ושלא לברך לא יברך."

"Where they are accustomed to recite a blessing, one should recite the blessing. Where the custom is not to recite a blessing, one need not recite the blessing."

The Gemara in 21b amends this statement:

‎"אמר אביי: לא שנו אלא לאחריה אבל לפניה מצוה לברך."

"Abaye said: the Mishna taught that the blessing over the Megillah is a matter of custom only in regard to the blessing recited after the reading of the Megillah. But regarding the blessing recited before the reading of the Megillah, there is an obligation to recite a blessing and this is not a matter of custom."

The Gemara then asks:

‎"לאחריה מאי לברך?"

"For those who have the custom of reciting a blessing after the reading of the Megillah, what blessing does one recite?"

The Gemara replies:

‎"ברוך אתה ה' אלקינו מלך העולם הרב את ריבנו והדן את דיננו והנוקם את נקמתנו והנפרע לנו מצרינו והמשלם גמול לכל אויבי נפשנו. ברוך אתה ה' הנפרע לישראל מכל צריהם. רבא אמר: הא-ל המושיע."

"Blessed are You, Hashem, our God, King of the Universe, Who takes up our grievance, judges our claim and avenges our wrong. And Who exacts vengeance for us from our foes. And Who brings just retribution upon all the enemies of our soul. Blessed are you, Hashem, Who exacts vengeance for Yisrael from all their foes.

Rava, however, says the blessings should conclude with: 'The God Who brings salvation.' "

The Gemara then concludes:

"אמר רב פפא: הלכך נימרינהו לתרווייהו, ברוך אתה ה' הנפרע לישראל מכל צריהם הא-ל המושיע."

Said Rav Papa: Therefore we should say both 'Who exacts vengeance for Yisrael from all their foes' and 'the God Who brings salvation.' "

The question here is: what exactly is the issue that Rava and the *Tanna Kamma* (the first opinion) are arguing about?

II

A SEPARATE ENTITY?

Does this blessing relate to the *Megillah* and its reading, or are we to view it as a separate entity expressing gratitude to Hashem and recognition of the miracle He performed on our behalf, rather than being related to the *Megillah* reading. The truth is, there is a sharp disagreement among the Rishonim, the early commentators, regarding the rationale behind this blessing.

THE SOLUTION OF THE RAN

The Ran, in his commentary to this Gemara (דף י"ב מדפי הר"ן), asks the following question:

"יש לתמוה ברכה זו למה פותחת בברוך, שהרי היא סמוכה לברכה שלפניה...י"ל דהאי ברכה אחרונה לאו אקריאת מגילה אלא ברכה בפני עצמה שנתקנה על הנס."

He explains that there is a halacha concerning the makeup of a beracha, which is that in the event that two berachos follow each other, even if they do not follow each other immediately, the second beracha does not require a *prefix*, i.e., the beginning words, "ברוך אתה ה'" — "*Baruch atah Hashem*". The rationale for this is that the second beracha shares the prefix of the first. Therefore, one must ask here why the concluding beracha after reading the *Megillah* requires a prefix, when it should be seen as being a ברכה הסמוכה לחבירתה relying on the beracha recited at the beginning of the *Megillah* reading.

The Ran answers this question by asserting that the concluding beracha recited here is not related to the *Megillah* reading but rather, as we have pointed out, it is a beracha recited to praise the Almighty for bringing about miracles for the Jewish people.

The solution of the Ritba

The Ritba addresses the same question. Why do we need a prefix for this concluding beracha of the *Megillah* reading, for it is a ברכה הסמוכה לחבירתה and thus can rely on the previous beracha? The Ritba comes to the same conclusion as the Ran — "שברכה זו אינה על המגילה אלא ברכה של שבח על הנס". He maintains that this concluding beracha is unrelated to the *Megillah* reading, rather it is a general expression of thanksgiving.

However, the Ritba then refers to another solution which others maintain. They explain that since the concluding beracha is recited only as a custom which some follow, then it cannot be considered a ברכה הסמוכה לחבירתה, a beracha adjacent to an obligatory beracha. The Ritba points out that this answer is invalid, for we see that even though the concluding beracha of the Hallel is only a custom, מנהג, the law states that a prefix is not required, since it *is* viewed as being adjacent to the opening beracha of the Hallel. From this we can see that even for a beracha which is optional, we apply the law of ברכה הסמוכה לחבירתה.

THE SOLUTION OF THE RASHBA

The Rashba, on the other hand, disagrees with this position and maintains that indeed this concluding beracha is related to the reading of the *Megillah*. As for the question why it is not viewed as a ברכה הסמוכה לחבירתה, a beracha which is adjacent to an obligatory beracha, the answer given is that the lengthy reading of the *Megillah* constitutes an interruption, הפסק, and this negates the status of the ברכה הסמוכה לחבירתה here.

This position of the Rashba is applied to the beracha of ישתבח, the concluding beracha of the פסוקי דזמרה. Why does this beracha not require a prefix — the beginning words of "ברוך אתה ה'" — since it is said long after we began the פסוקי דזמרה with the beracha of "ברוך שאמר" the beginning beracha to this section? Similarly, this question can be asked regarding the concluding beracha of the Hallel. Why does it, too, not call for a concluding prefix, for wasn't it also said only after a lengthy recitation of psalms which make up the Hallel?

To this question, the Rashba answers that we can distinguish between these prayers and the concluding beracha recited after the *Megillah* reading, for the latter does indeed require a prefix. In the Morning Prayers of the פסוקי דזמרה everything which is said — including both the beracha and the contents of the פסוקי דזמרה — are concerned with one theme, which is to praise Hashem. Thus we apply here the principle of ברכה הסמוכה לחבירתה, and the prayer of ישתבח does not require a prefix.

The same is true for the Hallel, whose concluding beracha does not need a prefix. However, regarding the concluding beracha and the reading of the *Megillah*, there is no common denominator. For the reading of the *Megillah* concerns itself with relating the story of Purim, whereas the beracha is in praise of the miracle wrought on our behalf. This difference in intention means in effect that the *Megillah* reading constitutes an interruption, הפסק, between the opening beracha and the concluding one. Therefore it calls for a prefix before the final beracha.

Consequently, we see that the position of the Rashba is that the concluding beracha is related to the *Megillah* reading. Thus he had to find a justification for why we do not have here a ברכה הסמוכה לחבירתה, and he maintains that it is because the *Megillah* reading constitutes an interruption here.

III

CONSEQUENCES OF HOW WE VIEW THIS BLESSING

There are a number of issues that are affected if we view the concluding beracha of the *Megillah* reading as being an integral and related part of that reading, or whether it is seen as an independent entity, a beracha of praise to Hashem placed here at the end of the reading of the *Megillah*.

If for whatever reason one did not hear or read the *Megillah* on Purim day, is that person still obligated to recite this concluding beracha? If we adopt the view that this is an independent beracha, not related specifically to the *Megillah* reading, then it should follow that one should still be required to recite this concluding beracha even if he did not hear the reading of the *Megillah*. On the other hand, if we view this beracha as an integral part of the *Megillah* reading, then one would not be required to recite it without first hearing the *Megillah*.

And yet, HaGaon Rav Shlomo Kluger contends that even those who do not consider this beracha to be an integral part of the *Megillah* reading, still do not require one who has not heard the *Megillah* to recite it. The reason for this is that this beracha is viewed as a "ברכת השבח" — *"blessing of praise"*, and therefore it can only be recited after reading the *Megillah*, because the *Megillah* describes the miracle for which we are praising the Almighty. Thus one who has not heard of Hashem's great act of salvation on behalf of the Jewish people, will have no reason at that moment to simply recite a blessing of praise.

This can be compared to the law of "הרואה נר חנוכה", which is that one who did not kindle the Chanukah lights himself but only "sees" a

Chanukah light can still offer the beracha of "שעשה נסים" — *He Who wrought miracles*". However, if one did not light and did not even see a candle, he is not required to make this beracha.

If one spoke immediately after concluding the reading of the *Megillah*, before the recitation of the concluding beracha, whether or not this constitutes an interruption depends on the above distinction. For if we say that this beracha is to be viewed as part of the *Megillah* reading, then it is forbidden to engage in conversation before the concluding beracha is recited. Therefore, if one did converse, he may no longer make this concluding beracha. However, if we view this beracha as a separate entity, a ברכת השבח, then it could be said even after an interruption by means of conversation. In light of this, we could explain the disagreement between the בעל העיטור and the טור, cited in the טור או"ח סימן תרצ"ב ס"ק ב', where we find the following:

> "ובעל העיטור ז"ל כתב מסתברא כיון שברכה האחרונה במנהגא תליא
> מילתא, אין לגעור במי ששח בקריאה דלאו הפסקה היא, אלא בקריאה
> תליא מילתא. ואינו נראה דכיון שהוא מברך צריך שלא להפסיק, דמאי
> נפקא מיניה דתליא במנהגא, סוף סוף הוא מברך."

The ח"ב (*op.cit.*) explains the basis of this argument as follows. It is as if the concluding beracha, the ברכה אחרונה here is to be understood simply as an expression of praise — which is the contention of the בעל העיטור who therefore allows a beracha to be recited after an interruption. Whereas the טור is of the opinion that the beracha is an integral part of the *Megillah* reading and therefore no interruption is allowed. And if there is to be an interruption, then the concluding beracha is not to be recited.

IV

WHY USE THE PRESENT TENSE?

We can ask a question regarding the makeup of the beracha of "הרב את ריבנו". In the "על הנסים" prayer, said on Chanukah, we read:

”ואתה ברחמיך הרבים עמדת להם בעת צרתם, **רבת** את ריבם, דנת את
דינם, נקמת את נקמתם...“

*"You in Your great mercy stood up for them in the time of
their distress. You took up their grievance, judged their claim
and avenged their wrong..."*

In the beracha after the reading of the *Megillah* we say:

”הרב את ריבנו, והדן את דיננו, והנוקם את נקמתנו...“

*"Who takes up our grievance, judges our claim, and avenges
our wrong..."*

Why, in the "על הנסים"of Chanukah do we use the past tense:
"רבת, דנת, נקמת" whereas on Purim we use the present tense:
"הרב, והדן, והנוקם"? If indeed we include in our Purim prayers the concept
of "רבת, דנת, נקמת" then why are these terms not used as well in the
"על הנסים" of Purim? Why do we use these terms only in the beracha of
the *Megillah* and not in the "על הנסים"?

In the "על הנסים" we stress the miracle which brought about the defeat
of the wicked Haman and the frustration of his evil designs.

”ואתה ברחמים הרבים הפרת את עצתו וקלקלת את מחשבתו והשבתו לו
גמולו בראשו.“

*"In Your abundant mercy, You nullified his counsel and
frustrated his intention and caused his design to return upon
his own head..."*

Why do we speak here of the downfall of Haman's plan rather than
the overall defeat of the enemies of Yisrael?

The Rambam, in his introduction to the "מנין המצוות", the enumeration
of the mitzvos cited at the beginning of his *Mishna Torah*, writes:

”ויש מצות אחרות שנתחדשו אחר מתן תורה וקבעו אותם נביאים
וחכמים ופשטו בכל ישראל כגון מקרא מגילה וכו' אלא כך אנו אומרים

שהנביאים עם ב"ד תקנום וצוו לקרות המגילה בעונתה כדי להזכיר
שבחיו של הקב"ה ותשועות שעשה לנו והיה קרוב לשועתנו כדי לברכו
ולהללו וכדי **להודיע לדורות הבאים** שאמת מה שהבטיחנו בתורה ומי
גוי גדול אשר לו אלקים קרובים אליו וגומר."

*"There are also other commandments that were instituted after
the giving of the Torah. They were established by the Prophets
and Sages and spread throughout Yisrael; for example, the
reading of the Megillah...Instead we are saying that the
Prophets and the Courts ordained that the Megillah be read
in order to recall the praises of the Holy One, Blessed be He,
the salvation He wrought for us and His response to our cries,
so that we will bless Him, extol Him, and inform the future
generations of the truth of the Torah's promise (in Devarim
4:7): What nation is so great that it has God close to it."*

Thus we see that the mitzva of reading the *Megillah*, as well as being
a fulfillment of a commandment dictated to us, is also a reaffirmation of
the promise given by Hashem Himself that whenever we call out for His
help, He will be close to us and will rescue us from whatever precarious
situation in which we might happen to find ourselves. Consequently, we
may now say that the prayer of "על הנסים" and the concluding beracha
after reading the *Megillah* concerns itself with two different concepts.

The "על הנסים" was inserted in the Amidah prayer, in the
thanksgiving section — הודאה. Its recitation there fulfills our
obligation to express gratitude verbally for divine kindness performed
on our behalf. This is the reason the past tense is used here, for it is
only after we experienced these miracles that we are obligated to
express our appreciation for them. Thank you is usually said after a
kindness has been bestowed. However, the ברכה אחרונה, the blessing
recited after the reading of the *Megillah*, expresses our recognition
that Hashem is constantly watching over us. It is, as we have already
pointed out, an affirmation of the promise that He will always do so,
if we cry out to Him sincerely. Thus the present tense is used here, to
emphasize that He is watching over us now just as He did at the time
of the Purim miracle.

We can say that indeed this beracha is related to the *Megillah* itself. For as the Rambam has so convincingly explained, the real purpose of the *Megillah* reading is to reaffirm His promise to protect us. The use of the present tense underlines this, and makes us see once more that He protects us and saves us from dangerous situations now and forever.

V

"הא-ל": Is it part of the blessing?

The Rambam in Chapter 1, Halacha 3 of *Hilchos Megillah* quotes the beracha which is required here after the reading of the *Megillah*. "ברוך... הא-ל הרב את ריבנו".

The Rambam adds the word "הא-ל", although it does not appear in our text of the Gemara. (Even though it is mentioned in parentheses, most commentators insist that it should not be quoted.) Indeed, the Rif, the Rosh and the Shulchan Aruch also do not include it in the text of the blessing. The Tur, citing Rav Amram Gaon, explains the rationale for deleting it from the beracha. He explains that since the word "אל-היגו" — *"our God"*, has already been said, there is no reason to repeat "הא-ל". Thus the commentators question the decision of the Rambam to add this word to the beracha. In light of this rationale that it not be included, what is the Rambam's source for including it?

The ב"ח in סימן תרצ"ב (see ד"ה ולאחריה) gives the following reason for adding the word "הא-ל" here:

"אלא שמוסיפין כאן שם הא-ל לפי שבמזמור, על אילת השחר' שאמרה אסתר הזכירה שם, הא-ל' בתפלתה, א-לי א-לי למה עזבתני' והוא אשר נס זה על ידה היה בשם א-ל חסד א-ל כל היום. שגם ושכבר נגזר ונכתב ונחתם בבי"ד של מעלה להרוג ולאבד וגו' נהפוך היה שישלטו היהודים בשונאיהם, ואין זה אלא במידת חסד א-ל. ולכן גם בחתימה אומרים, הא-ל הנפרע וגו' לפי שלא היתה תשועתם שלימה אלא בשתי'. אחת, שנפרע לנו מאויבנו, ושני' שהושיענו מידם. וכל אחת משתים אלה לא היתה אלא במידת חסד א-ל, כי לא היה הדור זכאי..."

"This psalm was said by Queen Esther, and it was she who included the key word here of 'הא-ל' when she said: 'My God, my God, why hast Thou forsaken me?' The miracle of Purim came about through her initiative, when she invoked the attribute of 'הא-ל' which alludes to divine mercy. For it was through this divine attribute that the Jews were saved, even though that generation was really not worthy of being saved. Therefore we include this attribute of 'הא-ל' in the blessing."

This rationale helps us understand the justification for including the word "הא-ל" in the Rambam's text. But there is a difference of opinion among the commentators regarding the makeup of the beracha to be recited here. One opinion states: "הרב את רבנו וכו'", and Rava maintains: "הא-ל המושיע".

It would seem that the disagreement is over what exactly we must stress here. The first opinion contends that we must stress the retribution brought upon our enemies. Rava, on the other hand, maintains that we should rather stress the role of the Almighty in bringing about our salvation. However, in light of the Rambam's words, in his commentary at the beginning of "יד החזקה", he contends that the miracle of Purim is a reaffirmation of the promise given to Klal Yisrael of Hashem's constant protection. And this is the reason that we use the present tense here: "הרב, הדן, הנוקם" — to emphasize that it is an ongoing process of divine intervention in our lives. Thus this beracha of "הרב" is an expression of praise to Hashem for His constant protection.

Rava, however, maintains that we must explicitly point to His personal involvement in our lives — "הא-ל המושיע" — *"The God Who brings salvation"*. Thus, when Rav Papa concludes: "We should say both", we now also adopt the thinking of Rava, that we should explicitly stress the role of Hashem. And so we now add the word "הא-ל" to the beginning of the beracha, to emphasize this requirement. This explains the Rambam's justification in adding the word "הא-ל", even though it does not appear in the Gemara.

VI

HAMAN'S PLAN WAS FRUSTRATED AND NULLIFIED

We can understand why, in the Purim prayer of "על הנסים" we stress the matter of "הפרת...וקלקלת", that Haman's diabolical plans were "nullified and frustrated", rather than placing our emphasis on "רבת, דנת, נקמת", that Hashem *waged our battles*".

This distinction is defined by HaRav Chaim Yaakov Sofer, in his sefer (סימן יז) "פרי טוב", where he delineates the difference between "עצה" — "nullified his *counsel*" and "מחשבה" — "frustrated his *intention*". "מחשבה" alludes to what a person thinks about by himself. Such a thought comes to a person from his own mind. "עצה", on the other hand, refers to ideas one receives from others.

We know that the wicked Haman desired two things, to hang Mordechai and to destroy Yisrael. How he was to carry out his plans was conveyed to him by others — his wife Zeresh and his friends, who did not hesitate to advise him.

"ותאמר לו זרש אשתו וכל אהביו, יעשו עץ גבוה חמישים אמה ובבקר אמור למלך ויתלו את מרדכי עליו וגו'." (אסתר ה:יד)

"Then his wife Zeresh and all his friends said to him: let a gallows be made, fifty cubits high, and tomorrow morning speak to the king and have them hang Mordechai on it." (Esther 5:14)

His thought — the wish to destroy Yisrael — was his own, even though in reality it never passed the planning stages. Esther intercepted his plan, as we read in the *Megillah* (אסתר ח:ג-ה):

"ותוסף אסתר ותדבר לפני המלך וגו' להעביר את רעת המן האגגי ואת **מחשבתו** אשר **חשב** על היהודים וגו'... ותאמר... יכתב להשיב את הספרים **מחשבת** המן בן המדתא האגגי אשר כתב לאבד כל היהודים."

"Esther yet again spoke to the king...and begged him to avert the evil intent of Haman the Agagite and the scheme which

he plotted against the Jews...Let a decree be written to countermand those dispatches devised by Haman..."

And so it is written in Esther 9:24:

‏"כי המן בן המדתא צרר היהודים **חשב** על היהודים לאבדם."‏

"For Haman... enemy of all Jews, had plotted to destroy the Jews..."

Thus the Purim story involves the *thoughts and plans* of Haman the wicked. Fortunately, his plan never got off the ground, in contrast to the events of Chanukah, when we were obliged to fight an actual battle against the Syrian Greeks. On Purim, however, Hashem frustrated and nullified Haman's wicked plans before they took effect, and this accounts for the fact that in the "‏על הנסים‏" prayer we emphasize this aspect of "‏הפרת...וקלקלת‏", that Hashem did not let his evil plans reach fruition.

On Chanukah we stress the actual battle: "‏רבת, דנת, וכו'‏", and offer gratitude for our victory as a result of God's help and for the miracle wrought on our behalf. This is true for "‏על הנסים‏"; however in the beracha following the reading of the complete story of the events of Purim, we do indeed mention "‏רבת, דנת, וכו'‏", for many is the time that we were called upon to defend ourselves against our enemies and with divine help we were able to prevail.

VII

SIX EXPRESSIONS OF DEFEAT

The Avudraham points out that we find in this beracha six expressions alluding to the defeat of our enemies; and this corresponds to the six heroes who undertook to defeat Amalek. These six heroes and their associated verses are the following:

1) Yehoshua: (in *Shemos* 17:13)

הרב את ריבנו — על ידי **יהושע** שנאמר (שמות יז:יג) ויחלוש יהושע את **עמלק** ואת עמו לפי חרב.

2) Ehud (in *Shoftim* 3:13 - 3:15)

והדן את דיננו — על ידי **אהוד בן גרא** בן הימיני שהרג את עגלון מלך מואב, והיו עמו עמון **ועמלק** שנאמר (שופטים ג:יג) ויאסף אליו את בני עמון ועמלק וילך ויך את ישראל. וכתיב (שם ג, טו) ויקם ה' להם מושיע את אהוד בן גרא.

3) Gideon (in *Shoftim* 6:33)

והנקם את נקמתינו — על ידי **גדעון** שנאמר (שם ו,לג) וכל מדין **ועמלק** ובני קדם נאספו יחדיו.

4) King Saul (in *Shmuel I* 15:1)

והנפרע לנו מצרינו —על ידי **שאול** שנלחם **בעמלק**.

5) King David (in *Shmuel I* 30:1)

והמשלם גמול לכל אויבי נפשינו — על ידי **דוד** בצקלג, שנאמר (שמואל א' ל:א) —**והעמלקים** פשטו אל נגב ואל צקלג.

6) Mordechai and Esther (in *Megillas Esther*)

והחתימה **הנפרע לעמו ישראל מכל צריהם** — כנגד הנס של **מרדכי ואסתר**. **הא-ל המושיע** —לימות המשיח.

Perhaps this expanded list draws our attention to the ever-growing desire of Amalek to destroy Yisrael and Hashem's constant protection of the Jewish people from Amalek, as promised in *Devarim* 4:7. To protect us, Hashem provided us with heroes throughout the ages who, acting as His agents, were able to defend us from our enemies in time of need.

Salvation and Miracles

All the ends of the earth have seen the salvation of our God. — "ראו כל אפסי ארץ את ישועות אל-הינו".

The Gemara in *Megillah* 11a comments on this *pasuk* by saying: "When did all the ends of the earth see the salvation of our Lord? In the days of Mordechai and Esther."

Rashi explains this statement as follows. The letters which were sent out all over the world with the news of the salvation of the Jews made everyone in the world aware of Hashem's power to protect the Jewish people.

The commentator Bnai Yissachar, however, has a different explanation of the Gemara (see also the sefer, "שערי ציון" מהרב בן-ציון אב"ד בילסק, דרוש לפרשת זכור). On the surface the statement seems to be contradicted by the facts. For the miracles which Hashem performed on behalf of the Jewish people were previously well-known by all the nations of the world, and they readily acknowledged them. This included the Ten Plagues, the Exodus from Egypt and the Crossing of the Red Sea by Bnai Yisrael. According to Chazal, the world was completely aware of these facts. How, then, can the Gemara claim that only in the days of Mordechai and Esther did the world see and acknowledge Hashem's miracles on behalf of the Jewish people?

To answer this question, the Bnai Yissachar distinguishes two kinds of miracles: *open miracles* — "ניסים גלוים", which defy the laws of nature, and *hidden miracles* — "ניסים נסתרים", which take place within the laws of nature. He contends that until the time of Mordechai and Esther, all

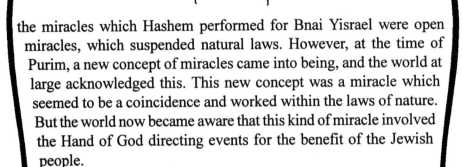

the miracles which Hashem performed for Bnai Yisrael were open miracles, which suspended natural laws. However, at the time of Purim, a new concept of miracles came into being, and the world at large acknowledged this. This new concept was a miracle which seemed to be a coincidence and worked within the laws of nature. But the world now became aware that this kind of miracle involved the Hand of God directing events for the benefit of the Jewish people.

With this in mind, we can now understand why Hallel is not recited on Purim. The Gemara in *Megillah* 14a suggests three possible reasons for this. (We will discuss this in greater detail later.) Why did not the Gemara simply say that Hallel may be recited only for a miracle beyond the laws of nature? For only then can all the world attest to Hashem's greatness. But because the miracle which took place on Purim was within the laws of nature, Hallel is not required.

Perhaps hidden miracles do not require Hallel because they cannot be discerned by the human eye, and therefore not everyone is aware of the Hand of Hashem at work in the world. However, in the Purim story, the whole world saw the miracle, from one end of the earth to the other: "ראו אותו כל אפסי ארץ".

But this fact might lead us to expect that Hallel should be recited. And this is why the Gemara found it necessary to give the reasons it does to explain why we do not say Hallel on Purim.

CHAPTER NINE

No Hallel on Purim

I

The Gemara gives three reasons

Hallel is usually recited on every holiday and whenever a miracle was performed for the sake of Klal Yisrael. Yet on Purim Hallel is not said. Why? Chazal address this question in *Mesechtas Megillah*, 14a, where they give three reasons why there is no Hallel on Purim. The Gemara asks: "?הלל נמי נימא" — *"Shouldn't we should also say Hallel on Purim?"*

And Rashi comments: "If it was appropriate to utter a song of praise upon the deliverance from Egyptian bondage, then surely Hallel, which is also a song of praise, should be recited on Purim in commemoration of our salvation from annihilation."

The Gemara answers:

"אמר ר' יצחק: לפי שאין אומרים הלל על נס שבחוצה לארץ."

"Hallel is not said on Purim, because we do not recite Hallel for a miracle which occurred outside the land of Yisrael."

The Gemara then asks:

"יציאת מצרים דנס שבחוץ לארץ היכי אמרינן שירה?"

"If so, how may we sing a song of praise for the Exodus from Egypt, which was a miracle that occurred outside the land of Yisrael?"

Why, asks the Gemara, do we recite Hallel on the first day of Pesach to thank Hashem for our deliverance from slavery in Egypt? The Gemara suggests the following answer:

"כדתניא: עד שלא נכנסו ישראל לארץ הוכשרו כל ארצות לומר שירה,
משנכנסו ישראל לארץ לא הוכשרו כל הארצות לומר שירה."

"As long as the children of Yisrael did not enter the land of

Yisrael, all the other lands were appropriate venues for singing shirah, a song of praise for Hashem's miracles that occurred therein, However, once the children of Yisrael entered the land of Yisrael, all the other lands were no longer appropriate venues for reciting a song of praise for Hashem's miracles that occurred therein."

Since the Exodus from Egypt occurred before Bnai Yisrael entered Eretz Yisrael, it is appropriate to recite Hallel on Pesach for the miracle of the Exodus, even though the miracle of the deliverance of Bnai Yisrael occurred outside the land of Yisrael. However, since the events of Purim took place after the people entered Eretz Yisrael, a song of praise, Hallel, is inappropriate, since the miracle took place outside Eretz Yisrael.

The Gemara offers a second reason for not reciting Hallel on Purim:

"רב נחמן אמר: קרייתא זו הלילא"

"Rav Nachman said: Reading the Megillah on Purim is equivalent to reciting Hallel."

Rav Nachman maintains that reading the Megillah on Purim is tantamount to saying Hallel, since it publicizes the miracle and causes everyone to praise Hashem (see Rashi above in his commentary on the Gemara 4a, ד"ה יזמרך כבוד).

Rava offers another answer:

"רבא אמר: בשלמא התם, הללו עבדי ה' ולא עבדי פרעה, אלא הכא,
הללו עבדי ה' ולא עבדי אחשורוש, אכתי עבדי אחשורוש אנן."

"Rava said: Granted that there, regarding the Exodus from Egypt, it is appropriate to say Hallel, because we are able to recite the verse, 'Give praise, you servants of Hashem.' (Psalms 113:1) Thus the verse implies that at the moment of salvation the Jews became servants of Hashem and were no longer servants of Pharaoh. But here, regarding the miracle of Purim, how can we say, 'Give praise, you servants of Hashem', when we still remained servants of Ahashveros, even after being saved from Haman's evil decree?"

II

Looking deeper: why not acknowledge a miracle outside Yisrael?

"אין אומרים שירה על נס שבחוצה לארץ"

Why do we not acknowledge a miracle beyond the laws of nature performed for the benefit of the Jewish people outside the land of Yisrael? For if they were saved from a precarious, life-threatening situation in the Diaspora, why aren't we obligated to praise Hashem for His great kindness? We might suggest two possible answers.

The view of HaRav Leibele Pomaranchik, in his sefer *Emek Beracha*

We are obligated to praise Hashem whenever we witness His might and power — "גבורות השם", within the miracle that was wrought on our behalf. However, if this miracle is obscure or not complete, then we are not obligated to say Hallel. We can say that only a miracle which happened in the land of Yisrael calls for Hallel, for only in Eretz Yisrael are miracles completely open and visible to everyone.

In the Disapora, however, when miracles occur they are hidden within the laws of nature — "...מכוסה קצת בדרך הטבע". For this reason Hallel is not called for.

"וביאור הדבר נראה, משום דארץ ישראל הרי היא ארץ אשר השם דורש
אותה, ותמיד עיני השם בה, והיא המרכז של ההשגחה הפרטית כדאיתא
בספרי: והלא כל הארצות הוא דורש אלא אינו דורש אלא ארץ ישראל
ועל ידה דרישתה, נדרשות כל הארצות. וע"כ יש חילוק בהנהגות השם
בין ארץ ישראל לחוץ לארץ, וגם בהנהגה הניסית כשהשם עושה נס, אינו
דומה נס שבארץ ישראל לנס שבחוצה לארץ, כמו שאנו רואים באמת בנס
פורים שהי' מכוסה קצת בדרכי הטבע, וע"כ לא היתה בו הכרה שלמה
בגבורות השם, וע"כ אין אומרים שירה על נס שבחוצה לארץ..."

THE VIEW OF HARAV CHAYIM ZIMMERMAN

Hallel is said by Klal Yisrael only for a miracle which was wrought on behalf of a congregation — "ציבור", the congregation of Yisrael. It is only the Jews who reside in the land of Yisrael who constitute the congregation of Klal Yisrael. We learn this from the *parashah* of "פר העלם דבר של צבור".

The law reads: if the majority of Bnai Yisrael erred in certain mitzvos, they are obligated to bring only one sin offering. To determine if a majority erred, a census is taken to see if in fact a majority of the people erred. This census is taken from the population that resides within the boundaries of Eretz Yisrael (see הוריות ג', א'). Those Jews who live outside these borders are not counted, even though they too may have erred.

From this we see that the "congregation of Bnai Yisrael" consists only of those who live in Eretz Yisrael. Thus if Hallel is to be recited for a miracle wrought on behalf of the "congregation of Klal Yisrael," this means that it can only be said for a miracle that happened in Eretz Yisrael and not outside the land (see שו"ת אבני נזר, אור"ח ח"ב, סימן שי"ד אות ד').

אכתי עבדי אחשורוש אנן"

Hallel is recited whenever we can say, after the miracle, that we are now servants of Hashem alone. This was the situation of Bnai Yisrael after the Exodus from Egypt. On Purim, however, after the miracle has transpired and the Jewish people are saved from annihilation, they cannot honestly say, "הללו עבדי ה'", for they remain subservient to Ahashveros. They were still in bondage to the Persian king and this is one reason why they do not recite Hallel.

A second reason is that, because they are still in bondage, we can not view the miracle as complete, and therefore Hallel can not be recited. The sefer *Emek Beracha* maintains that these two possible views reflect a difference of opinion between the Talmud Bavli (the Babylonian Talmud) and the Talmud Yerushalmi (the Jerusalem Talmud).

In the Bavli, according to the text found in the Rif, we read:

"אלא הכא היכא נימא."

"How can we justifiably state 'we are servants of Hashem',
when we are still under te jurisdiction of the Persian king?"

Thus it would seem that as far as the miracle is concerned, we should be able to say Hallel, but we are prevented from doing so by this statement of "הללו עבדי ה'"

From the Yerushalmi, on the other hand, in פרק ערבי פסחים (הלכה ו'), the reason we do not say Hallel is because we were not completely liberated and we did not achieve self-determination, מלכות, and therefore we view the miracle as being incomplete, and thus not requiring the recitation of Hallel.

"קרייתא זו הלילא."

This statement is puzzling. Does it mean that by reading the Megillah it is as though we are fulfilling the requirement of praising Hashem, and therefore we need not recite the actual Hallel, for it would be a repetition of that praise? Or are we to understand this statement to mean that although we are not verbalizing the words of the Hallel, we are nevertheless expressing our appreciation for the miracle by reading the Megillah, and this appreciation would ordinarily be accomplished by reciting Hallel.

III

IF ONE DOESN'T HEAR THE MEGILLAH CAN HE RECITE HALLEL?

Is there a practical application to the question of why we do not recite Hallel on Purim? If one did not attend a public or private Megillah reading and has no Megillah from which to read on his own, would such a person be required to recite Hallel?

If we adopt the first two views, then it would seem that we are not required to recite Hallel on Purim as a substitute, even if we missed the Megillah reading. The third view, however, is that a Megillah reading is equivalent to the recitation of Hallel, "קרייתא זו הלילא".

From this it would follow that one who does not possess a Megillah should recite Hallel in order to fulfill his obligation to praise Hashem for His miracles. This view is expressed by the Meiri in his commentary on the *Megillah* 14a:

"דבר ידוע הוא שאין אומרי' הלל בפורים. אבל טעם מניעתו נחלקו בגמרא, והוא שאחד מהם אומר שקרייתא זו הלילא. ונראה לי לטעם זה שאם הי' במקום שאין לו מגילה שקורא את ההלל, שהרי לא נמנעה קריאתו אלא מפני שקריאת המגילה במקומו..."

However, the Meiri's view seems to be rejected by the poskim, based on the following considerations:

If we adopt the view that Hallel can replace the Megillah when we are unable to read the Megillah, then why does the Gemara say that if Purim falls on a Shabbos, we read the Megillah on Friday? Why couldn't we simply recite Hallel instead? The reason must be that we can not and do not substitute Hallel for the Megillah reading.

The reason for this is that the Megillah reading consists of two separate mitzvos: "קריאת המגילה" — the actual reading of the Megillah, which in itself constitutes a mitzva, and reciting the Hallel (the song of praise), which is contained within the Megillah.

Therefore we must say that Hallel can never replace the Megillah reading. For if we were to substitute the recitation of Hallel, one would not be fulfilling one's obligation of reading the Megillah, which is an indispensable mitzva on the holiday day of Purim. However, if one has no possibility of reading the Megillah, and thus has no way to fulfill this mitzva, one should at least fulfill the mitzva of praising Hashem on this day by reciting Hallel. This is the contention of the Meiri.

But this is so only in a situation in which one cannot obtain a Megillah, for to establish or substitute another day for the Megillah reading would not be realistic. However, when an entire congregation (צבור) cannot read the Megillah now, for example, when Purim falls on a Shabbos, then rather than reciting Hallel and thereby forfeiting the mitzva of the Megillah reading, we substitute another day for reading the Megillah. When we do this, the entire congregation benefits in two ways: all fulfill the mitzva of reading the Megillah, and all fulfill the mitzva of Hallel, praising Hashem, which is contained within the reading of the Megillah. This option is preferable to reciting Hallel on Shabbos day, because it does not sacrifice either of the special mitzvos of Purim.

IV

Two Gemaras: two different answers

This issue of why Hallel is not said on Purim is discussed with a slightly different emphasis in two separate Gemaras, in *Megillah* 14a and in Arakhin 10b. The question presented and the answers suggested are similar in both places, yet there is a difference in the structure of the two texts, which provides a focus for a new insight which affects the halacha here.

As we have said, there are three clear-cut reasons why we do not say Hallel on Purim:

1) According to Rav Yitzchak, we do not say Hallel for a miracle which took place outside the land of Yisrael.

2) According to Rava, since we remained slaves of Ahashueros we cannot honestly declare "הללו עבדי ה'".

3) According to Rav Nachman, the reading of the *Megillah* itself constitutes Hallel.

In the Gemara *Megillah* a question is asked of Rav Nachman: "קריאתא זו הלילא", and of Rava: "אכתי עבדי אחשורוש אנן".

According to their answers, it would seem as though the miracle required us to say Hallel, but we do not recite it because of the qualification which Rav Nachman spelled out and similarly, because of Rava's consideration. But why are their reasons necessary? Why not simply state the general rule that Hallel is never said for a miracle which took place outside the land of Yisrael, and therefore there is no question of reciting Hallel in this case?

The Gemara answers this by saying that since we were exiled to Persia, we revert to the status we had before we entered the land of Yisrael, which was that Hallel could be said for miracles which took place in any land.

However, in the Gemara *Arakhin*, this question why the reason we do not say Hallel for a miracle which took place outside the land of Yisrael is not enough, is asked only of Rav Nachman and not of Rava. How do we account for this change? (See שו"ת חתם סופר, אור"ח, סימן קצ"ב.)

In the Gemara *Megillah* 14a we read:

"בין **לרבא** בין **לרב נחמן** קשיא, והא תניא משנכנסו לארץ לא הוכשרו כל הארצות לומר שירה..."

And we read in *Arakhin* 10b:

"**לרב נחמן** דאמר קרייתא זו היא הלילא, התניא משכנסו לארץ לא הוכשרו כל הארצות לומר שירה..."

An unusual answer is suggested in the sefer "אמרי דוד" (חלק ב') by HaRav Dovid Milanovsky, of blessed memory. Based on the previous question as to whether the statement of "אכתי עבדי אחשורות אנן" means that we simply cannot justifiably recite this psalm which states "הללו עבדי ה'", or is it that the miracle of Purim is viewed as incomplete, because we remained in servitude to Ahashueros, and therefore we do not say Hallel for a miracle which was incomplete?

The Gemara in *Arakhin* maintains that this statement of "אכתי" is to be taken to mean that Hallel is not called for because the miracle was incomplete. Thus Rava, who offers the answer of "אכתי" agrees that Hallel is not required and is to be viewed as saying that Hallel is not warranted since the miracle was not complete. This is the reason Rava agrees that Hallel should not be recited on Purim, since it was not a complete miracle.

Only Rav Nachman is of the opinion that Hallel should be recited on Purim. And the Gemara directs its question to him, asking: Purim celebrates a miracle which took place in the Diaspora, and we know that miracles which happened outside the land of Yisrael do not require Hallel; why then does Rav Nachman maintain that Hallel should be recited?

The Gemara in *Megillah*, though, has a different question. There we are told that "אכתי" means only that we are unable to read this psalm, but the miracle itself justified a recitation of Hallel. And so both Rav Nachman and Rava maintain that Hallel should be read on Purim, were it not for the qualifying reason which each of them gives. Therefore, the Gemara directs its question to both of them. This question is how one can require the recitation of Hallel when we have a halacha that Hallel can not be recited for miracles which took place in the Diaspora, and Purim involved such a miracle.

We might account for the difference between these two Gemaras in the following way. The *sugya* of each Gemara deals with a different issue. The Gemara in *Arakhin* serves as the source for the formula set down here, as to when we are obligated to recite Hallel. Two prerequisites must be met: work must be forbidden on that day, and the day must be referred to as "מועד". Thus Hallel is not said on Shabbos, because even though work is forbidden, the Torah never calls Shabbos a "מועד".

The Gemara continues by raising the following issue: "Then it should follow that Chanukah should not require the recitation of Hallel, for these two prerequisites do not apply to Chanukah."

The Gemara answers this charge by saying: "Chanukah requires Hallel to be said, because a miracle transpired at that time."

To this the Gemara asks: "If so, why don't we say Hallel on Purim, for a miracle happened at that time?"

The Gemara answers: "אכתי עבדי אחשורוש אנן". In effect, the Gemara is telling us that there was a "flaw" in the miracle, and that is why no Hallel is required.

And so, the only one who maintains that the miracle of Purim warrants the recitation of Hallel is Rav Nachman. Therefore, the question that this miracle took place in the Diaspora is directed to him alone.

The Gemara in *Megillah*, however, deals with the issue from another perspective. There it is maintained that Hallel should be said, not because of the miracle that took place, but because Bnai Yisrael were saved from annihilation, and based on a קל וחומר. To this the Gemara answers: "אכתי עבדי אחשורוש אנן". And this means that we do not recite Hallel.

This leads the Gemara to ask, why do we need any other reason than that the miracle took place outside the land of Yisrael? Isn't this enough to obviate the need for reciting Hallel? This question is directed to both Rav Nachman and Rava, for both maintain that Hallel would have been required on Purim were it not for the reasons that each of them put forward.

V

MORE QUESTIONS REGARDING HALLEL

"הלל נמי נימא" — *"We should also say Hallel"*. This statement in the Gemara raises two further questions:

The Bais Yosef in סימן ת"צ rules that we do not recite the entire Hallel on the seventh day of Pesach, the day when Bnai Yisrael crossed the Red Sea, because the verse says: "בנפול אויבך אל תשמח" — *"We are not permitted to rejoice in the downfall of our enemies."*

But if this is so, how could the Gemara ask why we do not recite Hallel on Purim, for surely the miracle of the Jews' salvation which happened in the time of Mordechai and Esther came about only as a result of the destruction of the Jews' enemies. Why do we not consider the same verse of "בנפול אויבך אל תשמח" when it comes to Purim?

The sefer "יד המלך על הרמבם" by HaRav Eliezer Landau, at the end of *Hilchos Chanukah* asks: "How are we to understand this question of the Gemara: 'if so, we should also say Hallel'? If it means that we should read the Megillah and also recite Hallel, then this is puzzling. For we never make two memorials for one miracle; why, then, should we do both on Purim?

Indeed, the source from which we try to prove that we should say Hallel is from the Exodus; and even there only the *shiras hayam* was said, and nothing else. And so we must ask why the Megillah was introduced as a commemoration of the miracle of Purim, when we could have simply recited Hallel? This is how we are to understand the Gemara's question of "הלל נמי נימא", namely, that we should also do as they did regarding the miracle of Crossing the Red Sea — recite Hallel — and that should have been a sufficient way of commemorating the miracle. Even the Megillah reading should not be required.

Perhaps the idea that we never make two memorials for a single miracle does not apply here, based on the following considerations. The Gemara attempts to find a source for this mitzva of reading the Megillah. The source it identifies is based on the following קל וחומר: If we sang when we were redeemed from slavery to freedom [at the time of the Exodus], how much more so should we sing when our very lives were spared [at the time of the Purim miracle]. This gives us a היתר, permission to add a new mitzva without transgressing the prohibition against "בל תוסיף" — adding to the mitzvos of the Torah.

This leads the Gemara to ask: "אי נמי" — *"if so..."*, which signifies that this concept of applying a קל וחומר to create a new mitzva of reading the Megillah is really acceptable. Because the salvation we experienced in the days of Mordechai and Esther makes it incumbent upon us to express our gratitude to Hashem by praising Him, and this is not a repetition of our first commemoration of the event by reading the Megillah, but rather a further and separate obligation to verbalize our sense of gratitude. Therefore it is perfectly in order for the Gemara to ask why we do not *also* recite Hallel on Purim. Thus the Gemara answers by saying: "קרייתא זו הלילא".

This means that over and above our obligation to read the Megillah, represented in the mitzva of "קריאה", we are also obligated, within the Purim story, to express our gratitude to Hashem for rescuing us from danger and to praise Him. We do this by articulating within the Megillah, how the Hand of Hashem worked, seemingly within the laws of nature, to bring about our salvation.

And we may even suggest an answer to the question how we can contemplate reciting Hallel on Purim when our salvation came about as a result of our enemies being destroyed. For we know from the experience of the Exodus that we are not permitted to rejoice at the downfall of our enemies.

We might conceivably distinguish between these two events. At the time of the Crossing of the Sea, a miracle occurred and the Jews crossed over safely while the waters of the Sea receded. The same miracle that saved the Jews drowned their enemies, when they pursued them into the dry sea bed and the Sea then resumed its natural shape. Because the Egyptians were drowned we can not say Hallel, but must apply the principle that we do not rejoice at the destruction of any of God's creatures: "בנפול אויבך אל תשמח".

In the Purim story, however, we can distinguish between two separate events: the evil decrees against the Jews were abolished, and the Jews took revenge against their oppressors. It was the abolishing of the evil decrees which called for gratitude and an expression of praise to Hashem, not the destruction of our enemies. Thus there is no prohibition against praising Hashem on account of our enemies having been destroyed, for that was an independent matter, and the rescinding of the evil decrees against the Jews would have been enough to warrant our praise and gratitude.

Another aspect which allows us to sing *shirah* and express our happiness at the destruction of our enemies is that those enemies descend from the seed of Amalek, and the Torah itself commands us to destroy this particular enemy. Thus we can justifiably verbalize our expression of Hallel when it comes to the destruction of Amalek (see the sefer ("ימי פורים" מהרב דוד כהן, עמ' קכ"א-ג).

CAN WE RECITE HALLEL INSTEAD OF READING THE MEGILLAH?

We have seen that the Meiri is of the opinion that if circumstances do not one permit one to hear the Megillah being read or to read it for oneself, he can fulfill his obligation by reciting Hallel instead. This is based on the concept of — "קרייתא זו הלילא" that reading the Megillah itself constitutes Hallel.

The ברכי יוסף, however, contends that the halacha does not follows this opinion of "קרייתא זו הלילא" of the Meiri, but rather the law follows the opinion of Rava, who maintains that we do not recite Hallel because *"we did not attain absolute freedom, for we remained servants of King Ahashueros"* — "אכתי עבדי אחשורוש אנן".

It is for this reason that Hallel is not justified on Purim. Thus it is clear that one can not make up for a missed Megillah reading by reciting Hallel. The reason Rava's opinion is the one we accept, is in keeping with the rule that whenever there is a difference of opinion among Amoraim, the law is always decided according to the opinion of the Amora who lived later: "הלכה כבתרה".

Since Rava was viewed as a later Amora than either Rav Yitzchak or Rav Nachman, who represent the other opinions mentioned here, therefore the halacha follows the opinion of Rava, which is that we do not recite Hallel because we did not attain complete freedom from all oppression, since we remained in bondage to the Persian king.

The Rambam, though, in *Hilchos Chanukah*, 3:6, decides the law in accordance with the opinion of Rav Nachman, which is that Hallel can in fact replace the reading of the Megillah: "קרייתא זו הלילא". Thus the Rambam writes as follows:

"ולא תקנו הלל בפורים שקריאת המגילה היא ההלל."

> *"The Sages did not ordain the recitation of Hallel on Purim, because the reading of the Megillah serves the purpose of Hallel."*

This decision of the Rambam leads us to ask several questions:

1) Why did the Rambam maintain that the halacha should have been decided according to the opinion of Rav Nachman, when we know that Rava was a "בתרה", a later Amora than Rav Nachman, and therefore the halacha should have followed his opinion?

2) Would the Rambam agree with the opinion of the Meiri, that when one cannot read the Megillah he should recite Hallel?

There were several reasons to explain why the Rambam decided the halacha according to the opinion of Rav Nachman rather than that of Rava.

In the text which the Rambam used, the reading was not simply "Rav Nachman", which would mean we are speaking of "Rav Nachman, the son of Yitzchak" — "רב נחמן בר יצחק" who lived before Rava, and therefore Rava is seen as the later Amora — בתרה. Rather, in his text the reading was: "רב נחמן בר יעקב".

This Rav Nachman lived after Rava. Therefore it is not Rava who is considered to be the later Amora, but rather Rav Nachman himself. And so the halacha will rightly follow his opinion.

Others say that in the text of the Rambam the reading was not "רבא", but rather "רבה", for we find that their names are interchanged many times in the Gemara. Thus "רבה" is not seen as the later Amora, the בתרה, and this explains why the halacha does not follow his opinion.

The commentators point out that even though the Rambam may be of the opinion that "קרייתא זו הלילא", nevertheless if one is not able to read the Megillah on Purim, he is still not obligated to recite Hallel. The reasons for this are the following:

The Rambam's text here reads: "ולא תקנו הלל בפורים" — *"The Sages did not ordain the recitation of Hallel on Purim."* This seems to indicate that the Megillah and only the Megillah was chosen as the proper text to articulate our gratitude for the miracle which occurred on Purim. From this we can conclude that Hallel was never meant to be said on Purim.

There are two kinds of miracles: *open miracles* — "נסים גלויים", and *hidden miracles* — "נסים נסתרים". Hallel is recited only for an open miracle, one which all can see and attest to and which occurs beyond the laws of nature. Purim, however, is viewed as a hidden miracle, one which occurred within the laws of nature. Thus Hallel is not required for this type of miracle. In fact, the reading of the Megillah itself, where the miracle seems obscure, best represents the particular form of praise which is called for to commemorate this kind of miracle (see "פחד יצחק" על פורים, ענין ל"ג).

Although the miracle which occurred on Purim did not happen beyond the laws of nature, yet by piecing the events together in their true perspective one can sense the Hand of Hashem at work here within the seemingly natural events. Only the Megillah is the proper vehicle to convey to us the miracle as it gradually unfolded within the heart of natural events. It is for this reason that Hallel cannot be equated with the reading of the Megillah. For in Hallel we sing out the praises of Hashem's actions, as they are visible to everyone. In the Megillah, however, the disclosure is more subtle (see "קונטרס ימי פורים" מאמר י"ט).

"קרייתא זו הלילא" is not to be understood in the sense that by reading the Megillah one is actually reciting the Hallel, but rather the intention of this principle is that reading the Megillah affects a person emotionally and spiritually motivates him to offer praise to the Almighty. However, our Sages never considered instituting the actual recitation of Hallel on Purim. This was not their intention. And this is why Hallel cannot serve as a substitute for reading the Megillah.

"דאין כוונת הגמ' בזה שהקריאה היא ממש במקום הלל. וכאילו איהי
גופא ההלל, וזה וזה שוין, אלא רצה לומר, שקריאת המגילה היא סוג
הלילא כזו אשר בחובה טמון סגולה וכוונה אשר על ידי קריאתה יזכרו
בנס ויתנו על ידי כך שבח והודאה לשם יתברך על מה שקרה להם
במיוחד בימים ההם... אבל גדר של הלל ממש לא קבעו בזה חז"ל
בתקנתם." (שו"ת ציץ אליעזר, חלק י"ז, סימן ס"א)

We might suggest the following explanation of this matter. The *Behag*, one of our greatest halachic sages (בה"ג: בעל הלכות גדולות) maintains that the recitation of Hallel is dictated by the Torah itself. However, the Rambam, in the first section of his *Sefer HaMitzvos* dismisses this theory by asking: how can we say that Hallel is biblically dictated, when the Psalms recited as an integral part of Hallel are from the Book of Psalms, which was composed by King David? From this fact he seeks to prove that Hallel is not dictated by the Torah.

The Ramban, on the other hand, taunts the Rambam by asking: What about *Tefillah,* prayer? It has no set formulation, and one can say anything he wishes. Even though this is the case, certainly prayer is biblically dictated,. Why, then, can't Hallel fall into the same category, even if it does use phrases from King David's Psalms? In this way the Ramban proves that the Rambam's argument against the Behag has no basis.

But some commentators defend the Rambam's position. For example, Rav Eliyahu Levin, in his sefer "דברי שירה, פסח", contends that we must differentiate between prayer and Hallel. Although prayer can be said in any manner, and one can petition Hashem as he wishes, yet Hallel must follow a set format. Only the appropriate chapters from the Book of Psalms are acceptable. Hallel calls for "קריאה", recitation, and this is only realized when it is read from a book of *Kisvei Hakodesh.*

In addition, we find many prayers and chapters included in the Book of Psalms which were in existence even before King David's time. In fact, Moshe Rabbenu was the author of many of the psalms included in the Book of Psalms (for example, the psalm referred to as "תפלה למשה").

Yet it was only after King David incorporated them into the Book of Psalms that they assumed the status of *Holy Writings* — כתבי הקודש, and פרקי תהילים — *"Chapters"* from the *"Book of Psalms"*. And we find in *Mesechtas Pesachim* that Hallel was said at the time of Moshe Rabbenu, when Bnai Yisrael crossed the Red Sea, as well as by Yehoshua and other early leaders. Yet the Hallel which they recited was the kind of Hallel we refer to as "הלל דשירה" — *a song of praise* recited at the very moment of the miracle, and this is not fixed into any special formulation.

The kind of Hallel we are speaking of here, however, is that which falls into the category of "הלל דקריאה", which has a definite and fixed formulation and must be recited every year on the anniversary of the miracle (see *The Commentators' Haggadah*, pp. 198-200). There the reading has to be from the prescribed chapters of the Book of Psalms. This proves that this kind of Hallel must be ordained by the rabbis, דרבנן, rather than dictated by the Torah itself.

Thus we might ask, if the obligation of reciting Hallel is only fulfilled by reading from the appropriate chapters from the Book of Psalms, how can we possibly say: "קרייתא זו הלילא", that reading the Megillah is the same as reciting Hallel?

We must therefore say that our Sages never really intended that the actual Hallel be recited on Purim, but rather they chose the *Megillas Esther* to be the appropriate chapters of the *Kisvei HaKodesh*, the Holy Writings, that were meant to serve as our recitation of Hallel on this day. For they are the ones which properly fulfill our obligation to praise Hashem for His miracles on our behalf.

Thus the Megillah alone can serve as the "Hallel" for Purim day, and the regular chapters of Hallel were never meant to be recited. Thus we can conclude that if one lacked a Megillah on Purim he could not fulfill his obligation by reciting the regular holiday Hallel.

Esther and the Sages

This Gemara (*Mesechtas Megillah* 11a), which tells us that all saw and acknowledged the miracle which Hashem wrought for the Jewish people, makes it difficult for us to understand the rationale behind the following Gemara. In *Mesechtas Megillah* 7a we read:

"שלחה להם אסתר לחכמים: קבעוני לדורות. שלחה לה: קנאה את מעוררת עלינו לבין האומות. שלחה להם: כבר כתובה אני על דברי הימים למלכי מדי ופרס."

"Esther submitted the following request to the Sages: 'Establish me for generations' (i.e., establish an everlasting name for me by mandating a festival of Purim and the reading of the Megillah). They sent her the following reply: 'You will incite the wrath of the nations against us, for they will say we rejoice at the remembrance of their downfall.' Esther replied to the Sages by saying: 'I am already written in the chronicles of the kings of Persia and Medea.' "

Rashi explains her answer to mean that the nations of the world can find out what befell them at the hands of the Jews by looking into these historical documents (the chronicles of the Persian and Medean kings).

But why were the Sages so afraid that the nations of the world would find out about the Jews' victory over one of them, for do we not say here that "all the nations of the earth have seen and acknowledged the salvation of the Jews by the hand of Hashem"? This implies that they were all

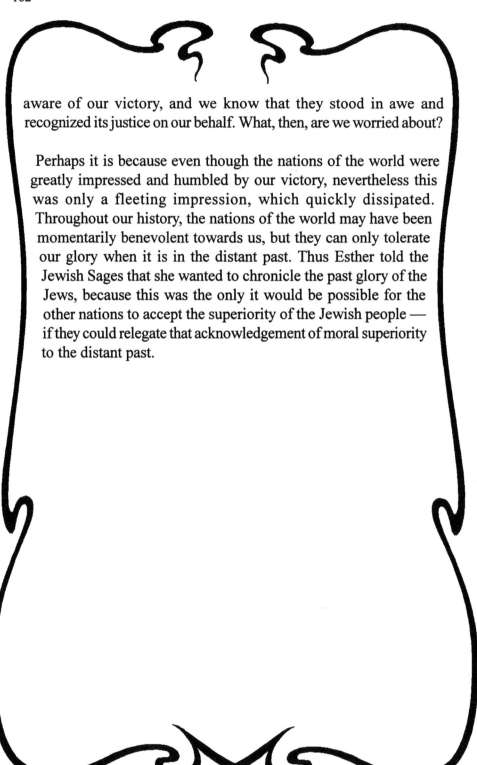

aware of our victory, and we know that they stood in awe and recognized its justice on our behalf. What, then, are we worried about?

Perhaps it is because even though the nations of the world were greatly impressed and humbled by our victory, nevertheless this was only a fleeting impression, which quickly dissipated. Throughout our history, the nations of the world may have been momentarily benevolent towards us, but they can only tolerate our glory when it is in the distant past. Thus Esther told the Jewish Sages that she wanted to chronicle the past glory of the Jews, because this was the only it would be possible for the other nations to accept the superiority of the Jewish people — if they could relegate that acknowledgement of moral superiority to the distant past.

CHAPTER TEN

Women are also obligated

I

"אף הן היו באותו הנס": EXPLORING THIS CONCEPT

In three places Rav Yehoshua Ben Levi brings up the subject of women being obligated in certain mitzvos.

1) In *Megillah* 4a, we read:

> "ואמר ר' יהושע בן לוי: נשים חייבות במקרא מגילה, שאף הן היו באותו הנס."

> *"And Rav Yehoshua ben Levi said: 'Women are obligated in the reading of the Megillah, for they too were involved in that miracle."*

2) In *Pesachim* 108a, we are told:

> "ואמר ר' יהושע בן לוי: נשים חייבות בארבעה כוסות הללו שאף הן היו באותו הנס."

> *"And Rav Yehoshua ben Levi also said: 'Women are obligated to drink four cups of wine on Pesach night, since they were also involved in that miracle.'"*

3) And in *Shabbos* 23a:

> "דאמר ר' יהושע בן לוי: נשים חייבות בארבעה כוסות הללו שאף הן היו באותו הנס."

> *"For Rav Yehoshua ben Levi said: 'Women are obligated to kindle Chanukah lights, for they too were involved in that miracle.'"*

There is a difference of opinion between the Rashbam and the Ba'alei Tosafos over how and to what extent women were involved in these three miracles — those of Purim, Pesach and Chanukah.

The Rashbam writes in *Mesechtas Pesachim* (*op. cit.*):

"כדאמרינן (סוטה דף י"א) בשכר נשים צדקניות שבאותו הדור נגאלו. וכן גבי מקרא מגילה נמי אמרינן הכי דמשום דעל ידי אסתר נגאלו. וכן גבי נר חנוכה במסכת שבת (כג')."

"These miracles were realized due to the women. The Pesach miracle occurred in the merit of the righteous women of that time. The miracle of Purim was due to the initiative of Esther and also the miracle of the Chanukah lights was due to a woman, Yehudis."

Tosafos, however, contends that their obligation is not due to the fact that they played principal roles in these events, but rather because they too were in danger. Tosafos writes:

"דבירושלמי גריס שאף הן היו באותו ספק, משמע באותה סכנה דלהשמיד להרוג ולאבד."

He contends that women are obligated in these particular mitzvos because they too shared the same danger as did the men.

Rashi, though, maintains that in each of the above mitzvos there is a different rationale, and thus he combines the opinions of the Rashbam and Tosafos. Rashi writes in his commentary on *Mesechtas Megillah* here:

"שאף על הנשים גזר המן להשמיד להרוג ולאבד מנער ועד זקן טף ונשים וגו'."

"Haman's decree to kill the Jews included the women, as the verse states: 'to destroy, to slay and to exterminate all Jews, young and old, children and women.'" (Esther 3:13)

The common element here between the miracles of each of these holidays is that the women were in jeopardy along with the men, and they were saved by the same miracle.

However, in *Pesachim* (ק"ח), he cites the same reason given by the Rashbam, that the women were instrumental in bringing about the miracle. In *Mesechtas Shabbos* (כ"ג,א) he gives both reasons: they were in the same jeopardy as the men, and it was because of them that the miracle came about.

Rashi writes here:

"שגזר יוונים על כל בתולות הנשואות להיבעל לטפסר תחלה. ועל ידי
אשה נעשה הנס."

How then, are we to reconcile the positions of Rashi, Tosafos and the Rashbam? We might suggest the following:

How were these three statements of Rav Yehoshua ben Levi made? Did he initially make one sweeping statement that women are obligated in the mitzvos of Purim, Chanukah and Pesach based on the concept that they too were involved in the particular miracle? And then, when each of these three separate mitzvos was discussed in detail in each particular Gemara, can we assume that Rav Yehoshua ben Levi's statement was then quoted? Or did he rather make his statements independently, at each of these three particular times, in *Mesechtos Shabbos, Megillah and Pesachim?* The practical difference here would be that if he made a single statement to cover all three cases, then this would imply that there is really only one rationale for all three mitzvos. However, if in each instance Rav Yehoshua voiced a particular principle, we might say that each case has its own unique explanation.

From this we can see that Rashbam and Tosafos both hold the opinion that Rav Yehoshua made one sweeping statement, and therefore a single rationale applies to all three mitzvos. And so Rashbam and Tosafos give only one reason for including women in these mitzvos. Rashi, on the other hand, maintained that Rav Yehoshua ben Levi dealt with each of these mitzvos separately and therefore he gave different reasons for the different mitzvos. And in one case, that dealt with in *Mesechtas Shabbos* 23a, Rashi understood that according to Rav Yehoshua both reasons were applicable.

II

Women's obligation: a new mitzva?

The HaGriz HaLevi questions this concept of "אף הן היו באותו הנס". How are we to understand its meaning? Is it that under ordinary circumstances we would say that the women are exonerated from these mitzvos, because they are time-bound: "מצות עשה שהזמן גרמא".

However, under the circumstances, because of the element of "אף הן היו באותו הנס", do we now say that a *new mitzva* has been created for them, so that women too could commemorate the miracle which happened to them as well as to the men? If so, then we might say that although the women were not obligated in the initial mitzvah, because it was time-bound, yet because of an innovation, arising from the fact that this too was "their" miracle, they were now equally obligated to acknowledge the miracle by performing the same mitzva as the men: namely, reading the Megillah on Purim, drinking the four cups of wine on Pesach, and kindling the lights on Chanukah.

Or, on the other hand, does the consideration of "אף הן היו באותו הנס" serve to neutralize the consideration that these mitzvos are time-bound? This would mean that even though women are normally exempt, because they too were saved by the miracle, we transcended the time-bound element, and women are now equally obligated to perform the mitzvos because of the special circumstances.

Thus we have two possible approaches:

1) Either women were instrumental in bringing about the miracle, or they were in equal jeopardy with the men.

2) Either a new mitzva was created for the benefit of the women, or the time-bound element was superceded.

These two approaches have their respective practical consequences. There is a basic difference of opinion between the Behag and Rashi regarding to what extent women are obligated in the mitzvah of Megillah. The Behag maintains that women are only called upon to "hear" the Megillah but not included in the obligation to "read" the Megillah. Therefore a woman cannot fulfill the obligation for a man, since her obligation is a different one. That obligation is to "listen" to the story of the miracle. A man, on the other hand, also has the mitzva to read the Megillah.

Rashi, however, is of the opinion that "אף הן" means that both men and women are equally obligated in this mitzva. How are we to reconcile these two positions?

The Behag holds that "אף הן" creates a new mitzva for women and therefore men and women have different obligations, and consequently, women can not fulfill the obligation for a man. And Rashi's position, which is that "אף הן" neutralizes the time-bound element, and thus both men and women share an equal obligation.

There is a halachic question which discusses whether the obligation of reading the Megillah applies to a non-Jewish bondsman, עבד כנעני. Such a person, a *"Canaanite servant"*, was an indentured servant who had undergone the process of circumcision and that of immersion in a mikvah. Although he is not technically Jewish, after he has undergone these ritual procedures his status in Jewish law is similar to that of women. This means that he was obligated to adhere to all the negative commandments and those positive commandments which are not time bound?

The Bais Yosef, in סימן תרפט maintains that according to the Rashbam — who stated that miracle came about in the merit of the women — it would follow that slaves are not obligated, for they were not responsible for bringing about the miracle. Neither do we create a new mitzva for them. However, if we were to say that women were obligated because of the consideration of "אף הן" — that they were in the same danger as were the men — then a bondsman who was in jeopardy would be obligated in the mitzvos.

The Sfas Emes, in his commentary here, dismisses this claim by saying that even though women and bondsmen were both in danger, yet this consideration would not affect the status of a bondsman. For the obligation of women to fulfill the mitzva remains in effect today, because the women who were in danger in those days were the direct ancestors of Jewish women today; whereas bondsman cannot trace their ancestry back to the bondsmen who lived in the days of the Purim miracle, for we no longer have the concept of a bondsman in the modern world. Thus on account of the principle of "אף הן היו באותו הנס" women are obligated in this mitzva and bondsmen are not.

III

RASHI INTERPRETS "אף הן"

As we have previously discussed, it seems as though Rashi gives two different interpretations of the concept of "אף הן היו באותו הנס". Relating this concept to the mitzva of Megillah, he explains that women shared the same danger as did the men. On the other hand, when it comes to the miracle of Chanukah, he seems to emphasize the primary role of women in bringing about the miracle. HaGaon Rav Yerucham Perlman, the Minsker Gadol, addresses this question (See the journal "מוריה", שנה י"ד, גליון יא-יב, ניסן תשמ"ז).

The Minsker Gadol raises the question of the חות יאיר (שו"ת חות יאיר, סימן ט') as to why it was necessary to include women in the obligation of the mitzvos of Purim, Chanukah and Pesach. We know that they were involved because of the concept of "אף הן", which tells us that they were involved in these miracles. According to the opinion of the Rambam, though, all the later Rabbinic enactments took their source from the *pasuk* of "לא תסור", that we are not to deviate from the words of the Sages.

If this is so, then these three "new" mitzvos are based on this negative commandment ("לא תסור"), and this would imply that women are definitely obligated in these three mitzvos relating to the three holidays. But if this is the case, why do we need to justify this by the addition of another unrelated concept, that of "אף הן", to obligate them in these mitzvos?

To answer this question, the Minsker Gadol cites the position of the דרשות הר"ן (דרוש ז'), who qualifies the Rambam's statement that only those Rabbinic enactments which find support or are alluded to in the Torah itself are to be included in the negative commandment of "לא תסור". On the other hand, entirely "new" mitzvos, those enacted by the Rabbis, and which find neither support (סמך) nor a reference (עיקר) in the Torah, are not to be included in this negative commandment of "לא תסור".

"אין זה רק בדברים שיש להם עיקר וסמך בתורה."

According to Chazal, the mitzva of Megillah, which was written based on the *pasuk* of "כתוב זאת זכרון בספר" derives its justification from a verse of the Torah, and thus does not need the additional support of "אף הן" obligate them in this mitzva. However, when the Gemara includes women, it is on the basis of "אף הן" in order to neutralize the time-bound factor. For it would seem that the mitzva is very much a time-bound one, and therefore women would normally be exempt from its performance. But because the women shared the same danger as did the men, we therefore disregard this time-bound factor in this case.

In relation to Chanukah, however, there is no source or support from the Torah itself, and so, in order to obligate women in the mitzva of kindling Chanukah lights, we need to depend on the justification of "אף הן" and here this carries more weight than te fact that they were equally in danger, for Yehudis, a woman, was the main catalyst in bringing about the miracle. Consequently, women are responsible for the creation of the mitzva, and this is the essential reason why women are obligated in it.

With this in mind, we might now attempt to answer the question raised by the commentators. The Mishna at the beginning of the tenth chapter of Pesachim (99b) emphasizes the requirement to drink four cups of wine on Seder night. Rashi here explains the source of this obligation, based on its corresponding to the four expressions of redemption, ד' לשונות של גאולה (These four expressions are: והוצאתי, והצלתי, וגאלתי, ולקחתי).

On page 108a Rav Yehoshua ben Levi tells us, "Women are also obligated in the four cups of wine." The question here is why did Rav Yehoshua have to tell us this fact? For why isn't the obligation to fulfill this mitzva which is mentioned in the Mishna sufficient to obligate them? Based on our previous discussion, we might say that since the mitzva of the four cups can be viewed as an entirely new mitzva, one ordained by the Rabbis, we might think women are not obligated, since it is a time-bound mitzva. Thus we are specificically told "אף הן" — women are equally obligated in the mitzva, because they were equally in danger, and this factor neutralizes the time-bound element.

IV

OPINIONS OF THE RISHONIM

There is a difference of opinion among the Rishonim as to whether this concept of "אף הן היו באותו הנס" applies only to those mitzvos ordained by the Rabbis, מדרבנן, or even to those which were also biblically dictated, מן התורה. Tosafos in Megillah and in other places expresses the opinion that "אף הן" applies only to those mitzvos which are דרבנן. However, ר' יוסי איש ירושלים, a commentator cited by Tosafos in the Megillah, maintains that "אף הן" applies even to those mitzvos which are from the Torah, מן התורה.

The Chasam Sofer (in שו"ת חתם סופר אור"ח סימן קפ"ה) was asked the following question regarding the opinion that "אף הן" applies to mitzvos from the Torah.

The Gemara in Kiddushin 29a states that women are not obligated in those positive mitzvos (מצות עשה) which are time-bound. This halacha is based on the fact that just as women are not obligated to put on tefillin, because it is time-bound, so too are they freed from all time-bound positive mitzvos. The Chasam Sofer was asked the following question in this connection. Regarding the mitzva of tefillin, the Torah writes:

"והי' לאות על ידיך ולטוטפות בין עיניך כי בחוזק יד **הוציאנו ה'** ממצרים." (שמות י"ג, ט"ז)

"And it should be for you a sign upon your hand, an ornament between your eyes, that by the strength of His Hand did Hashem bring us out of Egypt."

If the commandment to wear tefillin is justified by its being a commemoration of the Exodus from Egypt, then we should apply the concept of "אף הן" to include women, for they too were an equal part of the Exodus. Thus it should logically follow that women should be obligated to wear tefillin, and subsequently, they should be obligated in all the other positive mitzvos, even if they are time-bound.

The Chasam Sofer answers that there are two classifications of the mitzvos related to the Exodus — זכר ליציאת מצרים. And of these is characterized by the mitzvos which result directly from the Exodus, and include such mitzvos as matza, maror and the Korban Pesach, which all stem directly from the history of the Exodus.

The second class of commemorative mitzvos are not directly related to the actual even of the Exodus, but rather the Torah requires us to remember the Exodus when we perform them. This class of mitzvos includes putting on tefillin. Tefillin itself has no obvious connection to the Exodus, but the Torah requires us to mention the Exodus from Egypt when we put on tefillin.

The practical difference between these two categories of memorializing the event of the Exodus is that in the first instance, because the mitzva came into being because of the actual Exodus, we can apply this principle of "אף הן היו וכו'", that women were equally involved in the Exodus process and therefore they too are obligated in the mitzvos. In addition, fulfilling the mitzva is considered as a separate mitzva; thus if one dons tefillin he fulfills not only the mitzva of donning tefillin, but also in addition it is counted as a separate mitzva — that of making a memorial to the Exodus. Whereas, in this second category of memorial, "זכרון", the particular mitzva now being done has no obvious connection with the Exodus, and thus we do not apply the principle of "אף הן" and credit for fulfilling the mitzva of making a memorial is not given.

This answers the question about the tefillin, which, as we have explained, is not due directly to the Exodus, but rather the Exodus was only added as an extra element, and we are asked *"also to remember the Exodus"* when we perform the mitzva. But we do not apply the concept of "אף הן" here in this case. This is how the Chasam Sofer answers this question.

HaRav Moshe Soloveitchik offers his own answer to the above question (See "מסורה", חוברת ב',תשרי תש"נ, עמ'י). If the mitzva was created because of a miracle, even such a mitzva which deeply affected and involved women, yet we apply the principle of "אף הן" only when the fulfillment of the mitzva constitutes פרסומי ניסא — *"publicizing the miracle"*. These instances include the following:

1) Reading the Megillah on Purim (See *Mesechtas Megillah* 4a).

2) Drinking the four cups of wine on Pesach night (See *Mesechtas Pesachim* 108a).

4) Lighting candles on Chanukah (See *Mesechtas Shabbos* 23a).

However, regarding the mitzva of tefillin, even though it was created because of the Exodus, yet when we don tefillin we fulfill only the mitzva of *putting on tefillin* but not that of *publicizing the miracle* of the Exodus. Therefore, women are not obligated in this mitzva, since it is a mitzva which is time-bound and, as we have mentioned, we do not apply here the principle of "אף הן".

We might suggest another answer to the question regarding tefillin and its relation to the principle of "אף הן", based on an insight offered by the HaRav Aryeh Zev Gurwitz of Gateshead, cited in his sefer "מאורי שערים" (עמ' שנ"ח בענין נשים בקריאת מגילה). Tosafos asked: If we apply the principle of "אף הן" to those mitzvos which are from the Torah, then why was it necessary for the Gemara to provide us with the source of why women are obligated in the mitzva of matzah, when we could simply apply the concept of "אף הן"?

HaRav Gurwitz replies that we are to understand the concept of "אף הן" to mean that because women were also the beneficiaries of the miracle, they too must express their appreciation and praise Hashem for His kindness. Thus "אף הן" creates a debt, that of verbalizing one's appreciation in the form of thanksgiving. And this implies that only those mitzvos which involve the concept of thanksgiving and praise, such as that of the Megillah reading on Purim, lighting candles on Chanukah and drinking four cups of wine on Pesach, can apply the principle of "אף הן". However, in the case of the mitzva of matzah, there is no basis on which to apply the "אף הן" principle.

We could also say in this regard that since the mitzva of tefillin is not based on the concept of expressing gratitude and praise, we do not apply the "אף הן" principle, and thus women are not obligated in this time-bound mitzva of tefillin.

V

DOES "אף הן" APPLY ONLY TO WOMEN?

The טורי אבן, in his classic commentary to *Mesechtas Megillah* 4a, ponders the question whether the application of this principle of "אף הן היו באותו הנס" applies exclusively to women, as the three statements previously quoted seem to indicate. Or does it apply to others as well, those who can identify themselves with this concept? For example, the טורי אבן asks whether a man who is obligated in Megillah — as dictated by the prophets, "מדברי קבלה" — can fulfill this mitzva by hearing the Megillah read by a woman — who is obligated through a dictate of the Rabbis, מדרבנן, because of the concept of "אף הן" — if he has no other possible way of fulfilling the mitzva?

This is a basic question, which not only concerns the mitzva of Megillah, but all the mitzvos of the Torah. That question is whether one who is obligated in a mitzva by virtue of a direct dictate from the Torah is also obligated in the same mitzva on the authority of the Rabbinic Sages. Since he is already obligated from the Torah, does the Rabbinic obligation also apply to him?

The Netziv, in his classic sefer, "מרומי שדה" (מגילה ד',ד' א'), is of the opinion that if one already has an obligation placed upon him by the Torah, then the injunction introduced by the Rabbis in this case does not apply to him. He presents the following proof for this, citing the Mishnah in *Succah* 3:12:

> *"Originally the lulav was taken in the Bais HaMikdash for seven days and in all other places outside the Bais HaMikdash only for one day, the first day of yom tov. However, after the Bais HaMikdash was destroyed, Rabban Yochanan ben Zakkai instituted the decree that the lulav and esrog be taken in the provinces all seven days, as a remembrance of the Temple,* זכר למקדש.*"*

At the time the Bais HaMikdash stood, all seven days of taking the lulav was a dictate from the Torah, and therefore a kosher lulav and esrog were required in order to fulfill this mitzva. Those considerations which were only from the Rabbis, מדרבנן, regarding the mitzva of lulav were not applicable in the Bais HaMikdash all seven days and in the provinces on the first day of the holiday.

Thus the question is raised: what if a person had only an esrog which was deficient (אתרוג חסר), if, for example, the tip (*piytum*) fell off, thereby disqualifying it for use on the first day of Succos? However, it would be acceptable on the other days, which are מדרבנן, dictated by the rabbis. Would such a person, even though he can no longer fulfill the mitzva of lulav as directly required by the Torah, still at least fulfill the mitzva as dictated by the Rabbis, which allows an esrog without a piytum, "אתרוג חסר"?

The Netziv concludes that since the halacha tells us that a deficient esrog, אתרוג חסר, is acceptable on the other six days of the holiday and a blessing can be recited over such an esrog, then we can assume that such an esrog is unacceptable only on the first day of Succos. And if one were to ask, why not, we could answer that although one can not fulfill the obligation called for by the Torah, at least one should fulfill the obligation decreed by the Rabbis, even with a deficient esrog. From this it should be clear that since on the first day of yom tov, the mitzva of esrog was already dictated by the Torah, therefore the obligation as ordained by the Rabbis was never instituted.

However, in the responsa of the Chacham Zvi (סימן ט'), we find that he holds the opinion that if one possesses only a deficient esrog, אתרוג חסר on the first day of Succos, although he can not fulfill the obligation set down by the Torah with such an esrog, at least he should take this esrog to fulfill the obligation of the Rabbis, מדרבנן. In the sefer "משנת יעבץ" by HaRav Bezalel Zolti, the author gives the same proof as does the Netziv, which was that since one is not allowed to make a beracha on the first day of Succos on an esrog which is invalid, "אתרוג ולולב פסול", this proves that there is no obligation on the first day. He also points out that this is the position of the Rambam, as cited in *Hilchos Lulav*, Chapter 8, Halacha 1:

"ובשעת הדחק או בשעת סכנה לולב היבש כשר אבל לא שאר המינים."

This would seem to indicate that the Rambam is also of the opinion that whenever we have a prior obligation to do a mitzva, dictated by the Torah itself, we do not apply the Rabbinic ordinance here.

We might suggest that this question of whether a Rabbinic ordinance is in place in a case where we already have an obligation set down by the Torah is a difference of opinion between the Rambam and the Ravad.

The Rambam holds the opinion that the matza eaten on Pesach night must be eaten with charoses. That is to say, not only the matza eaten as part of the Korech sandwich is to be eaten with charoses, but also the matza which is eaten to fulfill the mitzva of matza at the beginning of the Seder. The Ravad, on the other hand, disputes this contention of the Rambam's and maintains that the matza neenot be eaten with charoses.

The Rogatchover Gaon (צפנת פענח, הל' חמץ ומצה, פרק ח' הלכה ח') explains the unusual position of the Rambam here. The eating of the matza represents both the process of freedom (חירות) and the experience of slavery (עבדות). Both the maror and the charoses are symbols of slavery; thus when we dip the matza in the charoses and later in the korech (that is, in the maror and in the charoses), we have a complete symbol of slavery, סימן שלם.

When the Bais HaMikdash was standing, both the symbol of freedom

— matza — and the symbol of slavery were in use, and when one dipped the matza in the charoses, we created a complete symbol of slavery. However, after the Temple's destruction, when maror was only ordained by the Rabbis, מדרבנן, this meant that we were no longer obligated from the Torah, מן התורה, to supply a symbol of slavery. Therefore the matza no longer represented the aspect of slavery and thus did not have to be dipped in charoses to create a complete symbol of slavery.

But this might lead us to ask, even though the matza now no longer represented slavery from the Torah point of view, didn't it now represent the aspect of slavery from the point of view of the Rabbinic ordinance, סימן של עבדות מדרבנן? Even in the absence of the Bais HaMikdash, we still had to eat matza, as dictated by the Torah, and the matza now represented freedom rather than slavery. And for the matza we no longer apply the Rabbinic ordinance. Therefore we do not combine matza and charoses. This is the opinion of the Ravad. The Rambam, however, maintains that we still have to dip the matza in the charoses, even after the destruction of the Temple. Thus we see that although matza no longer represents the aspect of slavery from the Torah, yet it still represents the aspect of slavery as set down by the Rabbis. Therefore, we see that the Rambam is of the opinion that when we have an existing mitzva from the Torah we still can apply the call to fulfill the mitzva from the Rabbinic point of view, מדרבנן.

From this we can conclude that the issue as to whether we apply a mitzva from the Rabbis, מדרבנן, to a mitzva that already exists from the Torah, מן התורה, is a matter of dispute between the Rambam and the Ravad. Furthermore, the Rambam is of the opinion that we do not apply a mitzva derived from a Rabbinic ordinance to a mitzva that was originally dictated by the Torah itself. But this seems to contradict his position that one cannot take a deficient esrog, אתרוג ולולב פסול, on the first day of Succos, since we say that a mitzva from the Torah is in effect on this day, and therefore we can not also apply a mitzva from the Rabbis to that same mitzva.

To resolve this apparent contradiction, we might suggest the following. We can say that the Rambam believes that we can apply a Rabbinic ordinance to an existing mitzva from the Torah in certain cases. And his ruling as regards the issue of lulav and esrog seems to indicate that we do not take a deficient lulav and esrog on the first day of yom tov in this instance, even if they are the only ones available.

Here the Rambam is of the same opinion as the בעל המאור, who contends that the mitzva of lulav — which is a Rabbinic ordinance commemorating what was practiced in the Bais HaMikdash, זכר למקדש — only applies from the first day of chol hamoed. For since the first day of Succos is, according to all opinions, מן התורה even today, then there was no need to make a memorial to commemorate that period in which the lulav was taken all seven days of the holiday in the Bais HaMikdash.

This explains the rationale behind the Rambam's statement in *Hilchos Lulav* 8:1 that one should not make a beracha on a lulav that is invalid on the first day of Succos, for since there is no Rabbinic ordinance which involved a memorial to the Mikdash, זכר למקדש, on this first day, we cannot use a lulav which is not kosher on the first day. On the other hand, the Rambam does hold that a mitzva from the Rabbis is attached to a mitzva dictated directly from the Torah, and therefore a male who is obligated "מדברי קבלה" to read the Megillah is also obligated מדרבנן, based on the concept of "אף הן היו באותו הנס".

Mordechai's divine inspiration

Chazal comment on the verse: "ויודע הדבר למרדכי" — "And the matter became known to Mordechai" (Esther 2:22), by saying, in *Megillah* 7a, that this proves that the Book of Esther was composed with Divine Inspiration: "אסתר ברוח הקודש נאמרה". For Mordechai could not have known about Bigsan and Seresh's secret plot to assassinate the king unless he was under the influence of the Divine Spirit (see Rashi, *ibid.*).

The Gemara attempts to dismiss this proof for we know that when Bigsan and Seresh hatched their murderoscheme they did not try to prevent Mordechai from overhearing their plans. The reason for this was that they spoke to each other in their native tongue, Tarsi, which they assumed Mordechai could not possibly understand. However, because Mordechai was a member of the Sanhedrin, he was well versed in seventy languages, and Tarsi was one of them. Thus he was able to understand what they were saying without the help of the Divine spirit.

HaRav Moshe Leib Sachor defends the thinking of Rav Meir, however. He claims that Mordechai did in fact become aware of their plot through Divine inspiration. The reason for this is that Mordechai would have had to be completely certain that they would not back down from their plot or change their minds before he went to Esther with his suspicions and asked her to transmit this information to the king. For if he had had even the slightest doubt, he would have been risking his reputation by discrediting two trusted servants of the king.

In addition, his informing like this would have aroused hatred against Mordechai himself, and he would consequently now be seen as a

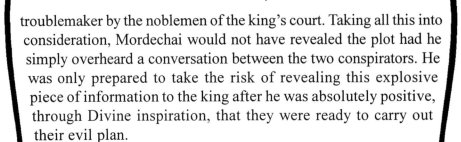

troublemaker by the noblemen of the king's court. Taking all this into consideration, Mordechai would not have revealed the plot had he simply overheard a conversation between the two conspirators. He was only prepared to take the risk of revealing this explosive piece of information to the king after he was absolutely positive, through Divine inspiration, that they were ready to carry out their evil plan.

Perhaps we can learn a lesson from this. Everything we think we know, and even things we are sure we know, do not always have to be revealed. Sometimes words spoken in haste can have unforeseen consequences, which may come back to haunt us.

We can see that the insight offered by HaRav Sachor is alluded to in the Torah. When Yaakov Aveinu began to sense that his father-in-law Lavan, could no longer look him in the eye, he felt that he was now unwelcome and he therefore planned to depart with his family and return home.

At this point, Yaakov calls his family together and informs them of the great injustice Lavan has done him and how he has consistently taken advantage of him, and how he never received any appreciation for his many years of devoted service to his ungrateful father-in-law. And he shares with them the information that Hashem has commanded him to return to his father's house.

We might ask why he went into such a detailed explanation and a recounting of all the insult and injustice he suffered at the hands of Lavan? Why didn't he simply say that Hashem had commanded him to return home?

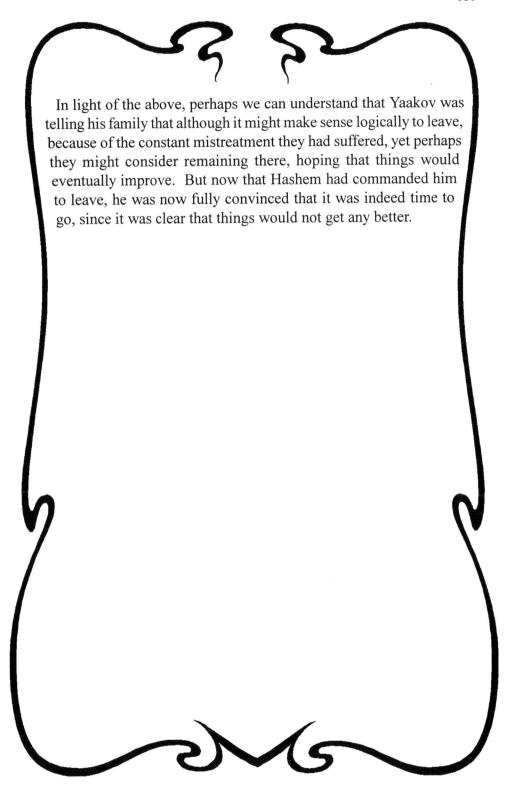

In light of the above, perhaps we can understand that Yaakov was telling his family that although it might make sense logically to leave, because of the constant mistreatment they had suffered, yet perhaps they might consider remaining there, hoping that things would eventually improve. But now that Hashem had commanded him to leave, he was now fully convinced that it was indeed time to go, since it was clear that things would not get any better.

CHAPTER ELEVEN

The Megillah reading takes precedence over Talmud Torah

I

IS READING THE MEGILLAH TALMUD TORAH?

In *Mesechtas Megillah* 3a we learn:

"כהנים בעבודתן ולוים בדוכנן וישראל במעמדן כולן מבטלין עבודתן
ובאין לשמוע מקרא מגילה, מכאן סמכו של בית רבי שמבטלין תלמוד
תורה ובאין לשמוע מקרא מגילה..."

*"The Kohanim engaged in their sacrificial service, and
the Levites on their platform, providing musical
accompaniment to the service, and the Israelites attending
the sacrificial service. All of them must abandon this
service and go to hear the Megillah reading. ... The scholars
of the school of Rebbe relied on this ruling to teach us that
one must abandon the study of Torah and go hear the
Megillah reading."*

A classic question is asked here. Why does the Gemara make the
statement: "מבטלין תלמוד תורה", that we are to abandon the study of Torah,
in order to listen to the Megillah; for doesn't the very reading of the
Megillah constitute a fulfillment of Talmud Torah, the mitzva of studying
Torah? For the Megillah is an integral part of Kisvei HaKodesh. Why
then, does the Gemara characterize the reading of the Megillah as an
abandonment of the study of Torah?

This question was posed by the eminent gaon, ר' יעקבקא לנדא, the son
of the נודע ביהודה, in the responsa of the "בית אפרים", by HaRav Ephraim
Zalman Margolis in סימן ט"ז. There we read the following:

"חייב אדם לבסומי בים הזה עד אשר לא אדע מה זה שאמרו של בית
רבי מבטלין תלמוד תורה ובאין לשמוע מקרא מגילה, הלא קריאתה זו
היא תלמוד תורה..."

The Bais Ephraim responds to this question by saying that in reality
the reading of the Megillah does not constitute an exercise of Talmud

Torah. Rather the real purpose of reading the Megillah is to fulfill the mitzva of *publicizing the miracle* — "פרסומי ניסא", by singling out the praises of Hashem for creating the miracle that saved the Jews from Haman's evil plot. We are commanded to make public the workings of Hashem's Divine retribution here. Thus we do indeed have here a situation of "ביטול תלמוד תורה", for we cancel Torah learning sessions in order to hear the Megillah.

"כשקורין בה [במגילה] אין בה רק משום מצות קריאה שהקריאה אינה כדי להתלמד רק למען יספרו לבניהם דור אחרון, אשר הגדיל ה' לעשות עמנו, ופרסום תקפו של נס. ואינו דומה לשאר נביאים וכתובים שנאמרו ברוח הקודש ומסרום לעם ה' בתורה דברי קבלה כדברי תורה ללמוד בהם ולתכלית זה זה הם כתובים ומסורים לעם ה' אלה, מה שאין כן במגילה שניתן לכתוב **לשם מצות קריאה** ואין מקיים מצוות תלמוד תורה בקריאתה רק מצות חכמים בקריאתה לבד..."

This rationale is cited in the קונטרס חנוכה מגילה, by HaRav Yehoshua Turtzin, in the name of the Brisker Rav, Rav Velvele (עמ' י"ב בהערה שם). The sefer "עטורי מגילה", a commentary on *Mesechtas Megillah* by הרב ר' אליקים געציל פשקש נ"י presents a beautiful example to illustrate this concept. The Shulhan Aruch (סימן מ"ז ס"ק ט) states that one should not read verses from the Torah without first reciting the *Bircas HaTorah*, the blessing on the Torah. We do not recite these verses in order to fulfill the mitzva of Talmud Torah, but rather as part of a petition to Hashem for mercy and Divine assistance.

Yet other commentators maintain that if the only reason these verses were said was for the purpose of prayer, then indeed the *Bircas HaTorah* is not required. In addition, we might say that even according to the first opinion that calls for a *beracha*, this is not considered a fulfillment of the mitzva of Talmud Torah. Rather the halacha requires that one who merely quotes verses from the Torah must make a *Bircas HaTorah*. This means that if a person reads the Torah not for the purpose of Talmud Torah, but rather because of other considerations, such as, when one reads the Megillah to publicize the miracle, then one has not fulfilled the mitzva of Talmud Torah.

With this in mind, we might perhaps now answer the question posed by the "משכנות יעקב" ("דבר אברהם" (in ח"ח ק"י, ט"ז, סימן ט"ז, ח"א). The "דבר אברהם" contends (in סימן ב') that the *Bircas HaTorah* is biblically dictated, מדאורייתא only when the *beracha* is recited in public — בצבור. This is what justifies the *Bircas HaTorah* recited prior to the reading of the Torah, even though one has already recited the same *beracha* in the early morning blessings. For that *beracha* is viewed only as a Rabbinically ordained blessing, מדרבנן, and insufficient to fulfill the obligation to recite a blessing for a public reading of the Torah.

This prompts the דבר אברהם to ask, why do we not recite the *Bircas HaTorah* prior to the public reading of the Megillah? For isn't the Megillah part of the *Kisvei Hakodesh*, the Holy Writings, from which one fulfills his obligation of Talmud Torah? His answer is the following. Since, according to the Torah there is no set formulation for this *Bircas HaTorah*, therefore the *beracha* of "על מקרא מגילה" constitutes a valid *Bircas HaTorah* and thus fulfills that requirement here.

However, in light of our previous discussion, which established that we read the Megillah for the purpose of publicizing the Purim miracle — פרסומי ניסא, rather than for the purpose of Talmud Torah, it is understandable why we do not recite a *Bircas HaTorah* prior to the reading of the Megillah. For as we have shown, we have not fulfilled the mitzva of Talmud Torah by reading the Megillah.

II

THE RISHONIM ADDRESS THIS ISSUE

The חזן יוסף רפאל מהרב "חקרי לב" (in סימן קפ"ז, חלק א') suggests that the Rishonim argued over this question, whether reading the Megillah constitutes the mitzva of Talmud Torah. As we have seen, the בה"ג (בעל הלכות גדולות) believes that women are obligated only in the mitzva of "שמיעה" — *"listening"* to the Megillah but not in "קריאה" — *"reading"* the Megillah.

He believes that either they should be exempt from the mitzva of both reading and listening to the Megillah because of its time-bound nature, or else they should be obligated in both and able to recite the *beracha*, "על מקרא מגילה". It is well-known that women are not obligated in the mitzva of Talmud Torah, and this is why they are not included in the requirement of reading the Megillah, which is essentially an exercise of the mitzva of Talmud Torah.

On the other hand, the requirement of *"listening"* to the Megillah, שמיעה, is based on the concept stated in the Torah: "הקהל את האנשים והנשים וגו'" — *"Gather together both the men and the women"*. Chazal explain that the men came to the assembled congregation *"to learn"*, whereas the women came *"to hear"* (See חגיגה נ', ב'). Therefore, the בה"ג holds that women do not recite the same *beracha* as men, because their obligation is a different one — to hear, but not to study.

And so the "חקרי לב" concludes that since all the other Rishonim, including Rashi, Rambam and the Ran, are of the opinion that women can and should recite the *beracha* of "על מקרא מגילה", it is clear that the reading of the Megillah does not constitute Talmud Torah, but rather it is an exercise in publicizing the miracle — פרסומי ניסא.

There is, however, a dissenting opinion. The "יד דוד", a commentary on *Mesechtas Megillah* by הרב יוסף דוד זיצהיים, questions (in ד',א') the position of the חקרי לב, that the mitzva of Talmud Torah is fulfilled with the reading of the Megillah. The יד דוד asks, if it is as the חקרי לב maintains, how can the Gemara make the statement that when we come to read the Megillah we abandon the study of Torah "מבטלין תלמוד תורה"?

There are several possible answers to this salient question, besides the one suggested by the בית אפרים. One is offered in the name of the Vilna Gaon. We are told that it was his opinion that if someone was deeply engrossed in a particular *sugya* and devoted all his energies to delving deeply into the topic, and then he was suddenly diverted to another topic, one which was much easier to understand and did not require such intense effort and concentration, this would be considered ביטול תורה — *"abandoning the Torah"*. Thus, for example, if the students in Rebbe's yeshiva, בית רבי, were deeply engrossed in their studies, and they were suddenly called away to hear the Megillah, this would constitute ביטול תורה.

A similar approach is expressed by the בעל התניא, who contends that if one does not exert all one's efforts and fails to penetrate to the depths of the subject matter, this too is an act of ביטול תורה. He gives proof of this by citing the Gemara in *Megillah* 3a, where we are told that an angel rebuked Yehoshua bin Nun for neglecting the study of Torah. Upon hearing this admonition we are told that Yehoshua bin Nun spent that night in the valley: "וילן יהושע בלילה ההוא... בתוך העמק".

Rav Yochanan explained this statement to mean that Yehoshua delved into the profundities of Torah law: "ר' אמר: מלמד שלן בעומקה של הלכה". (The word used in the Gemara for *"valley"* — עמק— means *"deep"*. Therefore, it is interpreted as *"profound"*.)

The בעל התניא points out that all Yehoshua had to do in order to rectify his neglect of Torah study was to immerse himself in its study. Why then does the Gemara stress that he "delved into the depths of the law"? He concludes that Yehoshua did not totally abandon the study of Torah even for a moment; yet because he did not concentrate on his studies to his greatest ability and reach his maximum potential in whatever he studied, this was viewed as an instance of ביטול תורה, abandoning the study of Torah.

This concept is actually alluded to in the words of the Gemara itself, according to Rav Yitzchak Weiss, in his sefer, שו"ת שיח יצחק, סימן שע"ב, when the Gemara makes the following statement:

"מבטלין תלמוד תורה ובאין **לשמוע** מקרא מגילה."

This statement alludes to someone one who was immersed in learning and then, all of a sudden, he stands passive and silent, listening. Because he ceased in his efforts, this is considered an abandonment of Torah.

According to the sefer "בית יצחק" על מסכת מגילה, the reading of the

Megillah fulfills the mitzva of Talmud Torah, and the expression "מבטלין תלמוד תורה" has a different connotation here, apart from its simple meaning. This is based on the words of the *Ba'alei Tosafos* here, who ask, how can we say that we call upon the Kohanim to abandon the service in the Bais HaMikdash, which is a fulfillment of a mitzva dictated by the Torah itself, in order to read the Megillah, which was only ordained by the Rabbis?

The *Ba'alei Tosafos* answer this by pointing out that we do not totally abandon the service here in the Bais HaMikdash, but rather we first read the Megillah and only afterwards return to complete the *Avodah,* the Temple service. This act of reading the Megillah taking precedence over the service in the Bais HaMikdash is referred to by the Gemara as "ביטול", abandonment of the Temple service.

Similarly, contends the בית יצחק, the fact that we first attend to the reading of the Megillah and only afterwards return to our formal study sessions in some sense constitutes "ביטול", even though the Megillah reading itself is also considered to be an exercise of Talmud Torah.

III

A DIFFERENT INTERPRETATION OF "ABANDONING TALMUD TORAH"

We might here suggest another consideration to confirm that reading the Megillah does indeed constitute a fulfillment of the mitzva of Talmud Torah. Thus we might see the statement of the Gemara, that reading the Megillah constitutes *"abandoning Torah study"* — "ביטול תלמוד תורה", in another light; in other words, perhaps it is not meant to be taken literally.

The commentators indicate that we two seemingly contradictory statements here in the Gemara. In one place we are told: "דורשין הלכות חג בחג", we are to engage in expounding the laws of each holiday on the day of the holiday itself. Yet elsewhere we find:

"שואלין ודורשין שלשים יום קודם החג" — that we are to engage in explaining the laws of a holiday thirty days before that holiday. This indicates that already a month before a holiday we must commence studying its laws. How are we to reconcile these two statements?

Several answers are offered by the Rishonim. The Ran, for example, contends that we do not really have a contradiction here, for in truth there is only an obligation to study and teach the laws of a particular holiday on the day the holiday begins.

What Chazal meant by the statement that we are to begin engaging in the laws of a holiday *thirty days earlier*, was that if a student has a question pertaining to a particular holiday, he should ask that question of his rebbe before the holiday commences. And this question takes precedence over any other, even those questions which relate to what is presently being studied. This shows us that there are times when one subject supercedes others in Torah matters.

In other words, every law constitutes a mitzva of Talmud Torah and one can study whatever one's heart desires. Furthermore, no one can force anyone else to study a particular subject or a particular section of the Torah. Yet here, in relation to Purim and the reading of the Megillah, if a class is studying a particular Torah topic and is called upon to stop and engage in reading the Megillah — which is also another aspect of Talmud Torah — one might ordinarily say that he would rather continue with what he was studying.

However, in this case, the Talmud Torah of reading the Megillah takes precedence over one's regular study, because it is the Talmud Torah of the hour, related to that particular holiday. In addition to this consideration, reading the Megillah also includes the mitzva of publicizing the miracle of Purim — פרסומי ניסא. Therefore we must cease studying the subject we were previously engrossed in, "מבטל", in deference to the Talmud Torah of the Megillah and its accompanying mitzva of פרסומי ניסא.

Thus, the statement of "מבטלין תלמוד תורה" does not allude to the abandonment of the mitzva of studying Torah, but rather the specific fulfillment of this mitzva through a particular subject, and instead we turn our attention to this mitzva of Talmud Torah in another direction — in order to fulfill the mitzva which is required at this moment, namely to read the Megillah.

Purim is mentioned five times in Megillas Esther

The first Mishna in *Mesechtas Megillah* reads:

"מגילה נקראת באחד עשר, בשנים עשר, בשלשה עשר, בארבעה עשר, בחמשה עשר, לא פחות ולא יותר."

"The Megillah may be read on the eleventh, twelfth, thirteenth, fourteenth and fifteenth days of Adar."

The חשק שלמה in his commentary on *Mesechtas Megillah* 2a, points out that the *Megillas Esther* itself alludes to these five time periods by the fact that the name of this holiday, Purim, appears five times in the *Megillah:*

(1) "על כן קראו לימים האלה **פורים**." (ט,כו)
"That is why they called these days 'Purim'."

(2) "וימי **הפורים** האלה לא יעברו מתוך היהודים." (ט, כח)
"And these days of Purim shall never cease among the Jews."

(3) "לקיים את אגרת **הפרים**." (ט, כט)
"To ratify this letter of Purim."

(4) "לקיים את ימי **הפרים** האלה בזמניהם." (ט,לא)
"To establish these days of Purim on their proper dates."

(5) "ומאמר אסתר קים דברי **הפרים**." (ט, לב)
"Esther's ordinance validated these regulations for Purim."

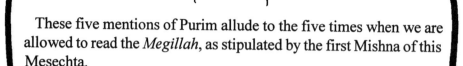

These five mentions of Purim allude to the five times when we are allowed to read the *Megillah*, as stipulated by the first Mishna of this Mesechta.

On closer observation of these five verses, we notice that in the first two verses, the word "פורים" is fully written, "מלא", with the letter vav "ו"; whereas in the other three verses it is written as "פרים", lacking the letter vav, "חסר".

This indicates that only on two of these days is Purim complete, with not only the *Megillah* being read but also the festive meal which is required on Purim, and the sending of gifts to one's friends and neighbors, משלוח מנות. On the other three days, however, the 11th, 12th and 13th of Adar, it is Purim only in regard to the reading of *Megillah*. This is the reason the *vav* is lacking in the spelling of the name of the holiday, because the other elements of the holiday are lacking.

Perhaps we can expand on this insight of the חשק שלמה and suggest that each of the five verses themselves allude to different time periods. For example, in the first verse, *"This is why they called these days 'Purim',"* where Purim is written fully with the *vav,* we can say that this alludes to the 14th and 15th of Adar. For only are these days Purim in the fullest sense, with all the accompanying mitzvos in place. On the other hand, the 11th, 12th and 13th of Adar are not called *"Purim"* at all, but rather only the reading of the *Megillah* is allowed on those days. This explains why the *vav* is lacking.

The second verse, which reads: *"And these days of Purim shall never cease from among the Jews"* also alludes to the 14th and 15th of Adar. For only these two days shall *"never cease"*. The other three days

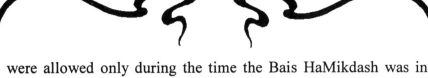

were allowed only during the time the Bais HaMikdash was in existence. In our days, though, following the Temple's destruction, one must read the *Megillah* in its proper time, which is on the 14th and 15th of Adar. (See *Mesechtas Megillah* 2a.)

The third verse, *"to fulfill this letter of Purim"*, is written חסר, without the *vav*. Here we allude to the *Megillah* itself, which, as we have said, may be read on all five days mentioned in the Mishna although the other mitzvos of the day are lacking — חסר.

In the fourth verse, "to establish these days *on their proper dates*", Chazal tell us (in *Megillah* 2a) that the additional days allotted for reading the *Megillah* are based on the key word here in this verse: "בזמניהם" — *"in their proper time"*. Chazal point out that this phrase is superfluous, and thus its use here was to refer to the additional days on which the *Megillah* could be read. Thus the verse indicates all those days, and spells Purim without the *vav*.

The fifth verse tells us that *"Esther's ordinance validated these regulations for Purim, and it was recorded in a book"*. Chazal explain (in *Megillah* 7a) that Esther requested from the Sages of her time that they include "her book" among the other Holy Writings. This is the meaning of the phrase, "ונכתב בספר" — *"and it was recorded in a book"*. Thus here we are referring, not to the holiday of Purim, but rather to the Book of Esther, which could be read on all five days stipulated in the Mishna. That is why this verse too writes the name of Purim without the *vav*, to allude to the fact that the *Megillah* can be read on any of these five days.

CHAPTER TWELVE

Holding the Megilllah with bare hands

I

Rabbi Parnach's harsh decree

We are careful to cover all the other scrolls of *Kisvei HaKodesh,* the Holy Writings of the Bible. The *Megillas Esther,* however, is left uncovered. Why do we treat this book of *Kisvei HaKodesh* differently? We can extend the question even farther and ask, if the practice of covering the scrolls of the Holy Writings is based on a halachic ruling, why does this not apply to *Megillas Esther* as well? To fully appreciate these questions, we must first examine the sources which call for the covering of the scrolls of the Writings.

Chazal, in *Mesechtas Megillah* 32a, tell us:

"אמר רבי פרנך אמר רבי יוחנן: כל האוחז ספר תורה ערום נקבר ערום.
ערום סלקא דעתך? אלא אימא נקבר ערום בלא מצות. בלא מצות
סלקא דעתך? אלא אמר אביי: נקבר ערום בלא אותה מצוה."

"Rabbi Parnach said in the name of Rabbi Yochanan: Anyone who grasps a Torah scroll with his bare hands will be buried bare, without shrouds."

The Gemara then asks: "Bare? How can it even enter your mind that the person should be punished so severely?"

Therefore the Gemara reinterprets the statement: "Say rather that the statement means: He will be buried bare, that is, without mitzvos."

The Gemara wonders at this reconstruction of the statement: "Without mitzvos? Can it even enter your mind that a person should lose all his mitzvos for this? Rather, said Abaye, the statement means he will be buried bare of *that* mitzva (i.e., he is not rewarded for the mitzva he did at the time he grasped the Torah scroll with his bare hands. For example, he grasped the Torah to read from it or to roll it closed, and he does not receive the reward of those particular mitzvos.)

Based on this law as set down here by Rabbi Parnach, Chazal tell us, in *Mesechtas Shabbos* 14a: "Among the eighteen decrees enacted by Bais Shammai (See *Shabbos* 13b), was that the Holy Writings rendered *terumah* unfit if it should come into contact with a Sefer Torah. The reason for this was that the priests stored the *terumah* alongside the scrolls of the Holy Writings, for they said, 'This (the Sefer Torah) is holy and this (the *terumah*) is holy', with the result that the mice which gnawed the *terumah* nibbled also at the scrolls. The object of this decree was to prevent this desecration. Holy Writings were thus declared to be in the second degree of impurity so as to render the *terumah* unfit."

The Gemara cites a Baraisa which teaches a different enactment regarding a Sefer Torah and the impurity which contaminates it from contact with a person's bare hands.

"אף הידים הבאות מחמת ספר פוסלת את התרומה משום דרבי פרנך,
דאמר רבי פרנך אמר רבי יוחנן האוחז ספר תורה ערום נקבר ערום..."

"Also hands that came into contact with a holy scroll are declared unclean and render terumah unfit on contact. This 'uncleanness of the hands' was legislated because of the decree of Rabbi Parnach. For he said in the name of Rabbi Yochanan: 'Whoever holds a Sefer Torah with his bare hands (i.e., when the Sefer Torah is uncovered) will be buried bare...'"

In order to strengthen the prohibition against touching a Sefer Torah without its cover, the Rabbis decreed that one rendered the Sefer Torah ritually unclean, "טמא", just by touching it.

Tosafos (*ibid.*) ד"ה האוחז writes that it seems that the law of Rabbi Parnach prohibiting touching a Torah scroll with one's bare hands applies not only to a Sefer Torah but to all the scrolls of the *Kisvei HaKodesh*.

Consequently, the question again arises: How do we justify holding an uncovered *Megillas Esther* , which is part of the *Kisvei HaKodesh*, with our bare hands?

The *Magen Avraham* address this question in סימן קמ"ז סעיף קטן א'.

There he writes:

"ומיהו במגילה שכתובה כדינא צריך ליזהר מדסתם הרמב"ם שם (הלכות
אבות הטומאה פרק ט') דלא קי"ל כשמואל דאמר אסתר אינה מטמאה
את הידים ע"כ.

*"If a Megillah was written properly, as prescribed by the
halacha, one should be most careful not to touch it bare-
handed. This is so since the law does not follow the opinion
of Shmuel, who contends 'the Megillah does not defile the
hands'. Therefore we regard the Megillas Esther as part of
the Kisvei HaKodesh and it renders the hands unclean."*

II

SHMUEL: THE MEGILLAH IS NOT DEFILED BY ONE'S BARE HANDS

The sefer (ו"ע סימן א' חלק) "שו"ת פנים המאירות", by the eminent Gaon
HaRav Meir Eisenstadt, cites this statement of the Magen Avraham and
concludes that the present custom does not require us to be careful when
touching a Megillah with our bare hands. He quotes a source to prove
that indeed the halacha follows the opinion of Shmuel, who maintains
that one's hands do not defile a Megillah. The Gemara in Sanhedrin (ק,א)
relates the following episode:

"לוי בר שמואל ורב הונא בר חייא חוי קא מתקני מטפחות ספרי דבי רב
יהודה, כי מטו מגילות אסתר, אמרי, הא מגילת אסתר לא בעי מטפחות."

*"Levi ben Shmuel and Rav Huna bar Chiya were once
repairing the mantles of the various sof Rav Yehudah. When
they came to the scroll containing the Book of Esther, they
said to Rav Yehudah, 'This scroll is not as sacred as the other
scrolls and it does not need a mantle'."*

From this we see that these Amoraim are of the opinion that the
halacha follows the opinion of Shmuel in that the scroll of Esther is not

to be considered part of the Kisvei HaKodesh. Furthermore, the scroll of Esther does not need a mantle or covering.

However, the consensus of opinion among the Achronim is that this source is not reliable. For all it proves is that these particular rabbis here followed the opinion of Shmuel, yet this does not constitute proof that the final halacha agrees with his opinion. On the contrary, the Rambam, as well as the majority of the commentators, agree that the halacha *does not* follow the opinion of Shmuel and that the *Megillas Esther* is indeed an integral part of the *Kisvei HaKodesh.*

Another reason we are lenient in this matter results from the decision rendered by the Rema in *Hilchos Kriyas HaTorah* (א' סק"ז קמ"ז סימן), where he appends his own amendment to the decision of the *Shulchan Aruch* which cites the prohibition against touching a Sefer Torah without first interposing a piece of material. The Rema writes as follows:

"ויש אומרים דהוא הדין שאר כתבי הקודש (אגודה ותוס' ס"ק דשבת)
ולא נהגו כן. וטוב להחמיר אם לא נטל ידיו..."

"Others contend that this law applies even to the other scrolls of the Holy Writings. However, the custom is not so. Yet one should be stringent if he did not wash his hands..."

And yet we find that in our days we are not stringent, and thus the question remains as to the rationale behind the fact that we do touch the Megillah without first interposing a piece of material. Why do we not take into consideration the strong statement of Rabbi Parnach?

III

VARIOUS RATIONALES FOR TOUCHING THE MEGILLAH

There are several rationales put forth to defend the practice of touching the Megillah with our bare hands. One of these is that of the Noda B'Yehudah.

The rationale of the Noda B'Yehudah

All the commentators who discuss this issue quote a classic responsa of the Noda B'Yehudah (מהו"ת סימן ז'), where this commentator attempts to prove that the position of the Rambam contrasts with that of the above-mentioned Tosafos, that this prohibition against touching a scroll that is not covered applies to the *Kisvei HaKodesh* as well. The Noda B'Yehudah maintains that the Rambam disagrees. It was only in relation to a Sefer Torah that this law of Rabbi Parnach was directed, and it does not affect the other books of the Kisvei HaKodesh. He attempts to prove this point and bases his opinion on the following statement of the Rambam (in הלכות אבות הטומאה, פרק ט, הלכה ה'):

> *"In earlier times they used to leave loaves of terumah besides the scrolls of the Scriptures saying: 'This is a hallowed thing* (ספר תורה) *and that is a hallowed thing* (תרומה). *But mice came and tore the scrolls. Therefore it was decreed that if loaves of terumah touch any of the Holy Scriptures, it* (כתבי הקודש) *becomes unclean... Thus all of the Holy Scriptures render terumah invalid as though they suffered a second grade of uncleanness.*
>
> *Moreover, if a man's hands are clean and he touches any of the Holy Scriptures, his hands become unclean with a second grade of uncleanness..."*

Thus, contends the Noda B'Yehudah, we see that since there is no mention of the law of Rav Parnach here, we can assume that the purpose of this decree declaring the hands unclean was not to prevent the holding of a Sefer Torah with bare hands, but rather as a preventive measure against placing *terumah* next to *Kisvei Hakodesh*. Although it would seem clear from what is stated in the Gemara in *Shabbos* 14a, that the hands were declared unfit due to Rav Parnach's law, we must say that they made this declaration only in relation to a Sefer Torah, but not for any other of the books of *Kisvei HaKodesh*.

Consequently, we see that although the *Megillas Esther*, which is part of *Kisvei HaKodesh*, defiles the hands, the reason for this is not to prevent one from holding a Sefer Torah bare-handed but rather to ensure that one does not place *terumah* and *Kisvei HaKodesh* together. Thus we may say that this decree applies to hands that were not previously washed; however, if one washed his hands there would be no decree of "טומאת ידים" — *"defiling the hands"*.

A SECOND SOLUTION

Another solution to justify not covering the *Megillas Esther* is offered by HaRav David Metzger, *shlita*, (קובץ שערי ציון" תשמ"ד מעמ' ס"ט" and "אורייתא", י"א, עמ' ס"ז). This solution is based on the previously discussed approach of the HaGriz HaLevi, that in relation to the Megillah one can apply two separate laws. There is a Megillah which is written and is meant to be included in the *Kisvei HaKodesh*. It was this kind of Megillah which the law of טומאת ידים, defilement of the hands, was intended for.

And then there is the Megillah that was written exclusively for the purpose of fulfilling the mitzva of reading it on Purim day. This type of written Megillah is not viewed as an integral part of *Kisvei HaKodesh*. Even the laws regarding the makeup of this type of Megillah is different than the laws of writing a sefer of the regular *Kisvei HaKodesh*. And thus the law of טומאת ידים does not apply to it. It is this type of Megillah which we read on Purim day, and therefore we do not have to be concerned with the matter of touching such a Megillah bare-handed.

A THIRD SOLUTION

A third solution is offered here in the sefer "עיטורי מגילה" on שע"ז עמ'. The author contends here that we are to understand the position taken by the Rambam as being different from that of the other Rishonim in this matter. This approach is based on the two following proofs: the sequence of the halachos cited here in regard to our subject matter, and the placing of this halacha in *Hilchos Sefer Torah*. In 10:6, he writes:

"לא יאחז אדם ספר תורה בזרוע ויכנס בו לבית-המרחץ או לבית-כסא
או לבית הקברות, אף על פי שהוא כרוך במטפחות ונתון בתוך התיק
שלו... ולא יאחז את ספר תורה כשהוא ערום..."

*"A person should not enter a bathroom, lavatory or cemetery
while holding a Torah scroll, even if it is covered by a mantle
and placed in its container... And one should not hold a Sefer
Torah when it is uncovered."*

We can conclude the following from these words of the Rambam:
Since he did not amend this law of holding a Sefer Torah uncovered by
saying that if one holds it with a mantle then it is permitted, this proves
that the prohibition here is not the result of touching a Sefer Torah when
it is uncovered, even if he held it with a mantle.

In addition, from the sequence of halachos here, we can see that these
laws concern the proper respect required in relation to a Sefer Torah.
'One should not enter a lavatory... hold a Sefer Torah when it is
uncovered.' All these laws deal with the proper respect due a Sefer Torah.

Therefore we can conclude that the law of Rav Parnach does not
concern itself with the matter of "touching a Sefer Torah", but rather
with "holding a Sefer Torah" when it is uncovered. Thus we see that this
law of Rav Parnach is exclusively concerned with a Sefer Torah and not
with *Kisvei HaKodesh*. Thus we have a *heter*, permission, to touch a
Megillah without being required to cover it with a mantle.

IV

IS MEGILLAS ESTHER PART OF KISVEI HAKODESH?

There is another possible solution regarding the law of טומאת ידים,
which does not apply to the *Megillas Esther* because it is referred to as a
"letter" — אגרת, rather than a book, ספר. This is based on the *pasuk* in
Esther 9:29, which states: "לקיים את אגרת הפורים הזאת." — *"And preserve*

this Purim letter." But such a solution will not work for the following reasons.

The Gemara in *Megillah* 7a raises a question regarding the statement of Shmuel that "the Megillah does not defile the hands". It would seem that Shmuel is of the opinion that the scroll of Esther was not written with Divine inspiration, רוח הקודש. If so, the Gemara asks, wouldn't this contradict the statement made previously by Shmuel himself that the scroll of Esther was indeed written with Divine inspiration? Thus we might ask (see תורת רבנו שמואל סלנט, חלק א', עמ' ע"ב) if we were to that טומאת ידים does not apply to the *Megillas Esther* because it is called אגרת rather than ספר, how are we to understand the Gemara's question here?

Shmuel contends that the answer here is obvious. The Megillah was written with Divine inspiration, רוח הקודש, yet it does not "defile the hands" because it is called a *"letter"* — אגרת. But why didn't the Gemara offer this simple solution instead of inventing an entirely new concept?

We regard the Megillah as a *"letter"* — אגרת, only in certain respects. For example, we read the Megillah folded as a letter. However, regarding other aspects of the Megillah, we consider this scroll to be a ספר. This is confirmed by the words of the Megillah itself, in 9:32, where we read: "ונכתב בספר" — *"And it was recorded in a book."* Thus the halacha requires that the Megillah be written with ink on parchment, etc., as is stipulated for a ספר, a *"book"*. Thus even though the Megillah is referred to as a *"letter"*, it still retains all the characteristics and the halachic requirements of a *"book"*, and therefore it is subject to the law of "טומאת ידים".

To answer these two questions, we might suggest the following. The Gemara in *Megillah* 7a quotes a *pasuk* from the Torah: "כתוב זאת זכרון בספר" to justify the writing of the Megillah and its inclusion in the *Kisvei HaKodesh*. And then the Gemara cites the opinion of Shmuel that the Megillah does not defile the hands. This seems to indicate that Shmuel believes that the Megillah is not part of the *Kisvei HaKodesh*. But why did Shmuel not say this explicitly?

We might assume that the Gemara here is really not primarily concerned with the laws of טומאת ידים, but rather from these laws we can deduce something significant about the Megillah — whether or not it is an integral part of the *Kisvei HaKodesh*. And so, when we are confronted with the contradictory statements of Shmuel, it would now not be such a straightforward matter for the Gemara to clarify the status of *Megillas Esther*. But this is the main concern of the Gemara and not the issue of when or where we apply the law of טומאת ידים. Thus the Gemara focuses on what Shmuel meant when he said, "*Megillas Esther* was written with Divine Inspiration" — רוח הקודש, and this statement is related to our requirement to read this *sefer*. Viewed from this perspective, we no longer have a contradiction, and the issue of טומאת ידים is left aside.

To answer the other question, we might say that even though the Megillah is referred to as a *"letter"* — אגרת, as well as a *"book"*, which calls for certain conditions to be fulfilled, yet the overriding view of this particular *"book"* is that it is in many ways considered a *"letter"* after all and this is essentially how it is to be treated, which accounts for the fact that it can be held barehanded.

V

The שערי תשובה CLARIFIES THE ISSUE

The commentator שערי תשובה in סימן תרצ"ה ascribes to this view that the prohibition against touching a Torah scroll because of the law of טומאת ידים does not apply to the Megillah, because it is called a *"letter"* — אגרת. He maintains this position in refuting the contention of Rav Yaakov Emden that one should be careful not to touch the Megillah with one's bare hands. The שערי תשובה writes as follows:

"ואין המנהג כדבריו...והיינו בפשיטות דברי הש"ס (מגילה י"ט, א')
דלענין זה אמרינן כיון דנקראת אגרת, בלא מטפחות סגי לה, ואף על גב
דנקראת 'ספר' היינו לענין הדברים שהם הכשר הכתיבה, כגון שירטוט,
והיקף גויל, אבל הדברים שאחר הכתיבה כאגרת דמי, ואף על גב
שמטמאת הידים, נטלה ערומה כמו תפילין."

"The custom is not as he contends...the reason being that since the Megillah is viewed as a 'letter', and even though it is also referred to as a 'book', this is only in regard to the manner of how it should be written. However, once it is written, it is referred to as a 'letter'. And although Chazal say that 'Esther defiles the hands', yet we are allowed to handle it in the same manner we handle the tefillin bare-handed."

Others contend, however, that this equating by the שערי תשובה of the Megillah with tefillin is really not a valid comparison. The reason being that in the case of tefillin we have no alternative but to handle it with our bare hands, for that was the way the mitzva was designed — "שאני תפילין דמצותן בכך ואי אפשר בענין אחר". Whereas, in the case of the Megillah, it is possible to hold it by means of some kind of interposing material.

We might use this contention of the שערי תשובה to defend our practice of holding the Megillah with our bare hands. However, the objection to his position is based on a misunderstanding of what he really meant. For we would say that since the Megillah is referred to as a *"letter"* — אגרת, this does not mean that we waive the law of טומאת ידים because it is viewed as a *"letter"*, but rather, since we must read the Megillah as if we were reading a letter, then just as one holds on to the edges of a letter as he reads, so too may we hold on to the edge of the Megillah as we read.

This is what justifies the comparison between the Megillah and tefillin, which is made by the שערי תשובה. Even though the law of טומאת ידים should apply in both these situations — i.e., that of the Megillah and that of tefillin — yet since we are dealing here with holy writings, כתבי הקודש, the mitzva itself calls for us to disregard the consideration of טומאת ידים, because we must handle these articles which contain "holy writings".

And so we can understand why in relation to the Megillas Esther, the Rabbis did not invoke this law of טומאת ידים, not only when reading the Megillah for the purpose of fulfilling the mitzva, but also after we have completed the mitzva of reading. Thus we are not required to cover the Megillah with a mantle, for in both cases the law of טומאת ידים was waived.

Not everyone praised Mordechai

A t the end of the Megillah we read of the prestige Mordechai attained: "He was a great man among the Jews, and popular with the majority of his brothers. He sought the good of his people and he was concerned for the welfare of his posterity" (*Esther* 10:3).

Chazal comment on this phrase: "The majority of his brothers, but not *all* of his brothers". We are then told that "some members of the Sanhedrin parted from him." Rashi gives the reason for this in his commentary on *Mesechtas Megillah*, 16b: "Because having become involved in government business, he neglected his study of Torah."

There is yet another possible way of explaining this phrase here, "the majority of his brothers, but not all" in light of the following insight of the eminent gaon Ha Rav Yehoshua Leib Diskin.

The Torah tells us that Moshe Rabbenu was 120 years old when he died. And we read that at his passing *"Bnai Yisrael mourned the loss of its great teacher and leader."* — "ויבכו בני ישראל את משה".

Rashi comments on this verse that "Bnai Yisrael" alludes to the *males*, and they were the only ones who cried. However, when his brother Aharon died we are told that *"all Yisrael cried"* — "כל ישראל". The reason for this was that Aharon was known as a peacemaker, who spent his life pursuing peace among the people. We are told that he constantly tempted to make peace between man and man and between man and wife. He was known

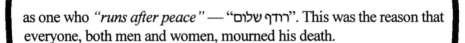

as one who *"runs after peace"* — "רודף שלום". This was the reason that everyone, both men and women, mourned his death.

One might wonder why it is, when the Torah comes to pay tribute to Moshe Rabbenu for his life's work at the end of *Parashas Zos HaBerachah*, it chooses to relate that not all the Jewish people cried at his death. Is this the highest praise to give the greatest leader of Klal Yisrael?

We can make a case for saying that the Torah here is indeed praising Moshe highly. For even though it is true that his brother Aharon, who pursued peace, was beloved by all, yet Moshe Rabbenu had a different role to fulfill for his people. He was their teacher and judge, and in fulfilling these functions he could not retain the love of everybody. For example, anyone who came before him to be judged and was found guilty would most likely feel offended. But this itself was actually the greatest praise which the Torah could offer concerning Moshe. The fact that not all the Jews cried proved that he had succeeded in his role as leader, even if it cost him the universal love of the people. As we know, a true leader will always inadvertently make some enemies.

In this vein, we might recall that the Sassover Rebbe, on Rosh Hashanah night, when eating the symbolic foods of the holiday, "סימנים", would pray: "May my enemies increase." When his Chassidim attempted to correct him by saying, "No, no, Rebbe, surely you mean, may our *merits* increase!" he would answer: "I know what I am saying. I pray that next year my enemies will increase, which means that I am '*somebody*'. For a '*nobody*' has no enemies."

This is the praise the Megillah gives to Mordechai here. He was a true leader in the fullest sense of the word. For if not everyone loved him, this proved that he had successfully met his challenge as the leader of his people.

CHAPTER THIRTEEN

Reading the Megillah in walled and unwalled cities

I

AN UNUSUAL MITZVA

The Mishna at the beginning of *Mesechtas Megillah* states:

"מגילה נקראת...בי"ד ובט"ו...כרכין המוקפין חומה מימות יהושע בן
נון קורין בט"ו. כפרים ועיירות גדולות קורין בי"ד..."

*"The Megillah is read...on the 14th [of Adar] and on the
15th [of Adar]... Residents of cities that were surrounded by
walls at the time of Yehoshua ben Nun read the Megillah on
the 15th of Adar. Residents of villages and large towns read
the Megillah on the 14th of Adar..."*

The following questions are raised by the Rishonim regarding the
laws laid down here in the Mishna:

1) Nowhere else do we find in regard to observing the mitzvos of the
Torah, that some do the mitzvos on one day and others on another
day. On the contrary, we stress the dictum of "תורה אחת" — that there
is one law for everyone. Indeed, if others have a different practice
than that of their fellow Jews, this can be considered an infraction of
the negative commandment against separate observance, which is
formulated as: "לא תתגדדו - לא תעשו אגודות אגודות".

In *Mesechtas Yevamos* 13b and 14a, the prohibition against "cutting
one's body" is interpreted as applying here to the "body of the nation"
as a whole. We are admonished not to "cut ourselves off into many
factions". Rather, we must remain united in the observance of Torah
law. Thus the question arises as to how we are to justify the observance
of this mitzva on two different days.

2) The actual law of reading the *Megillah* in walled cities on the 15th is
not spelled out explicitly in the *Megillah* itself. All that is mentioned
there in relation to the 15th of Adar is that the holiday of Purim was
observed on the 15th in the city of Shushan, as the verse tells us:

"But the Jews who were in Shushan assembled...and on the 15th they rested and made of it a day of feasting and gladness." (Esther 9:18). Consequently, although the *Megillah* itself mentions two days on which we are to celebrate Purim, there is no explicit mention of a walled city.

"להיות עשים את יום ארבעה עשר לחודש אדר ואת יום חמשה עשר
בו בכל שנה ושנה"

"To make the 14th day of the month of Adar and the 15th thereof every year." (Esther 9:21)

Since there is no mention of a walled city, what is the source for this halacha which calls for the *Megillah* to be read there on the 15th rather than on the 14th of Adar?

3) What is the source which requires a walled city to have been walled since the days of Yehoshua ben Nun? What indeed does he have to do with the Purim miracle at all?

THE ISSUE OF "לא תתגדדו"

Resh Lakish, in *Mesechtas Yevamos* 13b, addresses the question as to why we do not apply the law of "לא תתגדדו" here in relation to the two different days designated for reading the *Megillah* in walled and unwalled cities. The Gemara does not suggest an answer to Resh Lakish's question as to how we can justify the deliberate flaunting of this prohibition against establishing different observances of the same halacha.

The Rosh in his commentary to this Gemara (פרק א', סימן ט') explains why the Gemara chooses to ignore this question. The reason is that this practice of reading on different days was not the result of differing opinions as to how we should read the *Megillah* and thus apply the law, but rather it depended solely on where a person happened to be on the day of Purim and the following day. For indeed, if a resident of a walled city was in an unwalled city on Purim day, he would read according to the custom of that city in which he found himself, and the reverse situation would also apply — namely, if a resident of an unwalled city were to spend the night of the 14th of Adar in a walled city, he would be obliged to read the *Megillah* on the 15th of Adar along with the rest of the residents of that walled city.

Thus we see that this practice of reading the *Megillah* on two different days is not related to a difference of opinion as to how to apply the law, as we find, for example, in those arguments in the Gemara between Bais Shamai and Bais Hillel. Rather all agree that a resident of a walled city reads on the 15th and one who lives in an unwalled city on the 14th. Thus the prohibition of the negative commandment of "לא תתגדדו" does not apply here, and this is the reason why the Gemara does not find it necessary to deal with it.

One might ask that although we have here no infraction of the prohibition against "לא תתגדדו", yet how are we to account for the fact that two different days were established for reading the *Megillah*? And we might answer the general question by stating that it makes perfect sense for there to be two days established for the reading of the *Megillah*. For all the mitzvos dictated by the Torah itself are observed universally only for one day. Therefore it is legitimate to draw a distinction between Purim day, which is not biblically dictated, and those mitzvos which are dictated by the Torah. Thus our Sages established two separate days, to distinguish the holiday of Purim from those mitzvos of the Torah which must be observed universally on a single day.

II

Why "from the days of Yehoshua ben Nun"?

One might have thought that the determination of what constituted a walled city would have been made from the time of Mordechai and Esther, when the events of the *Megillah* took place, rather than from the time of Yehoshua ben Nun. For what is Yehoshua's connection to the Purim story? The classic commentators at the time of the Rishonim all address this question. However, for the present we will cite the opinion of only one of them — the Meiri — and we will leave the approach of the other Rishonim for a later discussion.

The Meiri gives the following reason for determining a walled city on the basis of the walls which existed during the period of Yehoshua ben Nun:

"ומה ראו לתלות הדבר בהקף שמימות יהושע, למדוה בגמרא (ב', ב') בגזרת שוה. כתיב הכא [במגילה], בערי הפרזות, וכתיב התם [בדיני בתי ערי חומה], לבד מערי הפרזי. מה התם מימות יהושע אף כאן וכו'.

ואף על פי שמקרא זה במשה כתיב, והי' לנו לומר מימות משה, אעפ"כ תלוי הדבר ביהושע, שהוא עיקר כיבושה של ארץ ישראל. ויש שפירשו הטעם מצד שנלחם יהושע עם עמלק, שהי' המן מזרעו. וממה שמצאו בהגדה זאת זכרון בספר ושים באזני יהושע...

ובתלמוד המערבי (מגילה הלכה א') פירשו הטעם כדי לחלוק כבוד לארץ ישראל שהיתה חריבה באותו זמן, ולא היו ערים שבה מוקפים חומה בימי אחשורוש. ואלו תלינו הדבר בימי אחשורוש, היינו דנים אותו כדין פרזי, ועכשיו נותנין להם דין כרכים ודין שושן..."

"The reason for determining walled cities from the period of Yehoshua ben Nun is based on the fact that the Gemara in Megillah 2b compares the law affecting the Megillah reading to the laws set down in the Torah concerning unwalled cities. In the Megillah (Esther 9:19) we read: 'על כן היהודים **הפרזים**' *— 'Therefore Jewish villagers who live in unwalled towns', and in the Torah we read (Devarim 3:5):* 'מערי הפרזי' *— 'aside from open [unwalled] cities.' Thus, just as the Torah refers to unwalled cities from the time of Yehoshua ben Nun, so does the phrase here in the Book of Esther allude to unwalled cities from the time of Yehoshua.*

In truth, this verse in Devarim alludes to Moshe Rabbenu rather than to Yehoshua ben Nun, and therefore we might expect that the walled cities in question would refer to cities which were walled at the time of Moshe. Yet we mention

*Yehoshua because he was the one who annexed the land of
Yisrael and sanctified it. And in addition, he initiated the battle
against Amalek. This emphasizes that the theme of the
Megillah relates to Amalek and his defeat, as Haman himself
was from the seed of Amalek.*

*The Yerushalmi explains why Eretz Yisrael was mentioned
in relation to the requirement of a walled city — because
the Sages wanted 'to give honor to Eretz Yisrael' —
'חלקו כבוד לארץ ישראל'. The Sages in this manner wished to
honor Eretz Yisrael, for at the time of the Purim miracle, the
land of Yisrael lay desolate. By determining the existence of
walled cities back to the time of Yehoshua, this served as a
reminder of the former glory of Eretz Yisrael."*

III

The opinion of the Ran

As we have previously discussed, the Rishonim dealt with the issue
of reading the *Megillah* on the 15th of Adar in walled cities whose status
was determined from the time of Yehoshua ben Nun. What emerges from
the various opinions of the Rishonim is a dispute regarding the following
matters: Why was this mitzva attached to the land of Yisrael? What about
walled cities outside the land of Yisrael? Did they have to be walled at
the time of Yehoshua ben Nun or would it suffice for them to have been
walled from the time of the Purim miracle?

According to the Ran, in his commentary on the Rif, the holiday of
Purim as a day on which we read the *Megillah* went through two stages
of development. At first, when the miracle took place, the Jews of that
time expressed gratitude that their lives had been spared. Those who
lived in open (unwalled) cities were saved on the 14th of Adar, whereas
those who lived in Shushan, a walled city, were saved on the 15th.

Consequently, those Jews who dwelt in open cities offered their thanks to God — הודאה, on the 14th, whereas the Jews of Shushan celebrated on the 15th of Adar. However, when Purim was established as a holiday for all time, the following considerations determined when Purim and the *Megillah* reading were to take place. All open cities — "ערי פרזות", throughout the world, where the vast majority of Jews lived, were to celebrate Purim on the 14th of Adar as the open cities did at the time of the miracle. But to ignore the 15th of Adar altogether was not justified, since the miracle also took place in the city of Shushan. Thus the city of Shushan was designated as a place where Purim was to be celebrated on the 15th.

To extend this line of reasoning, we might suggest that since Shushan was a walled city at the time of Ahashueros, it would have been fitting for all walled cities from the time of Ahashueros to have read the *Megillah* on the 15th as well. However, this way of determining the status of a walled city was not adopted, since it might seem to insult the land of Yisrael. For all Jews who lived outside the land of Yisrael and found themselves in a city that had been walled from the time of Ahashueros would read the *Megillah* on the 15th, whereas those who lived in the land of Yisrael would have had to read on the 14th, because all the walled cities in Eretz Yisrael had been destroyed by that time. This would have been degrading to the cities of Yisrael.

So as not to insult the Land, and to assure the dignity of the land of Yisrael, "לכבוד של ארץ ישראל" the law was established that cities which had been walled at the time of Yehoshua ben Nun (when Eretz Yisrael was in its glory) would read the *Megillah* on the 15th of Adar, even if they were no longer walled cities at the time of Ahashueros. And this meant that even though the land of Yisrael lay desolate, since the cities were once walled, they would read the *Megillah* on the 15th.

All other cities, however, even those which were walled, would read on the 14th of Adar, unless they had been walled cities at the time of Yehoshua ben Nun. Thus the Ran concludes: All cities walled from the time of Yehoshua ben Nun, even though they are no longer walled, were to read the *Megillah* on the 15th of Adar. All other cities, even if they are today walled cities, would read the *Megillah* on the 14th of Adar, if the city walls did not date from the time of Yehoshua ben Nun. This includes walled cities outside the land of Yisrael, even if their walls date from the time of Yehoshua ben Nun.

IV

The view of the Ramban

According to the Ramban, the difference between a walled city and an unwalled city as related to how we determine the date on which we celebrate Purim, involves a realistic consideration. The potential danger to an unwalled city was greater than that of one surrounded by a protective wall. Those who lived in an unwalled city were in jeopardy of genocide, God forbid. However, those who lived behind a protective wall felt a sense of security, for they were safe from an onslaught from outside by the presence of a fortified wall.

According to the Ramban, the establishment of Purim as a holiday went through two stages. At the time of the miracle, all Jews who lived in unwalled cities offered thanks to the Almighty on the 14th of Adar. Those who lived in walled cities, on the other hand, did not feel it necessary to offer special prayers of gratitude. Thus the city of Shushan was the only walled city to celebrate Purim on the 15th.

Later, however, when Purim was established as a holiday by the אנשי כנסת הגדולה — *the Men of the Great Assembly*, it was decided to draw a distinction between the two kinds of cities. The intention behind this distinction was to emphasize the situation which each kind of city experienced at the time of the Purim miracle. Thus those Jews who lived in unwalled cities celebrated on a separate day, the 14th of Adar, to focus on the specific danger they experienced on that day. And those Jews in walled cities celebrated, like the city of Shushan, on the 15th.

The reason that other walled cities apart from Shushan began to celebrate Purim later, even though they did not at the time of Ahashueros, was because Mordechai enlightened them that even though they may not have been aware of it, they too were in mortal danger. And thus, in order to honor Eretz Yisrael, the determining factor now became the presence of a wall around the city which had existed from the time of Yehoshua ben Nun.

In conclusion, we might summarize the opinion of the Ramban as follows: The difference between walled and unwalled cities was that unwalled cities were in greater imminent danger. After it was determined that walled cities also were required to celebrate the miracle of Purim, the criterion of determining the walled city was from the time of Yehoshua,. This affected all walled cities both in the land of Yisrael and *outside* the land.

UNDERSTANDING THE DISPUTE BETWEEN THE RAN AND RAMBAN

As we can see, there is a fundamental disagreement between the Ran and the Ramban regarding the status of walled cities outside the land of Yisrael from the time of Yehoshua. According to the Ran, we do not consider the walled cities outside of Yisrael at all, and thus they must read the *Megillah* on the 14th of Adar, like anyone else from unwalled cities. The Ramban, however, contends that the law of walled cities that applies to Eretz Yisrael — namely, that it be walled from the time of Yehoshua ben Nun — also applies to walled cities outside the land of Yisrael.

In order to reconcile these two opinions we might suggest the following. The Ran contends that the only reason Eretz Yisrael is considered at all, rather than only considering the status of the city of Shushan, is because we want to avoid insulting the land of Yisrael. For had we left everything dependent on Shushan, as we have previously explained, all of Eretz Yisrael would have read on the 14th of Adar, since all the walled cities had been desolated by Ahashueros' time. But because of this consideration, we consider a walled city to be so by virtue of it having originated in the days of Yehoshua ben Nun. But this involves only cities in Eretz Yisrael, whereas those outside it were not considered at all. And therefore Shushan is the only city in the Diaspora which reads on the 15th of Adar.

However, according to the Ramban, the reason walled cities were given special consideration was to emphasize that they too were in danger as were the unwalled cities. And this consideration affected all walled cities, both inside and outside the land of Yisrael. Since they are all considered equal in this respect, they are all determined as to whether or not they are walled from the days of Yehoshua ben Nun.

V

The position of the Rambam

The Rambam's position appears difficult to comprehend. In פרק א׳ מהלכות מגילה, הלכה ד׳ he writes as follows:

> "כל מדינה שהיתה מוקפת חומה בימי יהושע בן נון **בין בארץ ובין בחוצה לארץ**. אף על פי שאין לה עכשיו חומה קורין בט״ו באדר. ומדינה זו נקראת כרך.‏"

> *Any city which was walled from the time of Yehoshua ben Nun, whether in the land of Yisrael or outside the land of Yisrael, even though it no longer a wall, this type of city is called a 'כרך'.*

Thus we see that the Rambam considers walled cities outside of Eretz Yisrael and requires that they too must have been walled from the days of Yehoshua. This would seem to agree with the position of the Ramban, who also gives consideration to the walled cities of the Diaspora. Yet in the next halacha (הלכה ה׳), the Rambam writes:

> "שושן הבירה אף על פי שלא היתה מוקפת חומה מימי יהושע בן נון קורין בט״ו שבה היתה הנס. ולמה תלו הדבר בימי יהושע כדי לחלוק כבוד לארץ ישראל שהיתה חריבה באותו הזמן כדי שיהיו קוראין כבני שושן ויחשבו כאילו הן כרכים המוקפין חומה אף על פי שהן עתה חרבין, הואיל והיו מוקפין בימי יהושע. **ויהיו זכרון לארץ** ישראל בנס זה.‏"

> *"Shushan, the capital, even though it was not walled during the days of Yehoshua ben Nun, reads on the 15th of Adar, since the miracle occurred there. Why did they make the matter dependent on the days of Yehoshua ben Nun? In order to give respect to the land of Yisrael, which was desolate at that time. The inhabitants of those cities would thus be treated as were the people of Shushan, as though they were cities surrounded by walls, even though they are now in ruins. They would thus memorialize the land of Yisrael, while commemorating this miracle."*

Thus it would seem that the Rambam here gives the same reason as does the Ran as to why the law of walled cities refers to Yehoshua's time. Why, then, does he include the walled cities of the Diaspora and require them to read on the 15th, providing they were walled at the time of Yehoshua?

To explain the Rambam's position, we might say that he adopts the rationale of the Bais Yosef, as cited in his commentary in סימן תרפ"ח (and the Bais Yosef himself contends that his approach is also alluded to in the above cited Rambam). This rationale is that we attach this mitzva to the time of Yehoshua ben Nun not for the reasons given by the Ran or the Ramban, but simply as a memorial to the land of Yisrael — "זכר לארץ ישראל". This practice of adopting mitzvos as a means of memorializing the land of Yisrael and the Bais HaMikdash is required by our Sages in many instances, and so they applied here this same rationale in relation to reading the *Megillah*.

> "אלא היינו טעמא דכיון דמצוה זו הוקבע בזמן חורבן של ארץ ישראל ראו חכמים שבאותו הדור לעשות **זכר** לארץ ישראל בנס זה וכדאמרינן בפרק בתרא דראש השנה (ל.) דאית לן למיעבד זכר למקדש. ולפיכך תיקנו שמוקפין חומה מימות יהושע יקראו בט"ו ושאר העיירות בי"ד, ואילו לא הי' מחלקין ביניהם לא הי' לארץ ישראל **זכר** בנס. ויש קצת סעד לזה מדברי הרמב"ם, פ"א הל' ד-ה...**ויהיו זכרון לארץ ישראל**..."

And if one would ask, if so, it should follow that only walled cities in Eretz Yisrael should be considered and required to be walled from the time of Yehoshua. Why, then does the Rambam include walled cities outside Eretz Yisrael? We might answer this question by suggesting that when we include the walled cities of the Diaspora and demand that they too should be walled from the time of Yehoshua, that too serves as a memorial to the Bais HaMikdash — זכר למקדש. For only after Yehoshua entered Eretz Yisrael did walled cities gain their unique status in relation to laws pertaining to walled cities and only then did they come to be considered places of unique holiness.

Thus when we require that a walled city in the Diaspora be walled from the time of Yehoshua, we are essentially alluding to the unique sanctity of walled cities in Eretz Yisrael and thereby creating, in an indirect way, a memorial to the land of Yisrael, זכר לארץ ישראל.

VI

THE TORAH'S DISTINCTION BETWEEN WALLED AND UNWALLED CITIES

Perhaps one could make a distinction between open, unwalled cities and walled cities based on the differences set down by the Torah itself. In *Vayikra*, 25:29-35, we find halachic differences between walled and unwalled cities. For example, if one sold a home in an unwalled city the law is that it is to be returned to its owner on the Jubilee (50th) year, the *Yovel*, and in addition the seller has the power to nullify the sale for up to two years. However, if a home was sold in a walled city, the law is just the opposite. The seller has but one year to nullify the sale, and if he fails to do so the home remains in the possession of the buyer forever.

In regard to the sanctity of a walled city, a leper is required to leave such a city and is not allowed to dwell there. (See *Metzora*, 14:3, and Rashi there). Thus we might think that these considerations also affected the laws regarding the *Megillah* reading. Yet this would not be true, for we see that the conditions required for reading the *Megillah* in a walled city are different from those in an open, unwalled city. For example, if a city has the sea as its fourth wall, as does the city of Tiberias (see *Mesechtas Megillah* 5b), a halachic question arises which is whether the sea constitutes a "wall" and the city can thus be considered a walled city after all? On the other hand, regarding the laws as to what constitutes a walled city, as set down in the Torah in *Vayikra* 25, there is no question that Tiberias, a city "walled" by the sea, would not be considered a walled city. Consequently, we see that we do not equate the laws of reading the *Megillah* with those laws laid down by the Torah regarding what constitutes a walled city.

Yet we find that this question does not really pose a problem regarding the laws of reading the *Megillah* in relation to the laws as set down in the Torah related to what constitutes a walled city. This is maintained by the Ritba, when he addresses the question regarding the sanctity of the land of Yisrael. For if we say that the initial holiness of the land in the time of Yehoshua was lost with the destruction of the first Bais HaMikdash and the exile of the Jews to Babylonia, then we must say that there no longer exists any sanctity to the land of Yisrael at the time of the Purim miracle — "קדושה ראשונה קידשה לשעתיה ולא לעתיד לבוא".

If this is so, then how could we maintain that the law of a walled city was attached to the days of Yehoshua ben Nun "in order to give honor to Eretz Yisrael"? For if the land of Yisrael no longer retained its sanctity as a result of the exile of its people, how then could we attempt to give honor to a land which had no more inherent holiness than any other land? The Ritba answers this question in the following way:

"ואומר מורי נר"ו, דודאי טעמא דמלתא משום דכל מידי דהוה מדרבנן, סמכו לה אדין תורה כל מה שאפשר...והכי נמי כיון שהוצרכו נמי לחלק בין מוקפין חומה לעיירות, ומצאו שיש חילוק לענין בית בבתי ערי חומה בין מוקפין חומה לאין מוקפין חומה, אתו אנשי כנסת הגדולה **וסמכו תקנתם לאותו דין תורה** ומה להלן מוקפין חומה מימות יהושע בן נון, שהוא תחילת קיבוץ ארץ ישראל, אף זו מוקפין חומה מיב"ן...

וכי תימא והא **חזינן שאין דין שוה בשניהם**, שהרי לענין מקרא מגילה אמרינן כרך וכל הסמוך לו וכו' מה שאין כן לענין בתי ערי חומה, שאין נידון ככרך אלא מן החומה ולפנים. וכן טבריא אין לה דין מוקפת חומה לענין בתי ערי חומה, מפני שמצד אחד חומתה...ולענין מגילה, מספקי' לי' לחזקי'..."

ויש לומר דאף על גב דסמכו רבנן תקנתייהו אדברי תורה, לא הושוו
מדותיהן לגמרי בכל אלא דרך כלל. ועל הרוב חלוקים הן בפרטים..."

According to the Ritba, making a distinction between walled and
unwalled cities was based on the fact that we see that the Torah itself
makes a distinction between the two. And although we find several laws
that apply to one and not to the other, for example, all areas that are
deemed to be in close proximity to a walled city regarding the laws of
Megillah reading, are considered to be walled cities as well, even though
this does not apply to the laws of walled cities in relation to the laws of
the Torah.

Yet this is not really a problem, since we can say that the equation
was made according to the principle and not the particulars. And even
though the particular laws, the פרטים, are different, still Chazal saw fit to
base the laws of reading the *Megillah* on what the Torah regarded as a
walled city. And so, just as a walled city, with regard to the laws of the
Torah, was determined as a city which had been walled from the time of
Yehoshua, so too was this condition applied in relation to the *Megillah*
reading. Thus we speak of a walled city that was already walled from the
days of ben Nun.

From this we see that the law of *Megillah* reading was only equated
with the general concept of walled cities being different, as set down by
the Torah itself. However, the particular unique laws of "בתי ערי חומה"
do not apply to the *Megillah*.

VII

Rashi's opinion

According to Rashi, it would seem that, on the contrary, the laws of
reading the *Megillah* in a walled city are completely dependent on the
Torah laws that pertain to a walled city, "בתי ערי חומה". The Gemara in
Megillah states:

"אלא כל שתעלה לך מסורת בידך מאבותיך שמוקפת חומה מימות
יהושע בן נון, כל המצוות הללו נוהגין בה, מפני שקדושה ראשונה
קידשה לעתיד לבא."

*"But any city about which you have a tradition from your
ancestors that it was surrounded by a wall at the time of
Yehoshua ben Nun, all these mitzvos that pertain to walled
cities from that era apply in those cities, even if they were not
retaken by the returning exiles. This is so because the initial
sanctification was for its time and for all future time."*

Rashi comments on this as follows:

"כל מצוות הללו: הנוהגת בערי חומה שילוח מצורע, וקריאת מגילה
בחמשה עשר, והבית חלוט בה לסוף שנה."

*" 'All these mitzvos to be practiced in walled cities' alludes
to the laws of a leper is to be banished from a walled city, the
Megillah is to be read on the 15th of Adar, and the house
within a walled city which was sold may be redeemed only
during the first year of its sale."*

Thus it would seem that the law of reading the *Megillah* is equated
with all the particular laws enumerated in the Torah which pertain to
walled cities — "בתי ערי חומה". If so, then there seems to be a contradiction
in Rashi's position. For we find it stated in the Gemara, in 3b:

"אמר רב יהושע בן לוי: כרך שישב ולבסוף הוקף נידון ככפר."

*"A city that was initially housed, i.e. first settled and only
later was it surrounded by a wall, is to be treated as a village
[i.e., as an unwalled city]."*

Rashi comments here that this referred to the sale of houses within a
walled city. Thus, we can conclude from this statement of Rashi that in
regard to the *Megillah* reading there is no difference when the wall was
built, whether before or after the city was settled. In either case the
Megillah is to be read on the 15th (see Tosafos here, who disputes this
contention of Rashi).

Consequently, we see that Rashi does not equate the laws of reading the *Megillah* with the Torah laws concerning walled cities in general. This seems to contradict Rashi's assertion in 10b, that we do in fact equate these laws.

To resolve this apparent contradiction raised by the commentators, we must draw a distinction between the issues dealt with in these two statements. Rashi also agrees that in relation to the particular laws pertaining to a walled city, we do not always have to compare the laws concerning the reading of the *Megillah* to the laws of a walled city — "בתי ערי חומה". This is the position of the Ritba.

Therefore, in relation to a city which was first settled and only later walled, there is a difference between the laws pertaining to the *Megillah* reading and the laws regarding a "house within a walled city". The difference is that although in relation to the laws concerning walled cities — בתי ערי חומה, such a city is to be viewed as an unwalled city, yet when it comes to determining when such a city should read the *Megillah*, we give it the status of a walled city and it is required to read with all other walled cities on the 15th of Adar.

However, in the Gemara in 10b, the issue does not focus on whether or not we equate the laws of the *Megillah* reading to the particular laws regarding a walled city, but rather it centers on the question of how and when a wall retains its sanctity. For example, if a city was walled in the days of Yehoshua, even if that wall no longer exists, still we say that since the city had the original aura of sanctity at the time of Yehoshua, when the conquest of Eretz Yisrael took place — "קדושה ראשונה קידשה לעתיד לבא". For that city never loses its sanctity. And so, even though there may be no wall present today, the city retains the sanctity it had when a wall was present.

Rashi comments here that this would affect the following laws — reading the *Megillah*, banishing lepers from the city, and redeeming a walled city only in the first year. The reason for this is that just as the sanctity remains intact, so do these laws continue to apply. And this depends on the prerequisite that if the city had a wall, it was from the time of Yehoshua ben Nun.

To conclude we might say the sugyot of 3b and 10b deal with two distinct issues. In 10b that issue is whether or not the land of Yisrael retains its original sanctity even after its cities have been laid waste. In 3b, on the other hand, the focus is on what constitutes a walled city — "בתי ערי חומה", and what laws apply there, including the law of when to read the *Megillah*, whether on the 14th or the 15th. This is determined by whether or not the city meets the halachic requirements of a walled city as a result of its particular construction.

Thus Rashi agrees with the other commentators that the *Megillah* reading does not have the same requirements as a walled city in regard to the laws of "בתי ערי חומה", as set down by the Torah.

VIII

THE POSITION OF THE RASHBA

The Rashba appears to contradict this view that the *Megillah* reading on the 15th of Adar in a walled city is dependent on whether or not the original sanctity of the land of Yisrael from the time of Yehoshua is still intact, as a result of its never having been nullified.

The Rashba's view is cited by the Ritba in his commentary on *Mesechtas Megillah* 2a. There our earlier question is raised by the Rashba, who asks the following: If we say that the sanctity which Yehoshua gave to the land — "קדושה ראשונה לא קדשה לעתיד לבא" — only lasted as long as the Jewish people occupied Eretz Yisrael, and after they were exiled the sanctity of the land was nullified, then how can we say that at the time of Mordechai and Esther we sought to accord honor to the land of Yisrael by determining a walled city according to the criterion of whether it existed at the time of Yehoshua ben Nun? If the land of Yisrael no longer retained its holiness, what was the point of this ruling? And if the cities of Eretz Yisrael did not retain their inherent holiness, they would have been no different from any other cities in the diaspora.

Thus the intention to accord honor to the land of Yisrael would have been devoid of meaning, since the land no longer had any special sanctity attached to it. To this question the Rashba answered that although Eretz Yisrael no longer retained its original holiness, קדושת ארץ ישראל, yet since in the days of Yehoshua there did exist this special sanctity, therefore we attach our law of reading the *Megillah* to the matter of giving honor to Eretz Yisrael *of that period*, when Yehoshua did sanctify the land.

"אלא למאן דאמר קדושה ראשונה לא קדשה לעתיד לבא...אף לענין מגילה יהא כן. יש לומר, כיון דאזלינן בה בתר יהושע כדי לחלוק כבוד לארץ ישראל שהרי אנו דנין אותה לקריאתה כדינה שבימי יהושע ואפילו למ"ד לא קדשה לעתיד..."

This contradicts our contention that we attach the determination of the *Megillah* reading to the time of Yehoshua only according to the opinion that the sanctity of Yisrael was never nullified.

We might attempt to explain Rashi's position and that of the Rashba regarding whether or not the sanctity of the land of Yisrael remained intact after the destruction. Rashi contends that it did so, whereas the Rashba contends that even though the sanctity may have been nullified after the destruction, yet we still wish to accord honor to Eretz Yisrael in order to commemorate that earlier sanctity.

This difference of opinion is based on two different opinions as to what constitutes Eretz Yisrael after the first exile. The first is "שם ארץ ישראל". Once Eretz Yisrael was annexed by Yehoshua, this land was and always will be identified as "Eretz Yisrael", the land of Klal Yisrael, the congregation of Yisrael. Even though they were subsequently exiled and the agricultural mitzvos such as terumah and ma'aser — "מצוות התלויות בארץ" — no longer applies, nevertheless this land, שם ארץ ישראל, will always retain its identification with the Jewish nation.

The second opinion is קדושת ארץ ישראל. The agricultural mitzvos are to be practiced only if we contend that the original sanctity of the land of Yisrael continues to remain intact. However, according to the opinion that with the exile to Bavel, Eretz Yisrael lost its original sanctity,

"‎לא קדשה לעתיד לבא" the land of Yisrael came to be considered the same as any other place in the diaspora.

Thus we can say that this constitutes the basis for the different views of the Rashba and Rashi. The Rashba maintains that the issue of when to read the Megillah depends on the concept of "‎שם ארץ ישראל", and since Yehoshua did indeed annex the land for the sake of Klal Yisrael, this land will be identified with them forever.

Therefore, Mordechai justifiably sought to give honor to Eretz Yisrael and attached the law of the Megillah reading to the period of Yehoshua ben Nun. Rashi, on the other hand, believes that if we can say that the original sanctity of the land, ‎קדושת ארץ ישראל, remains intact, even after the destruction, then we can relate the reading of the Megillah to the necessity of according honor to Eretz Yisrael.

However, if the sanctity of Eretz Yisrael no longer exists, then there would be no need for us to honor the land of Yisrael. Therefore, Rashi maintains that the issue of whether or not the original sanctity of the land of Yisrael still applies — "‎קדושה לעתיד לבא" — determines when we read the Megillah. For we must make the effort to accord honor to the land of Yisrael by saying that the Megillah should be read on the 15th of Adar only in those cities whose walls date back to the days of Yehoshua ben Nun.

IX

THE LINK BETWEEN YEHOSHUA BEN NUN AND THE MEGILLAH

We must now return to our original question: Why did the Sages establish the prerequisite for a walled city to be a city walled from the days of Yehoshua ben Nun? For what does the reading of the *Megillah* have to do with that period, which preceded the miracle of Purim by many centuries? This question can perhaps be answered according to the following insights.

The *Meshech Chochma* asks: Chazal say that Bnai Yisrael were coerced to accept the Torah: "כפאו להם הר כגיגית" — "*He suspended the mountain over them and said: 'If you accept the Torah it is well; if not, you will be buried there.'*" But if this is so, couldn't we claim that we should not be punished for not observing the mitzvos and the teachings of the Torah, for we were forced even against our wills.

An answer is offered based on the following argument of the Rashba, cited in the sefer ז"ל, מהרב חיים צימרמן "אגרא לישרים". The Rashba explains his belief that the original sanctity of the land of Yisrael, קדושה ראשונה, by Yehoshua, was only temporary, and after the Jewish people were exiled from their land the sanctity of Eretz Yisrael was nullified. However, when it came to the "קדושה שניה", the sanctification of the land by Ezra and the exiles who returned with him from Bavel, we say that this sanctification was eternal: "קידשה לעתיד לבוא".

The Rashba explains this phenomenon by saying that that Eretz Yisrael belongs to the Jewish people as long as they keep the mitzvos. However, if they do not heed these mitzvos, they forfeit their entitlement to the land of Yisrael. Thus when Yehoshua conquered the land and Bnai Yisrael dwelt there, it was incumbent upon them to observe the commandments of the Torah, and they deeply desired to do this. However, the moment they were exiled, the claim of being coerced to observe the Torah re-surfaced.

Now, when they no longer considered observing the mitzvos to be obligatory, Eretz Yisrael no longer belonged to them, for entitlement to the land was contingent on their wholehearted and voluntary observance of the Torah and its mitzvos. Thus the sanctity imposed on the land by Yehoshua departed and became nullified. However, in the time of Mordechai and Esther, when the Jewish people once again willingly accepted upon themselves the Torah and its observance — "קימו וקבלו", they became entitled once again to lay claim to the land of Yisrael.

Thus when Ezra returned to Eretz Yisrael and sanctified the land, they now had an eternal claim to the land of Yisrael, as a result of their eternal commitment to the observance of the Torah. And so we see that at the time of the second conquest of Eretz Yisrael by Ezra,

"קדושה לשעתה ולעתיד לבא" — the sanctity now became eternal. This is how the Rashba explains this concept.

With this in mind, we can understand why reading the Megillah on the 15th of Adar became dependent on the period of Yehoshua ben Nun. For at the time of Mordechai, since the land of Yisrael now belonged to them eternally, the *Men of the Great Assembly* — אנשי כנסת הגדולה, attached the mitzva of reading the Megillah to the time of Yehoshua, which was when we first gained possession of Eretz Yisrael.

By linking the observance of the mitzva of reading the Megillah on the 15th to the willingness of the people to perform the mitzvos, we were reminded of how important was the willingness of the Jewish people to commit themselves to observing the Torah and its mitzvos in those earlier days of our national history. It was this commitment to Torah and mitzvos that we lay claim to Eretz Yisroel.

Rav Yonason Eybeshutz: the Purim Rav

When HaRav Yonasan Eybeshutz was a student in the yeshiva of the *Panim Meiros,* HaRav Meir Eisenstadt, he was chosen by his classmates to assume the position of "Purim Rav" and deliver an appropriate lecture. Here is an excerpt from that lecture:

The first Mishna in Bava Kamma reads: "ארבעה אבות נזיקין" — *"There are four categories of damages."* Tosafos asks, why is it that in other places, when the Mishna enumerates several items it concludes with the term "הן" — *"and they are these"* ? For example, in the first Mishna in Rosh Hashana we find: "ארבעה ראשי שנים **הן**" — *"There are four days of the new year."* And in *Mesechtas Shavuos* (49a) we read: "ארבעה שומרין **הן**" — *"There are four categories of guardians."* So why do we not add the word "הן" here in the Mishna in Bava Kamma?

The "Purim Rav" answered this question in the following way. The Gemara in *Pesachim* quotes various "sayings" that serve to protect us from dangerous situations. One of these is the following: "ניזהא דתורא הן הן" — *"If one wishes to chase away an ox, he should utter:* הן הן".

Thus we see that the word "הן" seems to tame a wild beast. Therefore the Mishna in *Bava Kamma*, which enumerates "potential damages", one of which is a wild ox, could not add the term "הן". For if we were to add this word, it would tame the wild beast, and he would then no longer be a danger; consequently, he would not be eligible to be mentioned in this Mishna.

We might add that "הן הן" not only serves to tame a beast with its wild instincts, but it also serves to tame the wild instincts of the human being. In order to "tame" man, Hashem gave us His Torah. Through its study, man is tamed and molded to become a truly civilized human being. The Mishna in *Pirkei Avos* 6:6 tells us: "והתורה נקנית בארבעים ושמונה דברים, ואלו **הן**." — *"The Torah is acquired by means of forty-eight qualities, **and they are these**…"*

CHAPTER FOURTEEN

Masquerading on Purim

I

The Halachos

Purim is the most festive of holidays in the Jewish calendar, with its feasting, merrymaking, drinking to the point of "not knowing the difference between Mordechai and Haman", wearing masks and costumes of clowns, buffoons, and characters from the Megillah and from the Bible. Indeed, merrymaking is the theme of the day. This leads the commentators to raise a number of halachic questions relating to this practice:

1) What is the source for masquerading on Purim?

2) Why aren't these practices an infraction of the prohibition against *"imitating the way of the gentiles"* — חוקת הגוים? For on their holidays they also dress up in costumes and engage in buffoonery. Aren't we copying their mode of celebrating?

3) When did the practice of masquerading begin? Neither the Gemara nor the writings of the Rishonim mention anything about masquerading on Purim.

4) Dressing in costumes usually means that one wishes to disguise one's true appearance, and indeed we find that on Purim many dress in costumes of the opposite sex. Men and boys dress as women and girls, and vice versa, with all the accompanying accessories to match. Isn't this an infringement of the prohibition from the Torah against dressing in clothes of the opposite sex? For we read in *Devarim* 22:5:

"לא יהיה כלי גבר על אשה, ולא ילבש גבר שמלת אשה."

"A woman shall not have upon her the apparel of a man, nor shall a man put on a woman's garment."

5) These costumes are often borrowed or rented and there is a likelihood that they may contain *shaatnes,* a mixture of wool and linen. Why aren't we concerned that this prohibition might be transgressed?

II

THE REMA EXPLAINS

The Rema, in סימן תרצ"ו, סעיף ח' tells us that masquerading in the clothes of the opposite sex is not prohibited on Purim because it is done purely for the sake of merrymaking, which is prescribed on the holiday of Purim. And even though some may wish to prohibit this practice, it has become a widespread custom in the Jewish world and is therefore permitted.

מה שנהגו ללבוש פרצופים בפורים וגבר לובש שמלת אשה ואשה כלי
גבר אין איסור בדבר מאחר שאין מכוונים אלא לשמחה בעלמא.
וכן בלבישת כלאים דרבנן. ויש אומרים דאסור. אבל המנהג כסברה
"...הראשונה

The Rema, in his commentary "דרכי משה" expands on this decision and gives several reasons why there is no infraction of the prohibitions against dressing in clothing of the opposite sex, "לא ילבש וגו'" and that of *shaatnes*.

The prohibition against wearing the apparel of the opposite sex applies when that apparel is the exclusive dress of either a man or a woman. However, if this kind of dress is customarily worn by members of both sexes, then there is no infraction involved. Thus on Purim, the "blouses" worn in the days of Mordechai and Esther were worn by both men and women. In addition, since on Purim both men and women customarily wear each other's apparel as costumes appropriate to the day, then this apparel is viewed as being the appropriate apparel of both sexes on this particular day.

Just as the Rabbis "looked the other way" and did not condemn frivolous behavior or levity on this day, even though this may have resulted in damage being done or in "stealing" food from friends in jest, yet this was not considered a transgression of the prohibition against stealing, "לא תגזול", because it was done for the sake of merrymaking, שמחה. So too did the Rabbis waive the prohibition against masquerading in costumes, even if this consisted of the clothing of the opposite sex and even if they contained *shaatnes*, which is only forbidden by Rabbinical decree, שעטנז דרבנן. This was the position of the Rema, as stated in his sefer "דרכי משה" (סימן תרצ"ו), where he writes:

"כתב מהר"י מינץ בתשובה י"ז, וזה לשונו: על דבר לבישת הפרצופין
שנוהגין בפורים, אם יש לחוש בזה משום 'לא ילבש גבר'... והאריך
בתשובה למצוא היתר לדבר משום דמאחר דאיש ואשה **שוין בו** לא
שייך משום 'לא ילבש'...

ותו דנמצא בשם רי"ב על הבחורים שחוטפין בפורים אפילו שלא
ברשות משעת מקרא מגילה עד סוף סעודת פורים... **אין בו משום** גזל
ואין להזמינם לדין על זה...הרי כתב **דמשום שמחת פורים** ליכא
למיחוש לאיסור 'לא תגזול' ולאיסור 'לא תלבש', עכ"ל התשובה.
ואפשר שמזה נתפשט המנהג ללבוש כלאים דרבנן בפורים ועושין
לשמחה, דהרי רואין דאפילו איסור דאורייתא דוחה כי לא מתכוין,
כל שכן כלאים דרבנן."

From this we see that much is allowed for the sake of the mitzva of merrymaking on Purim, yet the "דרכי משה" concludes:

"אבל טוב להחמיר ולעבוד את ה' בשמחה ולהיות גילה ברעדה"

"However, it is best to celebrate in a manner in which we need not fear that a transgression was involved in our merrymaking."

There is an interesting legend concerning the Rema which is relevant to our discussion here. In a footnote to the sefer "לב עברי", HaRav Akiva Yosef Shlesinger relates the following story:

"I heard that the Rema died at the age of 33, on the 33rd day of the Omer, and he wrote 33 books. The one who eulogized him cited 32 praises of the Rema and desperately sought to find one more praise in order to reach the number 33. An old man then pointed out that the 33rd virtue of the Rema was that on Purim, he wore a mask to disguise himself, and he went from house to house in order to announce that it was time for the Ma'ariv service."

III

WEARING MASKS

The above opinion of the "דרכי משה" makes us aware of the classic responsa of the מהר"י מינץ regarding the question of masks. This responsa is one of the first that mentions the practice of wearing masks and masquerading on Purim. This leads us to conclude that this practice of masquerading originated in Italy and this was the reason it was not mentioned earlier by the previous *poskim*.

At the beginning of this responsa the מהר"י מינץ emphasizes that he bases his own position concerning this matter on the opinion of "unimpeachable authorities, distinguished for their scholarship, who, in their personal behavior, go beyond the letter of the law." These authorities saw no objection in masquerading on Purim and in exchanging styles of dress between men and women. In addition, he writes:

"I have lived among great and pious persons, who were well aware that their sons, daughters, sons-in-law, and daughters-in-law wore masks and changed their attire from that of a man to that of a woman and vice versa... and since they did not protest, this indicates that they saw nothing wrong with this practice."

Although the מהר"י מינץ relies on the decision of the previous authorities he proceeded to add proofs to show that for the sake of the mitzva of merrymaking on Purim, שמחת פורים, we waive the above mentioned prohibitions. And he tells us the following:

For a man to look in the mirror is, according to Chazal, seen as an infraction of the prohibition against wearing women's clothes — "לא ילבש גבר שמלת אשה". Yet if one's hair is being cut by a gentile, one is allowed to look into the mirror in order to make sure that the corners of his beard are not shorn. And if, God forbid, we should find ourselves in danger, we may look into the mirror in order to save our lives. Thus we see that there are considerations which neutralize the prohibitions against לא ילבש. Similarly, we may say that the consideration of שמחה, can also serve to neutralize the prohibition.

Looking into a mirror on Shabbos is also forbidden, lest one see a loose hair dangling and come to remove it on Shabbos. And yet, if one will feel uncomfortable if he is not able to look into the mirror, he may do so, and the prohibition is waived. Thus we see that for relevant considerations it is possible to waive the prohibition against looking in the mirror, just as we can waive the prohibition against dressing in the clothing of the opposite sex on Purim for the sake of merrymaking.

Quoting the opinion of the ריב"א we are told that young people are naturally boisterous and if they should unintentionally grab food items in jest from their friends, this does not constitute a transgression of the prohibition against stealing, "לא תגזול". For the sake of celebrating the holiday of Purim, we may overlook these infractions.

IV

Opposition to masquerading on Purim

During the lifetime of the מהר"י מינץ this lenient ruling concerning masquerading on Purim went unchallenged. However, a century later, stiff opposition arose. For example, the בעל כנסת הגדולה, Rav Chayim Benveniste, in his classic sefer "כנסת הגדולה" dismissed all the proofs cited in the responsa of the מהר"י מינץ.

Although Chazal allowed a mirror to be used for self-protection or in order to relieve pain, yet they would never waive a prohibition for the sake of שמחה, fulfilling the mitzva of celebrating with joy, on Purim.

We might say that since both men and women shave and remove hair from under the arms as well as other areas of the body, therefore men should also be allowed to do this with the help of a mirror. When this happens, in no way is the negative commandment against men dressing in women's clothing being transgressed. Nevertheless, Chazal would not allow men and women to actually wear each other's attire and to revel in each other's company, because this manner of conduct was unheard of.

And if the Riva did not hold one responsible for rowdiness on Purim, and did not hold one responsible for an infraction of the prohibition against stealing, "לא תגזול", this relaxation of the rules applies only to monetary matters. When it comes to money we apply the principle of "הפקר בית דין הפקר" — the Bais Din has the jurisdiction in financial matters, even to make one's assets free for everyone, הפקר. However, in matters relating to prohibitions, איסורים, the Bais Din has no such jurisdiction to facilitate the celebration of Purim with the requisite joy.

THE ADMONITION OF THE SHELAH

The של"ה הקדוש expressed his displeasure regarding this practice of masquerading on Purim, for he believed that it violated the teachings of the righteous. His attitude was the following: "Be on guard, desist from this practice, for it leads to wearing garments that contain *shaatnes*, which is forbidden."

"בתשובת מהר"י מינץ סימן י"ז כתב דמותר ללבוש פרצופים אבל אני אומר לאו משנה חסידים הוא ושומר נפשו ירחק מזה ללבוש כלאים אפי' דרבנן או לחטוף מחבירו שלא ברשות כי זה הוא שמחה הוללות וכבר כתבנו לשמוח בשמחה של מצוה."

THE "MUSSAR" OF THE עוללות אפרים

In סימן ש"ט of the sefer עוללות אפרים by HaRav Shlomo Ephraim of Luntchez, this practice of excessive merrymaking on Purim was also attacked. He asks: "Is this the way we fulfill the will of Hashem and celebrate His holidays? Where is the source for this practice?"

V

RAV SHMUEL ABUHAV'S OBJECTIONS TO MASQUERADING ON PURIM

Yet another Italian gadol vigorously protested the leniency shown towards masquerading on Purim. Rav Shmuel Abuhav, in both of his seforim, "‫דבר שמואל‬" and "‫ספר זכרונות‬"dismisses the lenient ruling of the ‫מהר"י מינץ‬ regarding merrymaking on Purim, even though it is based on the dispensation of the ‫בעל כנסת הגדולה‬. In addition, he writes that he "cannot accept that wearing masks on Purim is a custom, ‫מנהג‬, because the Rabbis were more scrupulous in their views concerning what is forbidden by Rabbinical decree than they were regarding matters dictated by the Torah itself."

Secondly, he pointed out that the Rabbis were lenient only in regard to monetary matters (‫גזל‬), whereas they lacked the authority to permit what is forbidden by Rabbinic decree, ‫איסורים דרבנן‬, for the sake of ‫שמחת פורים‬ — joy on Purim.

However, in his responsa he adds another insight regarding why one should not allow masquerading. "The mask", he states, "portrays events of the Holy Scriptures and each mask is made according to one's inclination and intention." In other words, the construction of the mask and the costume which depicts a biblical character is left up to the imagination of the individual, and this might lead to gross distortions.

Masquerading followed certain trends in popularity. In some generations it was popular, and then it would suddenly disappear, and make its reappearance in another generation. Thus the *Aruch HaShulchan* writes: "Masks are not in vogue nowadays..." (See ‫סימן תרצ"ו אות קטן י"ב‬).

In our own day, this practice of wearing masks and masquerading in costumes on Purim has reached a peak of popularity both in the Diaspora and in Eretz Yisrael. Indeed the "Purim parade" in which people masquerade in costumes and masks is one of the highlights of Purim celebrations in Eretz Yisrael.

VI

THE CONNECTION BETWEEN MASQUERADING AND PURIM

Over time, the practice of masquerading became an integral part of Purim celebrations. But what does the idea of masquerading and wearing a mask have to do with the miracle of the holiday? Many explanations have been suggested to explain the meaning behind the mask or the masquerade. We will discuss just a few of them.

As previously mentioned, masquerading became the traditional manner of rejoicing on Purim, שמחת החג, which is a requirement of this day. The mitzva of merrymaking found its expression in dressing up in costumes, which would lead to merriment and laughter. A similar kind of merrymaking occurs at weddings, when one is required to bring joy to the bride and groom. People often wear masks in an effort to entertain and gladden the married couple, משמח חתן וכלה.

The אליהו רבה suggests another reason for wearing masks: To serve as a reminder of that which we read in the Megillah (*Esther* 8:15): "אפשר זכר למרדכי שיצא בלבוש מלכות" — *"And Mordechai left the king's presence clad in royal apparel."* Indeed, this verse serves as the source for our wearing holiday attire on Purim, בגדי יום טוב. This reminds us of the honor which was accorded Mordechai by King Ahashueros.

The מהר"י חגיז suggests that the reason we wear masks on Purim is based on the following incident recorded in *Mesechtas Megillah*, 12a: "The disciples ask of Rav Shimon ben Yochai: 'Why did the enemies of Yisrael [a euphemism for the Jewish people] of that generation deserve extermination?'

He said to them: 'You tell us the reason.' They said to him: 'because they derived pleasure from the feast of the wicked Ahashueros.' Rav Shimon ben Yochai said to them: 'If this is so, and Haman's decree was punishment for their enjoyment of the king's banquet, then only the Jews of Shushan should have been ordered to be killed, for they were the only Jews who took part in the feast.' The students then said to him: 'You tell us the reason.' He said to them: 'Because they prostrated themselves before an idol in the days of Nebuchadnezer.'

The disciples challenged the explanation of Rav Shimon: 'If indeed the Jews prostrated themselves before a golden image, should favoritism be shown in such a case?' He said to them: 'The Jews performed this act of prostration only outwardly because they feared Nebuchadnezer, but in truth their gesture lacked inner conviction. Similarly, the Holy One, Blessed be He, dealt with them only outwardly to frighten them into repenting. But He never actually intended to exterminate the Jewish people.' "

Thus we wear costumes to point out that how we look outwardly is not a true reflection of what we feel and how we look inwardly, in our hearts.

A beautiful explanation of why costumes were worn on Purim is given by another commentator:

"בכדי שלא יתבייש כל מי שצריך לפשוט יד ולקבל תמיכה להכין על פסח..."

"In order not to embarrass those who found it necessary to solicit charity on this day, not only for their needs for Purim day, but also to provide for their expenses for the upcoming Pesach holiday."

And although those who asked for help wore masks and one might suspect that they were simply posing as poor people, therefore we are told by Chazal that we are obligated to give on Purim day to all who stretch forth their hands — "לכל הפושט יד".

Masquerading also alludes to the miracle of Purim, which was "masked" within the laws of nature, even though it was really the Almighty Who was directing events. Even the name of the Megillah and its heroine, Esther, allude to what is "hidden" or "masked". The Gemara asks: 'Where is Esther's name alluded to in the Torah? And the answer given is that it is alluded to in the verse: "ואנכי הסתר אסתיר פני" — *"And I will surely hide*

My face." For this reason we wear masks to emphasize the symbolism of camouflage.

There are other possible allusions. We might offer a homiletic explanation of why we use the mask on Purim based on an idea we find in the Gemara of *Megillah*, 7a: "Esther made the following request of the Sages: 'Mandate the festival of Purim and the reading of the *Megillah.*' To which they sent her the following reply: 'You will incite the wrath of the nations against us, for they will say that we rejoice at the remembrance of their downfall."

From this we see that a Jew is not to flaunt his good fortune before the nations of the world, for this only serves to arouse anti-semitism. Thus we wear masks to disguise who we are and why we are celebrating on this particular day.

On the other hand, we might suggest that the mask simply became a customary form of celebrating Purim over the ages. Various conventions came to be practiced on this day, such as "hanging Haman", writing Haman's name on stones and then rubbing them together so that his name is "blotted out". Other customs include making bonfires and casting into them images of Haman, parading a rider on a horse dressed as Mordechai the Jew; while "Haman the wicked" leads him, shouting, "ככה יעשה לאיש" — *"thus should be done for the man whom the king wishes to honor!"*

Throughout the generations, the practice of wearing masks developed, as well as the use of the "grogger" — the noisemaker, and stamping one's feet whenever Haman's name is mentioned. From this we can see that masquerading and wearing masks on Purim was not a sudden innovation, but rather it developed slowly over time.

VII

DISGUISING THE TORAH

To "increase joy and merriment on Purim," Jews not only disguised themselves by wearing masks and costumes, but they also began to "disguise the Torah" itself. This was done by appointing a "Purim Rav" who was to deliver Divrei Torah, consisting of "pearls of wisdom" by connecting unrelated verses and subjects in an ingenious manner and thereby leaving the audience smiling, chuckling and even rolling with laughter.

The "appointment" of the Purim Rav was not a simple matter. A committee had to be formed of *ba'alei batim*, leading members of the community, who wrote and signed a "contract", in the presence of the real Rav, spelling out both the obligations of the Purim Rav and those of the *kehillah*. The Purim Rav could well be viewed as "king for a day" in the community.

The following incident was recorded as it occurred. Near the city of Rudnick, where the eminent gaon and tzaddik, Rav Chaim of Tzanz, lived as a young man, was a small town called Ulinov, אולינוב. One Purim, a new city commissioner was appointed.

This new city commisioner, together with the leading members of the community, sent a contract to the town of Ulinov informing the local Rav that he had been appointed as the Rav of Rudnick by Rav Chaim and all the leading members of the community. The "new Rav" was to assume his post on Purim day, and he was told that all the city was waiting impatiently for his arrival. When the Rav of Ulinov received this "letter of appointment" signed by Rav Chaim and the city commissioner, he packed all his belongings and traveled with his wife and family to take up the new position.

On Purim day, to the amazement of the citizens of Rudnick, he made his appearance in their city. To honor the "new Rav" a parade was organized and a Purim seuda arranged. At this seuda the new city commissioner ordered drinks for everyone and charged all the expenses to the real head of the city council, who had also joined in the festivities. After the *seuda* the bill was handed to him, and although he was a little tipsy, he refused to pay for the drinks and demanded that the matter be brought for judgment before Rav Chaim. When Rav Chaim was presented with this pressing issue, he declared that the final decision was to be based on the following Mishna on *Mesechtas* מכשירין. The law reads that food or produce of the soil only becomes impure if it comes into contact with water (see Leviticus 11:14, 37,38).

Accordingly, the first Mishna in מכשירין states: "any liquid which was desired at the beginning, though it was not desired at the end (i.e. the moistening of the produce by the liquid first pleased the owner, but afterwards displeased him) comes under the law of "כי יתן", "if water be put" and such liquid, when it has moistened the produce, renders it capable of contracting impurity by the touch of an unclean thing."

Thus when the head of the city council took part in the "liquid" (schnaps) at the beginning of the party, he was pleased about it, even though later, at the end of the party, when he was presented with the bill he was no longer pleased, yet still — "כי יתן" — he must pay for it. ("יתן" means *"give"*, in other words, *"pay"*).

Serving as the Purim Rav was not an easy task. One had to be well-versed in Tanach, Gemara, Shulchan Aruch, and the commentaries and one had to display a vast store of knowledge in order to be able to create a lecture which was both entertaining and brilliant. Thus the one who was appointed Purim Rav had to be someone who was recognized by everyone to be a superior scholar and worthy of being given this special honor. Indeed many future gedolim served as Purim Rav, and this included such luminaries as Rav Yonason Eyebeshutz.

The challenge of the Purim Rav was to invent divrei Torah which seemed plausible, but in reality was not true and never existed. The following incident is said to have really taken place.

A student was once appointed to serve as Purim Rav. He presented a difficult Rambam which seemed to be contradicted by the Gemara itself. However, the "Rav" offered an ingenious answer based on various quotations from the Gemara.

After Purim the "Rav" was summoned before the real Rav and Rosh

Yeshiva and sued for fraud. He was charged with having been appointed to create new divrei Torah to entertain his audience and instead he had delivered a genuine Talmudical discourse.

After hearing the claims and also the "divrei Torah" of the Purim Rav, the Rosh Yeshiva, who was adjudicating the matter, ruled in favor of the Purim Rav. When asked what was the basis for his decision, he replied as follows. "The Purim Rav lived up to the conditions expected of him. He did indeed create new divrei Torah, for in reality there does not exist such a Rambam, nor such quotations from theGemara. The Purim Rav created a fictitious Rambam and continued his "fraud" by creating a fictitious Gemara to answer a question which never existed.

VIII

THE DANGER OF PURIM TORAH TURNING INTO RIDICULE

Over time, the "lectures" of the Purim Rav began to turn ugly. Instead of delivering ingenious divrei Torah, the institution of the Purim Rav now took on a new dimension. It gave the student body, through the Purim Rav, the opportunity to vent their frustrations and express their anger against the Rosh Yeshiva, the faculty and the administration of the yeshiva. The students began to imitate the mannerisms of their teachers, which provoked laughter from the students and embarrassed individuals and insulted Rabbaim. This became in some instances true disrespect for teachers, "פחיתת כבוד הרב". Purim plays, which were once based on themes from the Tanach or the Talmud, now became take-offs of the mannerisms of one's teachers, and a way of showering them with sly, insulting remarks.

The reason for this deteriorating situation can perhaps be explained by the fact that the Purim Rav and the audience were no longer capable of appreciating the former highly skilled ingenuity of the Purim divrei Torah and people did not heed the injunction against embarrassing others in public, "המלבין פני חבירו ברבים". These Purim plays revealed deep-seated antagonism against one and all. I remember as a young yeshiva student that there was an older student who was taking exams for ordination from his *Yorah Deah* teacher. The exams were demanding and he was tested to his limits. On Purim he found an opportunity to "get even". This particular rabbi happened to walk bowlegged, and the yeshiva students howled with laughter when this boy imitated the rebbe's walk, in his "Purim spiel". Needless to say, the student paid a heavy price for his audacity when the holiday was over.

Indeed, these insults on the part of the Purim Rav caused much hurt and ill-feeling and it was even the cause of the demise of a certain gadol. In the biography of the eminent gaon HaRav Shimon Sofer, the Chief Rabbi of Cracow, the writer records that on the last Purim of Rabbi Sofer's life he was cruelly ridiculed by a group of Chassidim, and this had a fatal effect on the sensitive rabbi's health, to the extent that shortly after Purim he died.

These institutions of the *Purim spiel* and the *Purim Rav* met with stiff opposition on the part of many gedolim. In his biography of Rav Shlomo Zalman Auerbach, HaRav Nebeuzal writes that HaRav Shlomo Zalman once stated categorically that it would be better to put a lock on the door of the yeshiva on Purim day, than allow a Purim play to be presented which would hurt the feelings of others. "לדעתי, היו צריכים לסגור את **כל** הישיבות על מנעול ובריח בפורים".

In his responsa, יחוה דעת (חלק ה' סימן נ'), HaRav Ovadia Yosef, שליט"א, addresses this very question, and delivers scathing criticism against hurting other people's feelings for the sake of Purim joy, for this particular mitzva was never meant to be attained at the expense of others. He writes as follows:

שאלה: "בדבר המנהג שנתפשט לאחרון בחוגי הישיבות, שבחורי הישיבה בוחרים להם, 'רב פורים' אשר כטוב לבו ביין משמיע דברי ביקורת תוך כדי הטחת עלבונות אישיים בדברי היתול וליצנות על חשבון ראשי הישיבה והמורים והמחנכים. והשומעים ממלאים פיהם שחוק ומתבדחים בשומעם את דבריו, האם המנהג זה יכון על פי ההלכה?"

And he concludes by saying:

"ומצוה למחות בידם עד שיבטלו מנהג רע זה, שלא הותרה בפורים
אלא שמחה של מצוה ולא שמחה של הוללות וסכלות, **ואסור** אף...
להשתתף במושב לצים לזים זה."

*"It is a mitzva to protest such activities and one should see
that it ceases. Never was Purim joy meant to be achieved in
such a manner and it is forbidden to join in or be present on
such occasions."*

The Nahalat David: you never know when one act can tip the scales

After Mordechai received the message that Esther was to intercede on behalf of the Jewish people, Mordechai reprimanded her with these words (אסתר ד:יד):

"רוח והצלה יעמוד ליהודים ממקום אחר... ומי יודע אם לעת כזאת הגעת למלכות."

"Relief and deliverance will come to the Jews from another quarter...and who knows whether it was just for such a time as this that you attained this royal position."

Mordechai here is warning Esther that this is an historic moment for the Jewish people. If you do not take advantage of this unique opportunity to help your people, they will be saved by some other means, but you will have failed to seize the moment of your destiny.

Ha Gaon Rav David Tevel of Minsk, the famed author of the *sefer Nahalat David*, was a struggling rabbi in a small Russian town before he was appointed chief rabbi of the city of Minsk. The townsfolk in this small town were very poor and could not afford to pay their rabbi a decent salary. Thus there were times when the rav and his family did not have even a piece of bread in the house and many a Shabbos there was nothing to eat. In order to supplement his meager income, the rabbi took on the task of arbitrating financial disputes among wealthy businessmen. He would receive a small "bonus" for his wise advice and with this additional money he would supplement his small income. The business community was very satisfied with his counsel and they became his "regular customers".

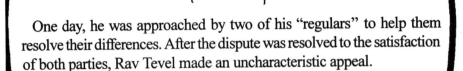

One day, he was approached by two of his "regulars" to help them resolve their differences. After the dispute was resolved to the satisfaction of both parties, Rav Tevel made an uncharacteristic appeal.

"You know that I have never asked you for a personal favor. All that I ever request is the fee I charge for arbitrating your business disagreements and delivering a just verdict. However, for the first time, I am compelled by circumstances to ask you gentlemen to help me out financially. My daughter has just become engaged to be married and I am obligated to provide her with a dowry. I do not have a penny to my name, and therefore I turn to you for help at this time of dire need. Could you please help me?"

"Rabbi", they replied, "We separate ma'aser (tithes) and give a good portion of our income for charitable purposes. We hand this money to our local rabbi and he distributes it to the needy of our town. As for you, Rabbi, we feel that it is the responsibility of your own congregants to take care of your needs and help you in your plight. We are very sorry."

The Nahalat David then turned to his "good friends" and said: "I would like to tell you a story. Once a very rich man died at an early age. Besides leaving a huge estate and vast sums of money, he also left a very precious pair of tefillin, worth a small fortune. The tefillin had been written by a famous scribe who had had great *yiras shamayim* (fear of heaven) and was an expert in all the laws of writing tefillin. He had been revered by all as a great and holy saint, and he understood the deepest secrets of Torah. The family decided that these special tefillin should be given to the youngest orphaned brother, who was about to become a bar mitzva.

The boy began wearing the tefillin and they remained in his

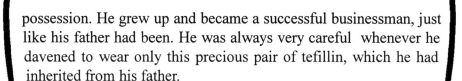

possession. He grew up and became a successful businessman, just like his father had been. He was always very careful whenever he davened to wear only this precious pair of tefillin, which he had inherited from his father.

One winter's day, it was necessary for him to travel to a small town on business. He arrived at a local inn and hoped to complete his business by nightfall and then return home. However, that afternoon a heavy snowstorm blocked all the roads and forced him to remain overnight at the inn.

In the morning when it was time to don tefillin, he was in a panic. Of course he had not brought his own tefillin with him, as he had not intended to remain there overnight. Where could he get a pair of tefillin in this tiny town, where there were only two Jews? He knocked on the innkeeper's door and asked him to help him. The innkeeper, who was a gentile, ventured out into the blizzard and borrowed a pair of tefillin from one of the town's Jews. The Jew gladly handed his tefillin over and the innkeeper delivered them to his relieved guest.

When he took the tefillin out of its bag, he was dismayed. For here was a very old pair of tefillin, which probably had not been used in ages and was perhaps not even kosher. Who could tell how reputable was the scribe who had written these tefillin? But since he had no other choice, he put them on and began to pray. He promised himself that as soon as he returned home he would put on his own precious pair of tefillin, just to be sure. However, when he finally returned home, he became caught up in several business transactions and he forgot entirely to put on his tefillin. For the rest of his life, he felt a sense of remorse whenever he remembered that he had missed putting on his holy tefillin one day in his life.

Years passed, and this man died and was brought before the Heavenly Tribunal to be judged. His record was opened and examined. The prosecuting angels presented a convincing case that this man be condemned to Gehinnom. The basis of their argument was a Gemara in *Mesechtas Rosh Hashanah* 17a, which states, "one who never wore tefillin in his lifetime is condemned to remain in Gehinnom forever." It turned out that the only pair of tefillin this man had ever worn in his life was the one inherited from his father, and it was *posul*, ritually invalid! Thus, he was to be viewed as a person who had never put on tefillin.

As he was being dragged by the angels to Gehinnom, suddenly a defending angel appeared out of nowhere and began to shout: "Stop, stop, he did put on tefillin *once* in his life!" And he proceeded to recount the time the man had borrowed a pair of tefillin when he was stranded in a small town in the middle of a snowstorm. It turned out that those tefillin were indeed kosher; whereas his precious ones were not! And so, this pair of tefillin, which the man himself had scorned as being so much below the level of his own tefillin, were the ones that saved his life."

The Nahalat David finished his story by telling his "friends": "It is true that you give charity, and you feel secure that this charity will serve you well in the world to come. However, if you were to help me marry off my daughter, who knows if *this* act of kindness will tip the scales, and accomplish for your souls much more than all the charity you have given the rest of your lives.

The moral of this story is the same point which Mordechai tried to make to Esther — we can never know what a seemingly insignificant act will do for us at the moment when we must stand in judgement before the Heavenly Tribunal.

CHAPTER FIFTEEN

The Mitzvos of
Purim Day

I

Shaloch Manos: a mitzva with no beracha

The Rema, in Hilchos Megillah (סימן תרצ"ה סעיף קטן ד') states:

"ואם שולח מנות לרעהו והוא אינו רוצה לקבלם...יצא."

"If one sends Shalach manos to his friend, and for whatever reason the friend does not accept them. Yet the sender has still fulfilled the mitzva of shalach manos [sending portions of food to his friends and neighbors]."

This leads us to ask the following question. One of the mitzvos over which we do not recite a beracha before we perform the mitzva is *tzedakah*, giving charity. The reason given for not making a beracha here, even though a beracha before doing a mitzva is usually required, is based on the following rule regarding berachos. We do not make a beracha on any mitzva whose fulfillment is dependent on someone else, for if the other person changes his or her mind and refuses to accept our mitzva, then we would have made a beracha in vain — ברכה לבטלה. Yet we might further ask, if the mitzva of shaloch manos is fulfilled even if the intended recipient refused to accept it, why not make a beracha before we send the shaloch manos?

The reason involves another rule which can be applied to the mitzva of tzedaka. The Rambam tells us that we do not make a beracha on tzedakah, for it is a mitzva which depends on the goodwill of others to accept our gift and that is a consideration impossible to predict. In *Hilchos Berachos* 11:2:

"וכל מצות עשה שבין אדם למקום, בין מצוה שאינו חובה בין מצוה שהיא חובה מברך עליה קודם לעשייתה."

"Every positive mitzva to Hashem, whether or not it is obligatory, requires a blessing to be recited before its fulfillment."

The "‏כסף משנה‎" here concludes:

‏"ודקדק רבינו לכתוב ,שבין אדם למקום לומר דמצוות שבין אדם לחברו‎
‏כגון עשיית צדקה וכדומה, אין מברכין עליהן."‎

"The Rambam was particular to point out that mitzvos beytween man and Hashem call for a beracha, which would indicate that mitzvos which pertain between man and man do not require a beracha."

Thus, since shalach manos is a mitzva between man and man it does not require a blessing. However, the Chasam Sofer (‏שו"ת או"ח, סימן קצ"ו‎) writes that this view of the Rema here — that even if the intended recipient does not receive the gift, the sender has still fulfilled his obligation in doing the mitzva — is not necessarily the view of all the commentators. For we can draw a distinction between two rationales for the mitzva of shalach manos.

The (‏קי"א‎) "‏תרומת הדשן‎" writes that the reason for this mitzva is to make available to those who do not possess them all the necessary provisions for the Purim meal.

‏"דנראה טעם דמשלוח מנות הוא כדי שיהא לכל אחד די וסיפק לקיים‎
‏הסעודה כדינא, כדמשמע בגמי פ"ק [ז,ב] דאביי ור' חנינא בר‎
‏אבין הוי מחלפין סעודותייהו בהדדי ונפקי בהכי משלוח מנות, אלמא‎
‏דטעמא משום סעודה היא..."‎

The second rationale for this mitzva is given by Rav Shlomo Alkabetz, in his classic commentary to *Megillas Esther*, entitled "‏מנות הלוי‎" (‏פרק ט', פסוק י"ט‎). There he explains that the purpose of sending these gifts to friends and neighbors is for the purpose of increasing good feelings among friends, in order to offset the evil reports the wicked Haman spread about the Jewish people, saying that they were *"scattered and dispersed"* — "‏מפוזר ומפורד‎".

There is a practical difference between these two possible reasons for giving shalach manos. For, if the reason is to increase friendship, then the mitzva is fulfilled of spreading love and friendship, even if the recipient does not actually accept the gift. However, if the reason for the mitzva is to provide provisions for the Purim meal, then if the gifts are not accepted and used for the actual meal, then the mitzva has not been fulfilled (see the sefer "מקראי קודש" מהרב צ.פ. פרנק, חנוכה-פורים, עמ' קנ"ג).

Finally, we might suggest another reason we do not make a beracha on the mitzva of shalach manos. On Purim we have three other mitzvos incumbent upon us, apart from that of reading the Megillah. Those other mitzvos are: משלוח מנות — sending gifts of food to friends and neighbors, מתנות לאביונים — giving gifts to the poor, סעודת פורים — eating the festive Purim meal.

On the surface, it would seem that these are three independent mitzvos, and there is no possible relationship between them. Yet on further examination we find that this is not so, and there is essentially one mitzva here, that of the festive Purim meal — סעודת ושמחת פורים. And the purpose of the other two mitzvos, those of giving gifts to the poor and sending portions of food to friends and neighbors, is to assure that all are provided for and can therefore partake of the festive meal on Purim day. By fulfilling these two other mitzvos and sharing what we have with others, we are in a sense having them join with us in our extended Purim feast. This concept is traced to the Rambam in Hilchos Megillah 2:15, where his words reflect this concept:

"כיצד חובת סעודה זו? שיאכל בשר ויתקן סעודה נאה כפי אשר תמצא ידו..."

"What is the nature of our obligation regarding this feast? A person should eat meat and prepare as attractive a feast as his means permit."

"וכן חייב אדם שתי מנות בשר...לחברו..."

"Similarly, a person is obligated to send two portions of meat...to a friend."

Thus we find that since the Rambam joined in the same halacha both the mitzva of סעודת פורים — the festive Purim meal and משלוח מנות —

the sending of portions of food to one another, this seems to indicate that there is an intrinsic relationship between the two.

And so the word used here, "וכן" — "and *so* one is obligated to send gifts", seems to indicate that this requirement is an extension of the previous halacha cited, that of סעודת פורים. In other words, in addition to the requirement of fulfilling the mitzva of סעודה, setting one's own table with delicacies, there is an additional requirement to fulfill, which is an integral part of our obligation to partake of a festive meal, and that is to see to it that others join us, if not in person, than by virtue of providing them with the means to enjoy a festive Purim meal of their own, and in this manner it is viewed as if they are part of our festive table.

Thus the mitzva of מתנות לאביונים is also an extension of the mitzva of סעודת פורים, as indicated in what the Rambam writes in halacha 17:

"מוטב לאדם להרבות במתנות לאביונים מלהרבות בסעודתו ומשלוח
מנות לרעהו, שאין שם שמחה גדולה ומפוארה אלא לשמח לב העניים..."

*"It is preferable for a person to be liberal with his donations
to the poor than to be lavish in his own preparations for the
Purim feast or in sending portions to his friends. For there is
no greater and more splendid happiness than to gladden the
hearts of the poor, the orphans, the widows, and the converts."*

One might wonder what the Rambam means here when he says that "it is *better* to increase gifts to the poor..." For don't we have here two separate mitzvos to fulfill? How then can we be told to skimp on one mitzva in order to fulfill a second mitzva? We never find such a precedent anywhere else which tells us to hold back our expenses in one mitzva in order to "better" fulfill another one.

We must say that giving gifts to the poor on Purim is also part of the mitzva of the festive Purim meal, סעודת פורים, since we are called upon to invite the poor to partake of our Purim feast. And although they do not actually join us at our table, by giving them money to provide for the needs of their own festive meal it is as if we actually invited them to our Purim meal. This explains what the Rambam means when he says that it is better to fulfill the mitzva of *seudas Purim* by providing for the needs of the poor than to spend lavishly on one's own seuda.

If giving gifts to the poor is considered part of the mitzva of the Purim seuda, then perhaps the recent practice of giving Purim cards in lieu of shalach manos to help charitable institutions is not fulfilling the mitzva unless the money donated is used specifically for the purpose of buying provisions for the Purim seuda. Perhaps we can now understand why we do not make a beracha on the mitzva of shalach manos. The שדי חמד (in his sefer "מערכת בברכות", סימן ג', ומערכת יום הכפורים, סימן א', אות ג') writes that we never make a beracha for things we do by ourselves. Rather, only in those instances when we act solely because Hashem dictated that we do so.

"לענין שלש סעודות שבת, שאין מברכין עליהן, משום שחז"ל לא תיקנו ברכת המצוה אלא על דבר שניכר בתוך מעשיו שעושה דבר זה מחמת המצוה אשר צונו הבורא יתברך, כגון שצונו לאכול מצה או מרור, אשר בלתי צוואת השי"ת היה יכול לאכול כל מה שירצה להשביע את עצמו, והוא יתברך צונו לאכול בדוקא מצה או מרור, בזה שפיר שייך לברך אשר קדשנו במצותיו וצונו, מה שאין כן סעודות שבת ויום טוב, או אכילת ערב יום הכפורים, הא גם בלתי צוואת הבורא יתברך היה גם כן אוכל...".

Thus if shalach manos and giving gifts to the poor are part of the mitzva of the Purim seuda, then just as we do not make a beracha for the seuda, based on what we have explained, so too, there is no beracha called for when performing these mitzvos since they are in effect an integral part of that mitzva of seudas Purim.

II

"Simcha" on Purim

The Shulchan Aruch in סימן תרצ"ה סעיף א' states:

"סעודת פורים שעשאה בלילה לא יצא ידי חובתן.".

"One who eats the Purim feast at night has not fulfilled his obligation."

The source for this halacha is to be found in *Mesechtas Megillah* 7b, where we find:

"אמר רבא: סעודת פורים שאכלה בלילה לא יצא ידי חובתו. מאי טעמא?
ימי משתה ושמחה כתיב."

"Rava said: one who eats the Purim feast at night has not fulfilled his obligation. What is the reason? For it is written (Esther 9:22), 'days of feasting and gladness', days and not nights."

Yet the Rema writes (*ibid.*):

"ומכל מקום ישמח וירבה קצת בסעודה."

"Yet one should rejoice and increase somewhat his meal at night."

This leads to the following question. If the Purim seuda is relegated to the daytime, as the *pasuk* states when it says, "*days* of feasting", why does the Rema tell us to "somewhat increase" our nighttime meal, and what mitzva do we fulfill when we do so? And where is the source for the Rema to require any kind of a special seudah at night? In the prayer "אשר הניא" recited after the reading of the Megillah at night, we say:

"קימו על יהם לעשות פורים ולשמוח בכל שנה ושנה."

"They undertook to establish Purim, to rejoice in every single year."

In the sefer "מאורי המועדים", which contains insights by Ha Rav Meshulam David Soloveitchik, שליט"א , the author asks:

"צ"ב מה דנקט מצות שמחה בפני עצמה, והלא כבר נכלל במצות
הפורים שהים ימי משתה ושמחה..."

"One has to wonder why 'simcha' alone was spelled out here, when indeed 'simcha' is part and parcel of the mitzva of Purim, as the verse states: 'days of feasting and gladness'. Thus, since the mitzva of Purim was already mentioned,

wouldn't this also include joy. Why, then, do we need to repeat this requirement on its own?"

In answer to this question, we might suggest the following. Chazal tell is in *Megillah* 7b:

"אמר רבא: מיחייב איניש לבסומי בפוריא עד דלא ידע בין ארור המן
לברוך מרדכי."

"Rava said: One is obligated to become intoxicated with wine on Purim until one does not know the difference between 'cursed is Haman' and 'blessed is Mordechai'."

In the sefer "עמק ברכה", the author quotes his rebbe, the Brisker Rav, Ha Rav Velvele Soloveitchik,who asks the following question:

"וממו"ר הגאב"ד דבריסק שליטא [זצ"ל] שמעתי שאמר, הא דנשתנה
שמחת פורים מכל שאר השמחות של מועדים, דלא מצינו בשום
שמחה דין כזה שיתחייב לבסומי בשתיית יין עד דלא ידע... משום שבכל
המועדות עיקר מצות שמחה אינו אלא לשמוח בהשם ובשר ויין אינו
אלא סיבה לעורר השמחה. וכמבואר ברמב"ם פ"ו מהל' יו"ט ה"כ...וכן
הוא במדרש רבה רבה שיר השירים פ"א, 'זה היום עשה השם נגילה ונשמחה
בו,' אינו יודע, עם 'בו' ביום או 'בו' בהקב"ה, תלמוד לומר, נגילה
ונשמחה **בך**. אבל בפורים כיון דכתיב, משתה ושמחה, נמצא שהמשתה
עצמה היא גוף המצוה בלי שום תכליתם של שמחה, ועל יסוד זה של
מצות משתה תקנו דין זה שחייב לבסומי עד דלא ידע וכו'."

"What is the difference between the 'simcha' of Purim and that of all the other holidays, that it alone calls for this means of 'simcha'—that one become intoxicated? We must say here that there is a basic difference regarding the mitzva of 'simcha' on Purim. For on all the other holidays, we express the mitzva of 'simcha' by rejoicing with the Holy One, Blessed be He, and feasting is only a means of reaching that state. However, on Purim, the feasting is an end in itself, without any other consideration or motive. This is why Chazal concluded that this feasting should reach the point of intoxication."

Perhaps this explains why in the prayer of "אשר הניא", the element of "simcha" is emphasized separately. For there are actually two requirements of "simcha" here. Firstly, we have the "simcha" of Purim which, as the Brisker Rav explained, is unique to this holiday, such that this kind of simcha is alluded to in the word "Purim", which includes all the mitzvos of the day. And secondly, there is the mitzva of "simcha" which is similar to the joy experienced on all the other holidays. This is the kind of "simcha" which is singled out in the prayer of "אשר הניא".

With this distinction in mind, perhaps we can understand what the Rema means when he calls for "increasing somewhat" the meal on Purim night. For even though halachically one does not fulfill his obligation of eating the Purim seuda if eaten at night, this obligation is part of that mitzva of simcha which pertains to Purim day alone — that unique act of feasting as an end in itself, and not as a means to increasing a feeling of joy.

The seuda at night, however, is related to the second aspect of 'simcha', which is common to all the other holidays as well. And because Purim begins at night and feasting in general increases the feeling of joy and celebration, it is therefore appropriate for one to "increase somewhat" his meal on Purim night in order to experience the joy of the holiday, just as one does on the night of the other holidays.

III

EATING MEAT AT THE PURIM FEAST

The Rambam in *Hilchos Megillah* 2:15 writes:

"כיצד חובת סעודה זו? שיאכל **בשר** ויתקן סעדה נאה כפי אשר תמצא ידו..."

"What is the nature of our obligation for this feast? A person should eat meat and prepare as attractive a feast as his means permit."

The מגיד משנה (*ibid.*) writes that the source for this ruling of the

Rambam is based on *Mesechtas Pesachim* 109a and several other places, where we find "אין שמחה אלא בבשר" — *"there is no happiness at a feast without meat"*. Thus, since both Yom Tov and Purim have the obligation of simcha, it therefore follow that one is obligated to eat meat at one's Purim seuda.

Yet other commentators maintain that the obligation to eat meat on Yom Tov was only because of the meat that was offered as a sacrifice on festivals. And since we no longer have sacrifices today, we are no longer obligated to eat meat at our festive meals. This means that 'simcha' in relation to a yom tov does not obligate one to eat meat. Yet why are we explicitly instructed to eat meat at the Purim feast? How is it different from the festive meals of the other holidays?

The distinction made by the Brisker Rav regarding the two different aspects of simcha may help to answer this question. As he has pointed out, the yom tov seuda is a means of increasing our joy and celebration and consequently bringing us closer to an appreciation of Hashem. Whereas the Purim feast is an end in itself, and this might be a sufficient reason for eating meat, for the importance of the meal as a mitzva in itself warrants that meat be included.

Even those commentators who maintain that the yom tov seuda calls for meat, do not obligate women to eat meat. The Rambam articulates this opinion in *Hilchos Yom Tov* 6:10-11:

"והנשים קונה להם בגדים ותכשיטין נאים לפי ממונו והאנשים אוכלין בשר ושותין יין, שאין שמחה אלא בבשר, ואין שמחה אלא ביין..."

Although the menfolk fulfill the requirement of 'simcha' on Yom Tov with the eating of meat and the drinking of wine, the womenfolk rejoice on Yom Tov by wearing new clothes and jewelry."

Thus it would seem that women do not have the obligation of eating meat on Yom Tov. Yet many *poskim* maintain that women are also obligated to eat meat at the Purim feast. Once again, we can ask what is the difference between Purim and the other holidays in this regard? The answer might again be supplied by the insight of the Brisker Rav, who maintains that on all the other holidays the mitzva is to experience simcha in order to bring us close to Hashem. For men this is achieved by eating meat and drinking wine, whereas women experience simcha on a festival by wearing new clothes and jewelry. On Purim, on the other hand, the mitzva called for is feasting as an end in itself. Thus women, too, are obligated in this mitzva on the holiday of Purim, and meat is required as part of that unique meal.

IV

THE RISHONIM ANSWER RAVA

As we have discussed, Rava, in the Gemara in *Megillah* 7b makes it clear that:

"אמר רבא: סעודת פורים שאכלה בלילה לא יצא ידי חובתו. מאי טעמא?
ימי משתה ושמחה כתיב."

"One who eats the Purim feast at night has not fulfilled his obligation. What is the reason for this? For it is written (Esther 9:22) 'days of feasting and gladness', days and not nights."

This halacha can be understood in three different ways. Although we read the Megillah and recite "על הנסים" in our evening prayers, this would seem to indicate that the holiday has already commenced, and this is so in regard to the mitzva of Megillah. Yet as far as the mitzva of *Seudas Purim* is concerned, this only commences the next morning. And so if one were to eat a festive meal at night, he has not fulfilled his obligation in this mitzva, for it is not yet considered to be Purim regarding this mitzva.

Or perhaps we might say that even though Purim commences in the evening, it might be possible to fulfill the mitzva of seudas Purim, except for the following condition, which is that the *Seudas Purim* must be eaten during the daytime. By day and not by night, as Rava tells us.

We could also perhaps say that the Purim seuda could be eaten at night except for the fact that the mitzva calls for "a *day* of feasting", and "a day" here means a continuous day of feasting, which extends both to the day and into the night. And so if one were to eat only at night and not also during the day, he would not have fulfilled his obligation.

In examining the various interpretations given by the Rishonim to this statement of Rava, we may conclude that each of these three explanations is based on one of these views.

THE VIEW OF THE ריטב״א

The Ritba comments on Rava's view by saying:

"הא כתיבנא לעיל שלא נצרכה אלא לילה של פורים שבו קורין את המגילה, דאילו לילה של מוצאי פורים, ולא יעבור נפקא..."

"We have previously explained that this halacha, that one cannot fulfill the mitzva of Seudas Purim at night, refers to the night that precedes Purim day, for the night that follows Purim is disqualified by the verse 'and it should not pass' (Esther 9:27), which teaches us that Purim can not be observed later than its prescribed time."

Thus it would seem that the Ritba subscribes to our first view above, that the night preceding Purim day is *not* the proper time for the Seudas Purim, for even though we read the Megillah at that time, yet in regard to the mitzva of the seuda, we say that Purim has not yet commenced. Purim commences, in regard to this mitzva, only the next morning. And the night *after* Purim is also ruled out as the appropriate time for fulfilling this mitzva, for it would be too late then.

THE VIEW OF THE מאירי

The Meiri comments on Rava's statement by saying:

"סעודת פורים אין **עיקר** שמחתה אלא **ביום**, שהרי נאמר, ימי משתה
ושמחה. ואם אכלה בלילה, לא יצא ידי חובתו, הן לילה שמחרתו יום
הפורים, הן לילה שעבר הפורים."

*"The main period of this Seudas Purim is during the day, as
the pasuk dictates: 'days of feasting and gladness'. Therefore,
if one ate the festive meal at night, whether the night preceding
Purim day or the night after Purim day, one would not have
fulfilled the mitzva."*

We see from the Meiri's commentary here that the main thrust of this
halacha stipulated by Rava is that the proper time for the seuda is during
the *day*. Thus, even if we consider the night after Purim as still part of
Purim, it is nevertheless ruled out as an appropriate time to eat the festive
Purim meal, based on the same reason why the night preceding Purim
day is ruled out, and that is because this mitzva can only be fulfilled
during the daytime period.

THE VIEW OF THE ראבי"ה

The מרדכי in סימן תשפ"ז cites the opinion of the ראבי"ה:

"סעודת פורים שאכלה בלילה לא יצא: פירש ראבי"ה, שצריך לנהוג כליל
שבת ויומו דומיא דקריאה, דכתיב, והימים האלה נזכרים ונעשים
ואין היקש למחצה."

The ראבי"ה explains the halacha to mean that the Purim seuda must
be eaten both by night and by day, just like the Shabbos meals, and just
as the Megillah is read both by night and by day. This is the meaning of
the verse which compares the obligation of "remembering" Purim by
reading the Megillah with the mitzva of "observing" Purim by making a
special seuda. We are obligated to carry this comparison through to the
end, and not just half-way.

Thus we see that the ראבי"ה adopts the view that Seudas Purim should
be a continuous process, beginning at night and continuing the next day.

ANSWERING THE ריטב"א

There are several possible answers to the Ritba's question as to why Rava found it necessary to mention that the night after Purim was too late to fulfill the mitzva of *Seudas Purim,* "ולא יעבור".

The Ran, in his commentary at the beginning of this Mesechta contends that the pasuk of "ולא יעבור" refers exclusively to the mitzva of reading the Megillah. However, regarding the mitzva of Seudas Purim, those who read the Megillah earlier than the 14th of Adar, that is, on the 11th, 12th of Adar, still celebrate with the Purim seuda on the 14th, and not earlier.

From this we see that even though the 11th or 12th may be the date for reading the Megillah in some places, yet the restriction of "ולא יעבור" does not apply to the seuda and is viewed as the proper time. So here too, "ולא יעבור" does not apply to the night following Purim.

The Yerushalmi contends if Purim comes out on a Shabbos day, we are to "מאחרין", delay the seuda to a later date, for the pasuk which relates to the seuda is "לעשות אותם ימי משתה ושמחה" — *to observe these days of feasting and gladness"* (*Esther* 9:22). We are called upon to *"create"* days of feasting, whereas Shabbos as a day of feasting comes to us without our having to do anything to bring it about. It has been "created" by the Almighty on the seventh day when He created the world. For it has its own sanctity, "קביעה וקיימה", which is set in motion by Hashem Himself.

Purim Torah

I t is an accepted custom to recite Kaddish after we read from the *Scroll of Ruth* on Shavuos, the *Song of Songs* on Pesach and the *Book of Ecclesiastes* on Succos. Yet after we read the *Scroll of Esther* no Kaddish is said. How are we to account for this difference? One answer suggested is that since all ten sons of Haman were killed, and therefore there was no son left to say Kaddish.

. . . .

It is customary to recite the names of all ten sons of Haman in a single breath. This indicates that they all expired at the same time. This practice led someone to remark, "Thank God that Haman had only ten sons; had he had twenty, we would have all expired!"

. . . .

There is a halachic question which the *poskim* were confronted with, and that was: which takes precedence, the reading of the *Megillah* or a circumcision which is due to take place on the 14th of Adar? One "scholar" pointed out that this question is really an ancient one. For Chazal tell us that Moshe Rabbenu was born on the 7th of Adar. Thus his *bris* should have taken place on the 14th of Adar. This means that already in Moshe's time the question arose as to which took precedence, the *Megillah* reading or the *bris*?

However, another "scholar" pointed out that since the city of Goshen,

where Moshe lived, was a walled city, the reading of the *Megillah* took place on the 15th of Adar. Therefore there was no problem regarding the *Megillah* reading usurping the *bris* of Moshe himself, which could have taken place as normal, on the 14th of Adar.

CHAPTER SIXTEEN

More Insights and Stories

I

WHERE IS ESTHER ALLUDED TO IN THE TORAH?

The Gemara in *Chullin* 139b cites a number of questions asked of the men of Pappunia:

1) "Where is Moshe Rabbenu indicated in the Torah?"

2) "From where do we derive Haman?"

3) "Where is Esther indicated?"

4) "From where do we derive Mordechai?"

Rav Matana answers each of these questions with a verse from the Torah. He tells us that *Moshe* is indicated in the verse in *Bereishis* 6:10: "בשגם הוא בשר והיו ימיו מאה ועשרים שנה" — *"For that he also is flesh"*.

How this is an allusion to Moshe is explained in the following way. "בשגם" has the numerical value of its letters, and this is equivalent to the numerical value of the name of Moshe, "משה", that is, 145. In addition, this verse adds: "Therefore shall his days be 120 years", and this corresponds with the years which Moshe Rabbenu lived.

Haman is derived from the verse in *Bereishis* 3:1, "המן העץ" — *"It is from the tree"*. The first word, "המן" can be read as "Haman", and the second, "העץ", refers to the gallows (tree) upon which Haman was hanged.

Esther is alluded to in the verse in *Devarim* 31:18: "ואנכי הסתר אסתיר פני" — *"I will surely hide my face"*. The second word here, "הסתר" is similar to the name of *"Esther"* — "אסתר" both in spelling and in sound. The verse in general foretells the many evils and troubles that will befall Klal Yisrael when they forsake the ways of Hashem, which was the situation at the time of Esther.

Mordechai is indicated in the Torah in the verse in *Shemos* 30:23: "מר דרור ומתרגמינן מירה דכיא". Here, too, the sound and the spelling of this word resemble the name "Mordechai" — "מרדכי".

Several questions can be asked here:

1) Why is the Gemara interested in tracing allusions to the names listed here; what is gained by doing this?

2) Why are these particular names listed here? What is the connection between Moshe, Mordechai, Haman and Esther?

3) The commentators ask why the name of Esther is derived from a *pasuk* which appears to have negative connotations. Why choose a verse which talks about Hashem hiding His face from His people rather than a more positive *pasuk*?

We would suggest an answer to these puzzling questions based on the following intriguing and profound insights given by HaRav Yosef Dov Soloveitchik. We read in the *Megillah*:

"ובכל יום ויום מרדכי מתהלך לפני חצר בית הנשים לדעת את שלום אסתר ומה יעשה בה." (אסתר ב', י-י"א)

"Every day Mordechai would walk in front of the courtyard of the harem to find out about Esther's well-being and what would become of her."

"בימים ההם ומרדכי יושב בשער המלך." (אסתר, ב', כ"א)

"In those days, while Mordechai was sitting at the king's gate..."

HaRav Soloveitchik makes the following observations. Why was Mordechai so inseparable from Esther? While Esther remained in the royal harem, Mordechai walked past that courtyard each and every day. In fact, the phrase "ובכל יום ויום" means not only once a day, but many times each day. Moreover, even after Esther was taken away and appointed Queen of Persia, Mordechai continued to remain at the king's gate. Why did he insist on persisting in his watch over his niece? What attracted Mordechai, so that he was unable to leave the king's gate, and continued to pace back and forth, listening, watching, trying to overhear something? What was he expecting. Surely he knew that Ahashueros would not release Esther, who was now his cherished queen. Why didn't he leave the royal courtyard and return home?

According to Chazal, Mordechai was a member of the Sanhedrin. He had more important affairs to attend to. Why didn't he return to his normal life and his many duties and responsibilities as a leader of the Jewish community in Shushan?

The answer can be found if we look between the lines of the Megillah, in the small invisible print. Somehow a mood of tense expectancy, of concentrated anticipation gripped Mordechai. As we read the whole story, a mood of foreboding pervades the whole Megillah, a sense of waiting for events to unfold and not knowing what to expect.

Mordechai did not regard the forced removal of Esther from her home to the royal palace and her subsequent ascent to the throne of Persia as a trivial event. Anyone other than Mordechai would most likely have interpreted such an event rationally and in practical terms.

He, however, understood with a deeper intuition born of his spiritual greatness, that it was not coincidental that a Jewish girl, a refugee and an orphan should rise to become the queen of Persia. He recognized the hand of Hashem, the Maker of History, in what was happening around him. He realized that this was setting the stage for the unfolding of a great historical and spiritual drama. And he was well aware that the destiny of the Jewish people was being determined by what was happening around him. This is what we might call an alertness to history, a sensitivity to the deeper meaning behind contemporary events. (See נוראות הרב, חלק שביעי, עמ' 62-65 edited by my nephew B. David Schreiber.)

Based on this profound insight of Rav Soloveitchik's, we can now attempt to explain the Gemara in *Chullin* 139b, and indeed show that this insight is alluded to in the words of Rashi there. Commenting on the question,

"Where was Moshe Rabbenu indicated in the Torah?", Rashi writes:

"מנין למשה רמז קודם שבא שסופו לבא"

"From where do we find an allusion to Moshe even before he appears in the Torah. From where do we know that he would ultimately appear on the scene?"

We are being taught in this Gemara a very important lesson. Hashem's Master Plan calls for man to appear on the scene in moments when history is to be made, and he is challenged to be instrumental in shaping events. Thus even before the history of Klal Yisrael begin to unfold, Hashem prepared for them a spiritual guide in the guise of a leader, Moshe Rabbenu, who is alluded to in the phrase, "and a man lived 120 years".

With this allusion to Moshe and his place in history, we are being taught here that life was given to man to shape his destiny and effect the course of events. This is the reason why the Gemara asks, "Where is Moshe Rabbenu alluded to in the Torah?" It is not possible that the one who is to guide Klal Yisrael as the redeemer of an enslaved and down-trodden people, and the giver of the Law, is not already anticipated by the Torah itself at the moment the history of humankind begins to unfold.

And so, too, we can understand why and how Esther is alluded to in the verse, "הסתרת פנים",which states that Hashem will hide His face from His people. He appears to shun His people, but in reality He has already begun to prepare the for the individual who will help redeem His chosen people. In the very verse which articulates the darkness of seeming rejection, salvation is already on the way. This is made clear by the allusion to Esther's name in the Torah.

II

WHERE IS HAMAN ALLUDED TO IN THE TORAH?

In the Gemara in *Chullin* 139b, the Pappunians ask Rav Matana a number of questions. Among them is: "From where do we derive Haman?"

Rav Matana answers each of these questions with a verse from the Torah. Among his answers is that Haman is derived from the verse in *Bereishis* 3:11: "המן העץ" — *"Is it from the tree?"* Here the first word: "המן", can be read as "Haman", and the second word, "העץ" — *"the tree"*, can refer to the tree or gallows upon which Haman was hanged.

Two questions arise here: Is there really an allusion to Haman in this *pasuk*? Why, in the first place, would we search for an allusion in the Torah to this wicked person, Haman?

The *Ba'alei Mussar* answer that we are not interested in Haman himself but rather in his personality and character traits, so that we can learn from them. The Gemara suggests that we find his personality traits indicated in the description of first man, Adam HaRishon. For Adam had everything, yet he was still not satisfied. Knowing that he was denied only the fruit from the tree of knowledge, עץ הדעת, he craved that as if he had nothing else. And this is what destroyed him.

The same can be said for Haman. He was the most powerful and influential person in the kingdom, except for the king himself, yet he was still not satisfied. He was irked beyond measure by the fact that an elderly Jew clad in sackcloth and ashes refused to bow down to him. This destroyed all his pleasure and contentment in everything he possessed. Haman gritted his teeth in rage and declared: "All this is worth nothing to me every time I see Mordechai the Jew sitting at the king's gate." This depiction of moral failing is the real reason for the allusion to Haman in the Torah.

After Haman returned from escorting the exalted Mordechai around town, he arrived home exasperated, and then his wife and his friends proceeded to inform him that his fate was sealed, and it was only a matter of time before he would be defeated by the Jews.

"אם מזרע היהודים מרדכי אשר החלות לנפל לפניו לא תוכל לו כי נפול תפול לפניו."

"If Mordechai, from whom you have begun to fall, is of Jewish descent, you will not prevail against him, but will undoubtedly fall before him." (Esther 6:14)

The question here is obvious. Didn't Haman know that Mordechai was Jewish? Doesn't the verse itself state that when Mordechai refused to bow down to Haman, he was told that Mordechai was a Jew (*Esther* 3:4): "אשר הוא יהודי".

The commentators explain this phrase: "מזרע היהודים" to refer to those people, such as Yehoshua, Saul, and the descendants of our Matriarch Rachel, before whom Amalek fell, since Haman was a descendant of Amalek. (See "דרשות צפנת פענח" ממהרי"ט, עמ' ק"ד and "זרע אמת" דרוש י"ב.)

The *pasuk* concludes: "While they were still talking to him, the king's chamberlains arrived and hurried to bring Haman to the banquet which Esther had arranged." (*Esther* 6:14)

This is to be understood in the following way. After hearing the advice of his friends and his wife about the Jews and his inability to overcome them, he decided to investigate whether or not Mordechai's ancestors were indeed those who traced their family lineage back to Rachel. If so, he planned to remove the gallows he had erected for Mordechai.

However, he was hurried off to attend the banquet and thus had no time to remove the gallows. The commentators point out that it was this "עץ", this gallows, that proved to be the undoing of Haman, for several reasons:

Had he not already prepared the "עץ", the gallows, he might have had a chance to survive. For even though the king was furious with him, if he had had to instruct his servants to build a gallows on which to hang Haman, there was a good chance that during the time it would take to construct the gallows, his anger might have cooled off. Thus, he may have reconsidered and Haman would have gotten off with a lighter punishment.

However, since the gallows were already prepared, he ordered that Haman be hung immediately, without any time for reflection.

Furthermore, Haman built the gallows without first getting permission to do so from the king. This showed his great arrogance and indicated that Haman was prepared to defy the king.

This set a pattern for his behavior and how it was perceived. And so, when Haman fell on the couch of the Queen a few days later, instead of being seen as an accident, that perhaps he had tripped, he was accused of another act of arrogance and audacity against the king. This reinforced once again how the construction of the gallows proved to be Haman's undoing.

This, then, is the allusion of "המן העץ" to Haman in the Torah. Its purpose is to teach us that "if a person is given enough rope, he will hang himself". The wicked are punished in this way, they bring their punishment upon themselves. Thus, it was necessary to point out exactly where Haman is indicated in the Torah, in order to emphasize this lesson of reward and punishment and to show how a person is capable of creating his own destruction. This serves as a warning to us to follow the Commandments, lest we be responsible for our own undoing.

III

BLESSED IS HE WHO SPEAKS AND DOES: "ברוך אומר ועושה"

We praise Hashem for fulfilling His promises to us. All the commentators question this. How could we possibly suspect Hashem of not keeping His promises? Perhaps we could answer this with the following story.

In the city of Brisk, the local officials issued a decree against the Jewish shopkeepers, nullifying the חזקה (a legal term denoting presumed title to property based on undisturbed possession during a fixed period, in cases where a claim to ownership cannot be established by other legal evidence). This decree caused panic among the Jewish shopkeepers of Brisk. They immediately called a meeting at the home of their spiritual leader, HaRav Yosef Ber Soloveitchik, which was also attended by the lay leaders of the community.

"This decree will ruin us," the shopkeepers complained to the rav. A decision was made by Rav Yosef Ber and the lay leaders that the only solution to the problem was to bribe the city officials who had issued the decree. Everyone agreed to try this approach, and a committee was set up to go out and collect a certain amount of money from each shopkeeper, and with that money they were to approach the city officials.

Jews are assured that "the gates of money [i.e., bribes] are never locked" — "שערי מעות לא ננעלו". Therefore the rav was confident that the community's bribe would surely be accepted and would yield positive results.

However, when the shopkeepers were approached, each one pleaded that at present he had no spare cash, and he was sure that the other shopkeepers would raise the amount needed.

When Rav Yosef Ber Soloveitchik was informed of the situation, he smiled and sent the shopkeepers the following message. "By your actions you have solved a question that has puzzled me for years. We read in the *Megillah* that Haman offered King Ahashueros ten thousand talents of silver as a bribe to advance his evil plan to exterminate the Jews. The question arises, Where were the Jews? Why didn't they take up a collection themselves and offer *twenty thousand* talents of silver to bribe those who were to carry out Haman's plan? Surely if they had offered double the amount of Haman's bribe, that would have frustrated his plan."

"Now I understand", concluded Rav Yosef Ber, "that indeed they embarked on a collection. However, when each Jew was approached to make his contribution, he replied, 'At the moment I have no money. Go to the other Jews!' "

Thus we see that even if one initially promises something and fully intends to keep his promise, yet an excuse always seems to crop up and justify one's inability to fulfill that promise. And because Hashem never looks for excuses not to keep His word, even when the Jewish people no longer deserve His generosity, we rightfully praise Him for keeping His promises to us. Indeed there is an aphorism that there is a *great distance* between "saying" and "doing".

IV

"מבני בניו של המן למדו תורה בבני ברק" — "THE DESCENDANTS OF HAMAN TAUGHT TORAH IN BNAI BRAK" (*GITTIN* 57B)

How is it possible that Haman's descendants merited to become *talmidei chachamin*? How could such a great enemy of Yisrael, who tried to annihilate the Jewish people, have the merit of grandchildren who converted to Judaism and taught Torah in the land of Yisrael? The answer offered to this question by the Maharal of Prague in his "חדושי אגדות לש"ס" explains this phenomenon in the following way.

Any one who sought to harm Yisrael and was in any way successful was empowered by Heaven itself with great potential. Although this was pure power, it was misused by an evil human being, and an enemy of Yisrael became contaminated, טמא. However, because this "great potential" was originally pure, the descendants of Haman were able to convert this potential into something positive and holy, and thus they became Jews and teachers of Torah in Yisrael.

This concept can be illustrated by the following story. HaRav Meir Shapiro, the Lubliner Rav, once approached an "enlightened" Jew (משכיל) for a contribution to his yeshiva. The man answered indignantly, "I don't have use for your yeshiva, and neither do my children. And I tell you that neither will my grandchildren ever study there. Thus I have no reason to contribute to your yeshiva!"

The Rav looked at the man and said, "It seems that you see yourself as a greater anti-Semite than even Haman." The man was highly insulted and asked HaRav Meir Shapiro what he meant by such a statement?

"Don't you understand?" Rav Meir replied, "The Gemara in *Gittin* tells us that "the grandchildren of Haman taught Torah in the city of Bnai Brak". From this arch-enemy of Yisrael were born children who converted to Judaism and became yeshiva students, and eventually became teachers in Yisrael. Yet you are so certain that neither your children nor your grandchildren will ever study Torah. Therefore, you are indeed a greater enemy of Yisrael than Haman ever was."

From this we see that although Haman himself misused his potential, yet his descendants took advantage of the opportunity to rectify his misdeeds. The "enlightened" Jew, on the other hand, not only deviated from the path of Jewish observance, but saw to it that his descendants would not have the chance to return to the true path. In this sense he was a greater enemy to the Jewish people than was Haman.

V

THE MANNER OF THE MIRACLE OF PURIM

From the very beginning of their existence, Bnai Yisrael have been the recipients of wondrous miracles. Whenever they found themselves in a precarious situation, Hashem performed for them miracles beyond the laws of nature — חוץ מדרך הטבע. In Egypt He saved them from danger by performing miracles which changed the course of nature. These included the Ten Plagues and dividing the Red Sea. When Sisera attacked them, they were rescued in a miraculous manner. When Sennacherib, the king of Assyria, engaged them in an all-out war in the days of King Hezekiah, a great miracle was wrought on their behalf to save them (*Kings* II 19:35)

This leads us to ask, why in the Purim story, when Klal Yisrael found themselves in imminent danger, didn't Hashem perform a miracle for them beyond the laws of nature, as He had done many times in the past for His chosen people? Why now did he bring about our salvation by seemingly natural means, נס בדרך הטבע?

The Ben Ish Hai suggests a beautiful answer to this question. He asks, why is Purim the only holy day celebrated with so much fanfare? We engage in merry-making and make noise every time Haman's name is mentioned. We never do this in the case of any of our other enemies. We masquerade and stage parades and a festive meal with music. All this is done, he suggests, to send a message to all the nations of the world, especially those nations which might wish to do us harm and destroy us.

This message is that although we no longer witness miracles that extend beyond the laws of nature, this does not mean that we have been forsaken by our God. He is forever watching over us, and even though we may no longer merit open miracles performed on our behalf, yet He will always come to our rescue *within the laws of nature*. Proof of this is the story of Purim. We were in danger and He saved us by seemingly natural means.

Therefore, we warn nations which contemplate our destruction not to dare to raise their hand against us, for we have a higher power to protect us. Therefore, we make noise to call this fact to attention and to remind the world that just as He saved us by a hidden miracle through the laws of nature, so will he continue to do so in the future. We celebrate this truth by our merrymaking.

VI

The Inclusion of the Megillah in Kisvei HaKodesh

What is the rationale for including the *Megillas Esther* in the Holy Writings, *Kisvei HaKodesh*?

The story is told that once the Brisker Rav, the Griz HaLevi, went for a stroll down David Yellin Street in Yerushalayim. Accompanying him was Harav Chaim Solomon. While walking, they were approached by an individual who demanded *tzedakah* in a loud and arrogant voice. Rav Solomon began fumbling in his pockets for some change. However, the Griz HaLevi motioned for him to stop searching for money. After continuing on their way, Rav Solomon asked the Brisker Rav why he did not feel it necessary to give the man something.

The Brisker Rav replied, "In the book of Proverbs, *Mishle*, we read: 'תחנונים ידבר רש ועשיר יענה עזות' — *'The poor man speaks beseechingly; the rich man's answer is harsh.'* Thus if one demands charity in a haughty manner, this indicates that the person asking really does not need the money. For if he were truly in dire need, he would be asking humbly and in a subdued manner."

As we have pointed out elsewhere, the purpose of the Miracle of Purim and the writing of the *Megillas Esther* was to reaffirm the promise given by Hashem Himself, that whenever we call out to Him He will answer. In the *Megillah* we are shown the way in which we must call out to Hashem. We read that Mordechai assembled the Jews of Shushan and they fasted and petitioned Hashem in a sincere and humble manner. This was the reason their prayers were answered.

This teaches us the importance of having the right attitude and thus justifies that the *Megillah* be included in *Kisvei HaKodesh*. In order to qualify to be included in the Holy Writings, not only must a *sefer* be written with prophecy and Divine inspiration, רוח הקודש, but it must also contain a message for future generations. The important lesson for all generations which the *Megillah* contains is that Hashem listens to our prayers only if we approach Him with humility. And so, just as the beggar in the story had an arrogant attitude and did not receive the *tzedakah* he demanded, so too must we be careful to have the right attitude if we wish our supplications to the Almighty to be answered.

VII

Haman's Gift

In the Megillah we read (*Esther* 3:9):

"And I will pay ten thousand silver talents into the hands of those who perform the duties for deposit in the king's treasuries."

This amount promised by Haman was an enormous sum, more than was required. Why, then, did Haman commit himself to pay such a large amount of money for the destruction of the Jewish people? Perhaps we can answer this with a story.

HaRav Ephraim HaLevi Bilizer was asked the following question. A father once promised a very large dowry for his daughter. In the end, though, he did not keep his word and he was severely reprimanded by the groom's family. They pointed out to him that not only did he lie, but what he did was strictly forbidden by the Torah.

The Rav tried to pacify the family of the groom by relating a parable. At the time when the Bais HaMikdash stood and sacrifices were offered, not all the sacrifices were of equal value. The wealthy offered more expensive sacrifices, such as bulls; whereas the offerings of the poor were more modest, consisting of a meager goat or a lamb.

Today, though, when we no longer have the Bais HaMikdash, we offer up in our prayers a description of the sacrifices instead of the actual sacrifices themselves. We recite: "ונשלמה פרים שפתינו" — *"Let our lips compensate for the bulls"* (*Hosea* 14:3). Now everyone is equal; there is no distinction between rich and poor. All say: "Let it be deemed by Hashem as if we offered a burnt-offering, peace-offering, thanksgiving offering, etc." For if all that is required is words, why should the poor person offer less than the rich man?

The lesson to be derived from this parable is that since we all know that which is promised is not always meant to be fulfilled, then why shouldn't a large amount be offered, in the same way as a poor person "offers" [in his prayers] the same sacrifice as a rich man.

To extend this reasoning to the story of Purim, Chazal point out that Ahashueros wanted to do away with the Jews as much as Haman did. Therefore, Haman surmised that Ahashueros would himself offer to cover the expenses (as he subsequently did). Therefore Haman rationalized, why shouldn't I offer a large amount. I will not have to pay for it anyway...

VIII

"לעשות כרצון איש ואיש" — *"THAT SHOULD DO ACCORDING TO EACH MAN'S PLEASURE."*

The king ordered that all the needs of his guests should be fulfilled and all that they required should be done. The Gemara tells us in *Mesechtas Berachos* that when Rabban Gamliel was impeached, the doors of the *bais medrash* were flung open "and many chairs were increased" within. Rabbam Gamliel was very careful to accept only a particular caliber of student, one who had the exalted quality of "תוכו כברו". Now, however, everyone was welcome.

HaRav Moshe Aaron Stern asked, why did the Gemara use this expression: "נתרבו ספסלי בית המדרש" — *"the chairs were increased"*? Why did it not simply say that there was a great increase of students, that the enrollment increased?

He answered that by using this phrase, the Gemara was indicating the diminished quality of the new enrollment. In the days of Rabban Gamliel, only those students who were of sterling character were admitted. Because of this, there was no need to accommodate everyone with chairs, for these outstanding students did not need to be pampered. Even if they had to stand, this was no problem for them. However, now that less worthy students were accepted and the enrollment requirements were lowered, these students needed to be pampered and they all must be accommodated with a comfortable place to sit. Thus the phrase used by the Gemara describes both the quantity and the quality of the students.

We can further explain the Gemara's use of the phrase *"there was an increase of chairs"* instead of *"there was an increase of students"* to teach us the responsibility an institution has to provide for the needs of its students. Every student must have his needs met, e.g. there must be enough chairs for everyone, in order that the students can function to the best of their ability. Being cramped and uncomfortable in a classroom without enough chairs can hamper the progress of the students in their learning. Thus it is the responsibility of the institution to see that these requirements are met.

My dear friend, HaRav Aryeh Leib Oschry, ע"ה once told me that when he became a teacher his first position was in Yeshivas Bais Yehudah in Detroit. The principal was Dr. Hugo Mandelbaum. One day Dr. Mandlebaum entered the classroom to observe how his new *rebbi* was faring. However, as soon as he opened the door, instead of paying attention to the lesson in progress, he headed straight for the window and opened it slightly. Later he told the young teacher that he had opened the window to provide fresh air for the room, which seemed to be stuffy. He remarked, "If you want your students to work to the best of their abilities, you have to provide an atmosphere conducive to learning."

Similarly, when Ahashueros made his feast, he wanted everyone to have a good time, and therefore he made sure that the desires of all his guests were fulfilled so that they could fully enjoy the feast.

IX

Celebration on Purim, but no Hallel

The similarity between Pesach and Purim is that our very existence was threatened in both instances. Yet we find that we express our appreciation for being saved differently on each of the two holidays. On Pesach we recite Hallel, yet we are not required to celebrate with a festive meal (Although we are obligated to have a festive meal on this holiday, just as we do on other holidays, this is not a festive meal in the same category as the "Purim Seuda".) On Purim, on the other hand, the opposite is true. We celebrate with a festive meal yet are not called upon to recite Hallel. How are we to account for this difference?

One explanation is that we are obligated to celebrate with a festive meal for this very reason — that we are not required to recite Hallel. If we do not mark the occasion with a festive meal, it would seem as if the miracle which saved us from destruction on this day was not significant. To counter this mistaken notion, a festive meal is required (see ‏"דרשות בן איש חי" לפרשת זכור, עמ' כ"ד‎).

Another observation offered by the Ben Ish Hai is that when we examine the two miracles — of Pesach and Purim — we find that indeed the miracle of Purim was greater, for although we were redeemed from slavery in Egypt on Pesach, yet we suffered numerous casualties while we were being saved. Chazal tell us that many Jewish children were cemented in the walls of the pyramids, many Jews died from overwork, etc. However, in the Purim story, although we were in mortal danger, we were saved to the extent that not one single Jew was harmed.

This insight might explain why on Pesach no special festive meal is called for, even though we do recite Hallel. For Hallel is an expression of gratitude offered in return for the gift of freedom from bondage and the opportunity we now have to serve Hashem alone, without any restriction being placed upon us. Yet we cannot wholeheartedly celebrate with a festive meal, for we remember those Jews who were left behind in Egypt and died in slavery.

On Purim, on the other hand, since we escaped unscathed, our joy and celebration is unbounded, and therefore we sit down to a festive meal. However, Hallel is not recited, for even though we were saved from annihilation, yet we remained subservient to Ahashueros, and

thus we were not able to fulfill our total commitment to Hashem —
"אכתי עבדי אחשורות אנן".

X

THE IMPORTANCE OF THE FESTIVE MEAL ON PURIM

The reason the commentators give as to why Purim requires a festive meal whereas Chanukah does not is that the miracle of Purim was related to the *physical* redemption of the Jews; thus we celebrate with a physical act — a festive meal. On Chanukah, on the other hand, the Jews were *spiritually* redeemed, and this is reflected in the *Al HaNissim* prayer, which states that the Syrian-Greeks wished to keep the Jews from learning Torah and the practice of mitzvos.

The question then arises: If indeed the *seudah* was celebrated because of the miracle of redemption, why does this not apply to Pesach as well? Shouldn't Pesach also require a festive meal, since it commemorated a miracle which reflected the very existence of Klal Yisrael.

The Ben Ish Hai answers this question with a parable. A lion had two cubs. They asked their father if they would have anything to fear if they were to venture into the wide world. He replied, "The lion is the king of the beasts, and need not fear anyone. It is rather all the other animals who must fear you!"

Fortified by this assurance, the cubs ventured out into the world, going fearlessly from city to city. One day they came to the gates of a large city and what they witnessed depicted on the city walls terrified them. They saw two biblical scenes. One was of King David ripping apart a lion; and the second was of Samson doing the same thing. They ran home in terror and confronted their father.

"You told us that a lion has nothing to fear. That he is mightier than anyone else. But lo and behold, the scene we saw showed two men who could tear apart a lion with their bare hands. How could you tell us that we have nothing to fear?"

"Fools!" replied the father lion. "What you saw was the greatest proof of what I told you, that you have nothing to fear. It was only in these two isolated cases, that a miracle transpired and a man was able to subdue a lion. That is why a painting was made to commemorate this exceptional event. For if a man was able to overcome a lion every day, do you think that they would bother to paint such a scene and display it on the city walls? Certainly not. Thus it is as I told you. You have nothing to fear; miracles do not happen every day."

This parable, contends the Ben Ish Hai, answers our question why Purim calls for a *seudah*, whereas Pesach does not. For the miracle which the Purim story relates appeared in the guise of an ordinary event. Thus a festive meal is called or, for if we do not celebrate in a festive manner, we might give the impression that nothing out of the ordinary happened on this day. And therefore to emphasize that something unique did indeed take place, we celebrate with a festive meal. On Pesach, however, when everyone is fully aware that miracle upon miracle took place, there is no need to emphasize the miraculous events by means of a festive meal.

We might suggest another reason why it is only the festival of Purim which calls for such an extremely joyous festive meal. In general all the mitzvos of the day, apart from being mitzvos in themselves, have the additional function of serving as reminders of the miracle of that particular day, זכר. For example, *matzah* on Pesach reminds us of what transpired in Egypt; the *succah* reminds us of the miracle of the ענני כבוד — *the clouds of glory*, which protected Klal Yisrael from the elements and other dangers during the time they wandered in the desert. So too do the Chanukah lights remind us of the miracle of the oil.

On Purim the mitzva of listening to the *Megillah* is only passive; and thus the mitzva of eating a festive meal is a positive *act* which commemorates the miracle. When we actively celebrate with wine and with joy we are remembering the unique events which took place in Shushan and brought about the salvation of the Jewish people. A festive meal is particularly appropriate on this holiday because it was by means of a *seudah*, the feast of Ahashueros, that the Jews of Shushan first committed a sin by attending that pagan celebration. And then there was the feast of Esther, during which the process of redemption was set in motion. Thus it is only Purim that the festive meal in itself serves as a symbol, a concrete reminder of the miracle, and that is why Purim is the only yom tov which requires such an elaborate festive meal.

XI

The Turnabout — "ונהפוך הוא"

The entire Purim story seems to involve a complete turnabout. At first the Jews were at the mercy of the evil Haman, but in the end they were victorious over their adversaries, as the *Megillah* itself delineates:

"להעשות ביום אשר שברו איבי היהודים לשלוט בהם ונהפוך הוא אשר
ישלטו היהודים המה בשנאיהם."

"On the very day that the enemies of the Jews expected to gain the upper hand over them — ...it was turned about."
(*Esther* 9:1)

Similarly, we find that the gallows which Haman prepared for Mordechai underwent a turnabout — "ונהפוך הוא", and in the end they were used to hang Haman himself. Another turnabout in the story was the execution of Queen Vashti and the ascension of Esther to the throne.

All these instances of turnabout follow the manner of punishment of the wicked which is described in the Torah: whatever our enemies planned for us was visited upon them in the end. However, there is one turnabout which seems strange, and that is the fact that the feast of Ahashueros, in which the Jews of Shushan took part, carried the danger posed by Haman. Yet that very feast led to our salvation, since it was at that banquet that Queen Vashti sealed her fate, and the way was cleared for Esther, the Jewess, to become the next Queen. This leads the Sfas Emes to remark:

"וזהוא פלא שבאותה סעודה נעשה ההצלה שנהרגה ושתי אז."

"And it was a wonder that at that very banquet, Vashti was done away with."

The Sfas Emes concludes that we see here the power of תשובה מאהבה repentance done out of love rather than out of fear of punishment. For when love is the motivation for repentance, even blatant sins are transformed into merits. "שזדונות נעשות לו כזכיות" — And because Hashem understood their repentance and anticipated it, He transformed the situation into one of salvation for His chosen people.

As we have discussed, Purim is celebrated as a joyous occasion commemorating the salvation of the Jewish people from the evil designs of Haman, and it serves as a reaffirmation of the promise given by Hashem to His people, that whenever they call out to Him, He will hear their prayers and bring about their salvation. How that salvation will come about is explained in classic Chassidic literature. The Prophet Jeremiah (30:6) says:

"ועת צרה היא ליעקב וממנה יושע."

"It is a time of distress for Yaakov, and from this he will be saved."

The manner of salvation springs from the distress itself, and the troubled situation will serve as the means of salvation. Thus, if the story of Purim serves to reaffirm the promise of salvation, then the troubled situation, "וממנה יושע", is also the catalyst for bringing about their salvation. Thus, just as the king's banquet caused all the trouble, so too did it serve to prepare the stage for the Jewish people's salvation, by bringing Esther onto the scene.

In honor of our dear parents

Mr. & Mrs. Howard D. Geller
Mrs. Frank Scher

Through your example we have been given an appreciation and love for Torah, synagogue and Israel.

May Hashem bless you with long life, health and much nachas from your children and grandchildren

—————∽∾∽—————

By your loving children
Marc & Debbi Geller and Family

In loving memory of our father

Mr. Frank Scher
אפרים בן ישראל הכהן, ע"ה

You brightened our lives, and instilled within us a dignity and courage that has shaped our lives.

May you always be remembered for all that you have done for us.

———— ❦ ————

By your loving children
Marc & Debbi Geller and Family

לזכרון עולם בהיכל ה'

לעילוי נפש

ר' אפרים צבי ב"ר יצחק מאיר רימל, ע"ה
מרת דבורה בת ר' יוסף מאניס, ע"ה

הונצח ע"י
הרב יוסף מאיר ושולמית רימל, נ"י

לעילוי נפש

הרב ירוחם פישל גולדפדר, ע"ה

הונצח ע"י בנו
ר' אברהם צבי גולדפדר, נ"י

לזכרון עולם בהיכל ה'

לעילוי נפש

ר' חיים יצחק בן מרדכי יהודה הלוי, ע"ה
Erdfruct

❧⟞⟝❧

הונצח ע"י נכדם
הרב שמואל וייוסיפה יבלון, נ"י
Rabbi & Mrs. Shmuel Jablon

לעילוי נפש

ר' יצחק יעקב בן יחיאל צבי, ע"ה
מרת מרים הידנא בת שמואל, ע"ה
ר' משה צבי בן נח, ע"ה

❧⟞⟝❧

הונצח ע"י
שמואל ושרה רוטא, נ"י